The Economics, Regulation, and Systemic Risk of Insurance Markets

The Economics, Regulation, and Systemic Risk of Insurance Markets

Edited by

Felix Hufeld, Ralph S. J. Koijen, and Christian Thimann

OXFORD
UNIVERSITY PRESS

OXFORD
UNIVERSITY PRESS

Great Clarendon Street, Oxford, OX2 6DP,
United Kingdom

Oxford University Press is a department of the University of Oxford.
It furthers the University's objective of excellence in research, scholarship,
and education by publishing worldwide. Oxford is a registered trade mark of
Oxford University Press in the UK and in certain other countries

First Edition published in 2017

Impression: 2

Published in the United States of America by Oxford University Press
198 Madison Avenue, New York, NY 10016, United States of America

British Library Cataloguing in Publication Data

Data available

Library of Congress Control Number: 2016943308

ISBN 978–0–19–878881–2

Printed in Great Britain by
Clays Ltd, St Ives plc

Contents

Part 3. Regulation

Part 4. Open Questions Going Forward from the Insurance Sector

List of Figures

List of Tables

List of Contributors

Viral V. Acharya is the C.V. Starr Professor of Economics in the Department of Finance at New York University Stern School of Business (NYU-Stern). He completed his Bachelor of Technology in Computer Science and Engineering from the Indian Institute of Technology, Mumbai in 1995 and his PhD in Finance from NYU-Stern in 2001. Prior to joining Stern, he was a Professor of Finance at the London Business School (2001–2008). His primary research interest is in theoretical and empirical analysis of systemic risk of the financial sector, its regulation and its genesis in government-induced distortions, an inquiry that cuts across several other strands of research—credit risk and liquidity risk, their interactions and agency-theoretic foundations, as well as their general equilibrium consequences. He is the recipient of the inaugural Banque de France-Toulouse School of Economics Junior Prize in Monetary Economics and Finance, 2011. He is the current PhD coordinator in the Finance department at Stern.

He is a member of the Economic Advisory Committee of the Financial Industry Regulation Authority (FINRA), the International Advisory Board of the Securities and Exchange Board of India (SEBI), the Advisory Council of the Bombay (Mumbai) Stock Exchange (BSE) Training Institute, and Academic Research Council Member of the Center for Advanced Financial Research And Learning (CAFRAL, India). He is also an Academic Advisor to the Federal Reserve Banks of Cleveland and New York, and, in the past, also to the Federal Reserve Banks of Chicago, Philadelphia and the Board of Governors, and to the European Systemic Risk Board.

Bo Becker is a Professor in the Department of Finance at the Stockholm School of Economics. His research is on corporate finance, especially corporate credit markets. Recent topics include, corporate bank lending through the business cycle, conflicts of interest in the credit ratings industry, the covenant structure of loans and bonds, and comparing out-of-court restructuring to bankruptcy. His research has been published in the *Journal of Finance*, the *Journal of Monetary Economics*, the *Journal of Financial Economics* and the *Review of Financial Studies* and other journals. Professor Becker has been awarded several prizes and grants, including the Standard Life Prize for best paper in the ECGI Finance WP series, the Nordea Price for Best Corporate Finance Paper at the European Finance Association's annual meeting, and the Lamfalussy Research Fellowship from the European Central Bank.

Professor Becker holds a Master's degree from the Stockholm School of Economics and a PhD from the University of Chicago. He previously worked at the University of Illinois and at Harvard Business School. He served on the board of directors of the Swedish National Debt Office until 2016.

Amélie de Montchalin is Vice-President for Public Policy and Regulation at AXA Group, where she works on transversal public policy questions relevant for insurance, with a special focus on the broader role of insurance in society and the economy, and on the economic aspects of global financial regulation.

She previously worked as Chief of Staff of AXA Group Head of Strategy, Sustainability and Public Affairs, and at Exane BNP Paribas as an Economist in charge of the Eurozone analysis, focusing on monetary, fiscal, and regulatory policies. She also worked at the European Commission at the time of the Lisbon Treaty signature and at the French Ministry for Higher Education.

Amélie de Montchalin holds a Bachelor's degree in History and Applied Economics from Sorbonne and Dauphine Universities, a Master's degree from HEC Paris, and a Master's in Public Administration from the Harvard Kennedy School.

Denis Duverne is the non-executive Chairman of AXA Group, after having been Deputy Chief Executive Officer of AXA, in charge of Finance, Strategy and Operations since 2010. He was the Chief Financial Officer of AXA and a Member of the Management Board from 2003 to 2010. Since He joined AXA in 1995, and assumed responsibility for supervision of AXA's operations in the United States and the United Kingdom and managed the reorganization of AXA companies in Belgium and the United Kingdom.

Prior to joining AXA, Mr Duverne was in the Crédit Lyonnais Group from 1991 to 1995. He started his career in 1984 as Commercial Counsellor for the French Consulate General in New York. He then worked for the French Ministry of Finance in various positions, including Deputy Assistant Secretary for Tax Policy from 1988 to 1991.

Denis Duverne is a graduate of the École des Hautes Études Commerciales (HEC), and the École Nationale d'Administration (ENA).

Andrew Ellul is Professor of Finance and Fred T. Greene Distinguished Scholar at Indiana University's Kelley School of Business. He joined Indiana University after completing his PhD at the London School of Economics and Political Science. His research interests focus on institutional investors' trading and risk management, empirical corporate finance, and market microstructure. He is a Co-editor of the *Review of Finance* and a Research Associate of the Centre for Economic Policy Research, the Center for Studies of Economics and Finance, the European Corporate Governance Institute, the Systemic Risk Centre, and the Financial Markets Group.

His research has been accepted for publication by various leading finance and economics journals, including the *Journal of Finance*, the *Journal of Financial Economics*, the *Review of Financial Studies*, and the *American Economic Review*, and presented at the top finance conferences in the United States and internationally. He teaches courses in corporate finance and investment analysis at the graduate (MBA) and PhD levels.

Daniel Hartley is a policy economist in the research department of the Federal Reserve Bank of Chicago. His primary research interests include insurance, urban economics, and labour economics. His current work focuses on neighbourhood housing market dynamics, crime, public housing, and the insurance industry. Prior to working at the Federal Reserve Bank of Chicago, he was an economist in the research department at the Federal Reserve Bank of Cleveland for almost six years.

Hartley holds a bachelor of science in electrical engineering from the Massachusetts Institute of Technology, an MBA from the University of Chicago, a master of engineering in electrical engineering and computer science from the Massachusetts Institute of Technology and a PhD in economics from the University of California, Berkeley.

John Hele is Executive Vice-President and Chief Financial Officer for MetLife, Inc. and has been a Member of the company's executive group since 2012. Prior to joining MetLife, Hele was Executive Vice-President, Chief Financial Officer, and Treasurer of Arch Capital Group Limited. He also served as Chief Financial Officer and a Member of the Executive Board of ING Group N.V., as Founder, President and Chief Executive Officer of Worldinsure, and he spent eleven years with Merrill Lynch in investment banking, marketing, and finance positions in the United States. Hele has been a Member of the CFO Forum in Europe, the Chair of the Chief Risk Officer Forum, and is a Fellow in the Society of Actuaries. He holds a Bachelor's degree in Mathematics from the University of Waterloo, Ontario, Canada.

Felix Hufeld is President of the German Federal Financial Supervisory Authority (BaFin) and member of the Supervisory Board of the Single Supervisory Mechanism (SSM) for the banks of the Eurozone. Previously he was Chief Executive Director Insurance Supervision at BaFin. Felix Hufeld was Chairman of the Executive Committee of the International Association of Insurance Supervisors (IAIS) from 2014 to 2015 and member of the Management Board of the European Insurance and Occupational Pensions Authority (EIOPA) from 2013 to 2015. Before joining BaFin he was Partner at Westlake Partners, a Private Equity firm. From 2001 to 2010 he served as Chief Executive Officer of Marsh Germany, Austria, and Northern Europe of Marsh & Mclennan Companies Inc.

Prior to joining the insurance sector, Felix Hufeld worked from 1999 to 2001 at Dresdner Bank as their Global Head Group Corporate Development. Prior to that, he worked at The Boston Consulting Group (BCG) for almost eight years, in the end as a Principal, primarily focusing on the financial services industry as well as Attorney focusing on corporate and tax law.

Felix Hufeld studied Law in Freiburg and received a Master's degree in Public Administration from Harvard University.

Chotibhak Jotikasthira is an Associate Professor of Finance at the Edwin L. Cox School of Business at Southern Methodist University. His research interests include financial intermediation, international finance, and fixed income, with a particular focus on trading behaviours of institutional investors and their impact on asset prices. Jotikasthira has written extensively on the effects of institutional frictions, including regulatory capital and accounting rules, on financial intermediaries' investment and trading incentives, which in turn shape the overall risk and interconnectedness of asset markets.

His research has been published in the *Journal of Finance*, the *Journal of Financial Economics, Economic Policy*, and the *Journal of International Money and Finance*. Jotikasthira received his PhD in finance from Indiana University in 2009. Prior to starting his doctoral coursework, he worked as a Portfolio and Risk Manager for the Bank of Thailand, where he managed $38 billion in foreign-exchange reserves invested in global fixed-income markets and developed quantitative models for formulating investment strategies.

Denis Kessler, a French citizen, is a graduate of HEC business school (Ecole des Hautes Etudes Commerciales), holds a PhD in economics and advanced degrees in economics and social sciences, and is a Fellow of the French Institute of Actuaries. He was Chairman of the Federation Française des Sociétés d'Assurance (FFSA), Senior Executive Vice-President and Member of the Executive Committee of the AXA Group and Executive Vice-President of MEDEF (Mouvement des Entreprises de France). He joined SCOR as Chairman and Chief Executive Officer on 4 November 2002.

Ralph S. J. Koijen is a Professor of Finance at the New York University Stern School of Business, on leave from London Business School. His areas of expertise are investments, health care and insurance markets, and financial econometrics. He is also a Research Fellow of the CEPR and Netspar.

Before joining London Business School, Ralph was a visiting Assistant Professor of Finance at New York's Stern University and an Assistant and Associate Professor of Finance at the University of Chicago's Booth School of Business. Ralph's research has been published in leading journals, such as *Econometrica*, the *American Economic Review*, *The Journal of Finance*, the *Review of Financial Studies*, and the *Journal of Financial Economics*.

He has received various awards for his work including the Richard A. Crowell Memorial Prize, the Roger F. Murray Prize, Swiss Finance Institute Outstanding Paper Award, the Glucksman Institute Research Prize, and the Amundi-Smith Breeden Distinguished Paper Prize.

Christian T. Lundblad is Edward M. O'Herron Distinguished Scholar; Professor of Finance, Kenan-Flagler Business School, University of North Carolina. He spans asset pricing and international finance, with a specialization in emerging market development. His research has been published in top academic journals such as the *Journal of Finance*, *Review of Financial Studies* and the *Journal of Financial Economics*. He is an Associate Editor for the *Journal of Finance*.

Professor Lundblad served as a financial economist at the Federal Reserve Board in Washington, DC, where he advised the Board of Governors on international financial market developments. He is the recipient of the MBA for Executives Teaching Excellence award. He received a PhD in Financial Economics and a Master's degree in Economics from Duke University. He earned his Bachelor's degree in Economics and English Literature with highest honours from Washington University in St. Louis.

Luca Pancaldi is a Partner from McKinsey Milan office with wide experience in banking and insurance. He has served primary financial institutions in Europe and Asia and he is one of the European leaders of the McKinsey Risk Management practice. In recent years, his work has focused mainly on risk appetite, ERM transformations, risk organization, and culture, capital optimization programmes.

Luca studied Management Engineering at Politecnico di Milano and he holds an MBA with distinction from INSEAD business school (Paris and Singapore).

Anna Paulson is a Vice-President and Director of financial research in the Economic Research department at the Federal Reserve Bank of Chicago.

Paulson's research focuses on insurance and systemic risk and how households cope with risk and incomplete financial markets. Her current research includes studies of the dynamics of entrepreneurship and how low interest rates are impacting the insurance industry.

Paulson's research has been published in scholarly journals, including the *Journal of Political Economy*, the *Review of Financial Studies*, and the *Journal of Financial Economics*. Before joining the Federal Reserve Bank of Chicago in November 2001, Paulson was an Assistant Professor in the Finance department at the Kellogg School of Management. She received a Bachelor's degree from Carleton College and a PhD in Economics from the University of Chicago.

Thomas Philippon is Professor of Finance at New York University—Stern School of Business. Philippon was named one of the 'top 25 economists under 45' by the IMF in 2014. He won the 2013 Bernácer Prize for Best European Economist under 40, the 2010 Michael Brennan & BlackRock Award, the 2009 Prize for Best Young French Economist, and the 2008 Brattle Prize for the best paper in Corporate Finance. He was elected Global Economic Fellow in 2009 by the Kiel Institute for the World Economy. He has studied various topics in finance and macroeconomics: financial distress, systemic risk, government interventions during financial crises, asset markets, and corporate investment. Recently his work has focused on the evolution of the financial system and on the Eurozone crisis.

He currently serves on the Monetary Policy Advisory Panel of the NY Federal Reserve Bank, and as a board member and director of the scientific committee of the French prudential regulator (ACPR). He was the senior economic advisor to the French finance minister in 2012–2013.

Philippon graduated from Ecole Polytechnique, received a PhD in Economics from MIT, and joined New York University in 2003.

Matthew Richardson is the Charles E. Simon Professor of Applied Economics in the Finance Department at the Leonard N. Stern School of Business at New York University. He currently holds the position of the Sidney Homer Director of the Salomon Center for the Study of Financial Institutions which is a leading financial research centre. Prior to being at New York University, Professor Richardson was an Assistant Professor of Finance at the Wharton School of the University of Pennsylvania. In addition, he is a Research Associate of the National Bureau of Economic Research.

Professor Richardson has done research in many areas of finance, including both theoretical and empirical work. His research has been published in the *American Economic Review*, the *Journal of Finance*, the *Review of Financial Studies*, and the *Journal of Financial Economics*, among other places. He was an associate editor of *The Journal of Finance, Review of Financial Studies*, and *Journal of Financial and Quantitative Analysis*. He recently co-edited two books on the financial crisis entitled, *Restoring Stability: How to Repair a Failed System* (Wiley, 2009) and *Regulating Wall Street: The Dodd-Frank Act* and the *New Architecture of Global Finance* (Wiley, November 2010) and is a co-author of *Guaranteed to Fail: Fannie Mae, Freddie Mac and the Debacle of Mortgage Finance* (Princeton University Press, March 2011).

Professor Richardson completed both his Bachelor and Master degrees in economics concurrently at the University of California in Los Angeles. He received his Doctor of Philosophy in Finance from the Graduate School of Business at Stanford University.

Richard J. Rosen is a Vice-President and Research Advisor in the Economic Research department at the Federal Reserve Bank of Chicago. In that position, he conducts research on issues relating to financial intermediation, insurance, bank regulation, mergers, and real estate and housing. In addition, he manages the Federal Reserve Bank of Chicago's insurance initiative.

Richard's research is published in numerous leading academic journals including the *Journal of Finance*, the *Journal of Financial Economics*, the *Journal of Business*, the *Journal of Money, Credit and Banking*, and the *Rand Journal*.

Prior to coming to the Chicago Federal Reserve, Richard taught in the Finance departments at the Kelley School of Business at Indiana University, the Wharton School at the University of Pennsylvania and the School of Business at Georgetown University. He has also worked at the Board of Governors of the Federal Reserve System.

Uwe Stegemann is a Senior Partner at McKinsey & Company and one of the senior leaders of McKinsey's Global Financial Institutions Group. After his return from the U. S. in 2006, he led McKinsey´s EMEA Banking Risk Practice from 2006 to 2011, co-led Asia Risk Practice from Singapore from 2011 to 2014, and is now leading McKinsey´s SREP Special Initiative and Enterprise Risk Management (ERM) service line globally. He has broad experience in enterprise risk, balance sheet and capital management, wholesale and retail banking, as well as regulation.

Christian Thimann is Head of Strategy, Sustainability and Public Affairs of the AXA Group and affiliated Professor of Economics at the Paris School of Economics. He is also an external member of the Council of Economic Advisers to the French Prime Minister and a Trustee of the Max-Planck Institute for Tax Law and Public Finance. Prior to joining AXA, he held senior positions at the European Central Bank (ECB), where he was Director General and Adviser to the President from 2008 to 2013. From 1995 to 1998, he worked at the International Monetary Fund in Washington, DC. He has published on international finance, insurance and macroeconomics and holds an MSc from the London School of Economics as well as a PhD from the University of Munich.

Motohiro Yogo is a Professor of Economics at Princeton University and a research associate of the NBER. Prior to joining Princeton in 2015, he was a research economist at the Federal Reserve Bank of Minneapolis and taught finance at Wharton. He earned a PhD in economics from Harvard in 2004 and an A.B. summa cum laude from Princeton in 2000. His fields of expertise are financial economics, insurance, and econometrics. His current research is on the impact of institutional investors on asset prices and on risk and regulation of the insurance industry. He has published in various economics and finance journals including the *American Economic Review*, *Econometrica*, the *Journal of Political Economy*, the *Journal of Finance*, the *Journal of Financial Economics*, and the *Review of Financial Studies*.

He has received various awards for his work including the Roger F. Murray Prize, the Swiss Finance Institute Outstanding Paper Award, and the Zellner Thesis Award in Business and Economic Statistics.

Introduction

Felix Hufeld, Ralph S. J. Koijen, and Christian Thimann

The insurance sector contains 13,000 small to very large companies in OECD countries. It directly employs around 4 million people (7 million including outsourced employees and independent intermediaries) and the aggregate balance sheet size is around $25 trillion in terms of assets—which is about half of the total GDP of the OECD. Given the long-term nature of insurance, insurance companies are an important group of long-term investors in global financial markets. Despite the importance of insurance in enabling individual and collective social, economic, and financial activities, discussions about the macroeconomic role and the risks of insurance markets have been surprisingly limited.

While insurance is part of the broader financial sector, the differences with other parts of the sector, and in particular banks, have been emphasized only recently. Insurance gained renewed attention from public and financial authorities since 2008 with the failure of AIG, the stress during the financial crisis in the insurance sector more broadly, and the subsequent low interest rate environment.

In response to these events, nine large global companies have been qualified as 'systemically important' and are facing new supervisory and prudential measures and standards, in addition to their long-standing national prudential regulatory frameworks. These new frameworks include centralized group supervision across international activities, preparation of Systemic Risk Management and Liquidity Management Plans, and the design of Recovery and Resolution Plans in coordination with supervisors. Moreover, capital surcharges (to be further defined) based on some specific, more systemically risky, activities are being contemplated.

As these new regulatory frameworks and qualifications are all extremely nascent, many conceptual and empirical questions remain open on the nature and intensity of systemic risk in the insurance sector.

Our core motivation for publishing this book is to bring together academics, regulators, and industry experts to provide a multifaceted array of research and perspectives on insurance, its role and functioning, and the potential systemic risk it could create. While these debates develop slowly and under public scrutiny, we hope that this book stimulates further research and debate to address the key questions and challenges faced by the insurance sector going forward.

The richness and depth of this book should not be just seen as the mere sum of the content of its 10 chapters, but as the result of an intense dialogue which has taken place since early 2014. A sequence of high-level, informal, and closed-door events took place, first in early 2014 in Bonn organized by the German Federal Financial Supervisory Authority (BaFin, Bundesanstalt für Finanzdienstleistungsaufsicht), then in September 2014 in Paris at the French Prudential Supervisory Authority (ACPR, Autorité de contrôle prudentiel et de résolution), and in September 2015 in London at the London Business School.

These meetings brought together regulators, insurance companies' senior executives, and academics in their individual capacities, with the sole aim to enhance our understanding of the insurance sector. The first three parts of this book largely cover the topics discussed in the various meetings. The first part discusses the macroeconomic role of insurance and how insurance differs from banking and general finance. Understanding the differences between the balance sheets of insurers and other financial intermediaries is essential in thinking about optimal regulatory frameworks. The second part of the book focuses on the risks of the insurance sector and the potential for systemic risk. The various chapters discuss the risks on both sides of the balance sheet of insurance companies, and the potential for risk mismatch. The third part of the book covers the impact of regulation on insurance companies. The discussions during the meetings often focused on the impact of existing, complex regulation on insurance companies' decision-making and functioning. The chapters also discuss the unintended consequences of various forms of regulation.

The book concludes with a summary of a survey that has been conducted in collaboration with McKinsey, where insurance executives have been asked about the risks and regulation in the insurance sector. The survey provides guidance for future research on insurance markets.

It should be stressed that all participants—regulators, academics, and industry executives—contributed only in their personal capacity as insurance experts and not on behalf of their affiliated organizations. In addition, this book has no commercial intent, but solely seeks to contribute to an enhanced interest and understanding of insurance by a larger audience and by the general public.

Part 1

The Economics of Insurance and the Macroeconomic Role of Insurance

1

What is Insurance and How Does it Differ from General Finance?

Christian Thimann

1.1 Introduction

What is insurance and how does it differ from general finance? What sounds a simple, perhaps even awkward, question is one of the most important issues in global finance at present. The reason is that global financial regulators at the G20 and the Financial Stability Board are trying to define if certain specific life insurance products, as well as advanced techniques of financial and risk management, could generate systemic risk in the financial system (IAIS 2011 and 2013). Regulators have for several years tried to identify such activities under the headline of 'non-traditional, non-insurance activities'. Addressing the challenge of defining the borders of insurance can only be achieved through an approach that methodically tackles the sources of the confusion arising from the appropriation of insurance terminology by general finance. Such an appropriation would be 'harmless' had the different meanings not led to an important misunderstanding of the very nature of insurance. This chapter seeks an understanding of the economics of insurance in the light of a conceptual delineation with general finance. The aim is to provide for a better understanding of insurance activities, both in terms of risk transfer and business models.

1.2 The Economics of Insurance

What is the economics of insurance, how does insurance differ from general finance and what is its deeper purpose?

1.2.1 *Insurance Versus Finance*

Insurance is the business of accepting insurable risks, managing them, and providing compensation for possible losses. This statement describes insurance with three qualifications:[1]

i. Insurable risks are faced by policyholders but beyond their control; they are not systematic but subject to the law of large numbers; and they are non-financial—that is, not directly related to the economic and financial cycle.[2]
ii. The managing of risk takes place through pooling or mutualization—that is, the aggregation of a large number of similar risks, linking the misfortune of the few to the fortune of the many; or it takes place through cession and diversification, which are the other ways to manage insurance risk.[3]
iii. Compensation takes place for losses that have actually occurred, not for hypothetical losses nor for events that may have caused losses.

These basic concepts of insurance pre-date modern economic theory and especially finance. But its key notions—especially that of risk—have been espoused by the economics profession from the 1920s onwards. They were transformed and popularized in particular by the development of financial economics in the 1950s and 1960s, and today they are omnipresent in economics, corporate finance, and even the everyday media commentary about financial markets. In this process, the notions that were longstanding insurance concepts received a very different meaning.

The concept of risk started to be used outside the boundaries of insurance in the early part of the twentieth century. Frank Knight brought it forcefully into modern economics through his 1921 treatise *Risk, Uncertainty and Profit*. The concept of risk was popularized through modern portfolio theory, which is based on a rational investor who seeks to optimize return for a given level of risk or to reduce risk for a targeted level of return. These ideas and related models have been firmly established in financial economics through the work of Markowitz (1952 and 1957), Lintner (1965) and Sharpe (1963 and 1964). Their work led to the capital asset pricing model, which describes the relationship between risk and expected return, and serves as a benchmark for the pricing of securities.

[1] Among the insurable risks, not every insurance company covers all risks; depending on their business line they may choose the types of risk they cover.

[2] Insurance companies can, however, themselves be exposed to financial risks, for example, when they provide guarantees on capital or interest rates in a wide range of life insurance contracts. The hedging of those risks is the main reason why insurance companies need derivatives.

[3] For example, insurers can cede risks to reinsurers or to the financial markets, or they can through reinsurance or hedging seek to eliminate the risk.

In the 1980s, the mixing of finance and insurance became even more intricate with a new strand of literature and market offer on 'portfolio insurance', which arguably could be obtained through combining the reference portfolio with riskless assets and various options (Leland and Rubinstein 1976; and Leland 1980). At that point, the literature had not only taken up the key terms of insurance into a new field but actually started to use the label of insurance itself—the confusion between insurance and finance became complete, and has lasted until today.

Unsurprisingly, the notion of risk is now omnipresent in this literature: risky assets, risk-free assets, risk-return trade-off, asset-specific risk and market risk, risk profile, risk tolerance, and risk reduction strategies, to name but a few, and the same holds true for the notions of values and losses.

It is therefore important to clarify the key concepts of insurance and contrast them with their meaning in finance.

In insurance, key terms have the following understanding:

- *Risk* is the possibility of actual damage, injury, liability, or loss of existing value or status (property, health, life) as a consequence of an external event.
- *Value* refers to an actual endowment regarding property, health, or life.
- *Losses* refer to the partial or total damage of the object insured or personal injury experienced by the policyholder.
- *Trading* of insurance contracts is generally not possible;[4] an insurance company may cede some of the risk taken to a reinsurer or the financial market, for example, via so-called Natcat bonds,[5] but itself remains fully liable vis-à-vis the initial policyholder.[6]

In finance, and specifically capital markets, these terms have a fundamentally different meaning:

- *Risk* means uncertainty or probabilistic change[7] in value over time. A financial asset is considered risky when the standard deviation of its

[4] An exception is the U.S., where some life insurance contracts are tradable in principle; here, there are policyholders who sold their life insurance contracts, mostly to investment companies, when faced with a critical illness and in need of cash.

[5] Natcat bonds are risk-linked securities that transfer a specified risk from an insurance company to investors. Such securities are a way to alleviate some of the risk that insurance companies take, especially in the context of natural catastrophes. Average issuances in recent years were below $5 billion, covering a small fraction of the insurance market.

[6] The difference in trading and tradability between insurance and finance contracts is yet one more argument making the marking-to-market of the full balance sheet of insurance companies compared to the partial marking-to-market of the balance sheet of banks (only the trading book that is typically a fraction of the balance sheet) more problematic. It is ironic that banks only have to mark-to-market their limited trading book, whereas insurers have to mark-to-market their full balance sheet even though insurance contracts are generally not tradable. This issue would warrant a separate study.

[7] Knight (1921) introduced the distinction between probabilistic change and changes where the probability distribution of outcomes was unknown; such distinction is however not essential here.

fluctuations over time is positive and/or when its return is not guaranteed;[8] the higher the standard deviation and the larger the possibility that the actual return is below the expected return, the riskier is an asset.[9]

- *Value* is the price of an asset or a portfolio at a given point in time. In principle, when prices follow a random walk or a random walk with a drift (Fama 1965; Malkiel 1973; Lo and MacKinlay 1999), the value of a financial asset is bounded from below at zero and it is unbounded from above.
- *Losses* are a negative change in the asset value over a given period.
- *Trading* refers to the exchange of contracts at varying prices, and is generally possible.

It is essential to clarify the fundamental distinction between risk in insurance and risk in finance. Risk materialization in insurance is a relatively rare event, happening exogenously 'out of normal'. By contrast, in finance and, more generally, in a market economy, risk materialization is endogenous, 'within normal', and happens all the time. Values in insurance are based on actual values, whereas value in financial markets refers to expected value. And losses in insurance are actual losses related to damage or injury, whereas losses in financial products reflect decreases in value, including to zero.

Consider these points in more detail: property and casualty insurance, health insurance, and life insurance exist because the threats to these values are relatively rare, 'out of normal' events and warrant protection. Specifically, property exists to serve its owners; thefts or destructions through fire or flood are events 'out of normal', and owners can therefore purchase property insurance against their consequences. Cars are made to ensure mobility, not to have crashes; owners can therefore buy insurance against the consequences of an accident. Life is made to last, not to end from accidents or disease at a young age; people can therefore buy insurance against the consequences of 'life accidents' (see Table 1.1).

In contrast, fluctuations in asset values leading to temporary or permanent price declines or 'losses' in value are 'within normal' and happen all the time in capital markets; they lie within the nature of financial markets, and it is not the purpose of insurance to provide protection against such losses. The permanent adjustment of prices over time is an intrinsic feature of financial markets, whose main function is to incorporate all relevant incoming information. Even

[8] The corporate finance literature often distinguishes between 'pure risk', which only refers to possible losses, and 'speculative risk', which can involve both a possibility of gain or loss (Merna and Al-Thani 2008). In this terminology, only pure risks are insurable.

[9] Accordingly, equities are typically seen as riskier than corporate bonds, which are typically seen as riskier than government bonds, which are seen as riskier for some countries than for others.

Table 1.1. Key concepts in insurance and finance compared

Concept	Insurance	Finance
Risk	Possibility of actual damage, injury, liability, or loss	Uncertainty in value over time
Risk materialization	Relatively rare occurrence, happening 'out of normal', as a consequence of an external event	Inherent feature 'within normal', happening continuously
Value	Actual endowment regarding property, health or life	Price of an asset or a portfolio at a given point in time
Loss	Partial or total damage of the object insured or personal injury experienced	Negative change in asset value
Purchase of protection	Possible only if an exposure to the risk exists	Possible also if no exposure to the risk exists
Trigger for payouts	Damage	Event
Compensation level	Determined by actual damage	Determined by product terms
Compensation differentiation	Case-by-case	Same for all instrument holders
Profits possible?	No. Insurance cannot create profits for policyholders (except for life insurance products); loss compensations cover at best the loss in full	Yes. Profits are possible; payouts can exceed a possible loss from event and even occur if there is no loss
Tradability of contracts	Generally not possible	Generally possible

Source: Author's compilation. For further explanations see text

complete losses in the value of assets are within the range of market outcomes and lie in the nature of a market economy. Arrangements that offer protection against such events 'within normal' are not insurance products but financial products.

Life insurance contracts with a savings component are closer to finance than pure risk life insurance products or property and casualty insurance products. In life insurance products with a savings component, the insurance companies often provide a guarantee of the paid-in capital (e.g. in France and many other countries) and/or a guaranteed minimum return (e.g. in Germany, where life insurance has been accompanied for almost 120 years by a guaranteed return, but might be abolished due to the ultra-low interest rates). The insurance company providing such guarantees exposes itself to financial risks and it needs to use derivatives to hedge such risk.

How do such contracts fit into the scheme outlined above? The purpose of such contracts is to provide the policyholders with a protection against the risk of longevity through life-long annuities or with a protection of the survivors in case of death. These are insurance risks, they are not risks related to the financial cycle. The financial guarantees are attached to such contracts in order to make the protection meaningful. And as a result of these guarantees, it is the insurance company that is exposed to financial risks, for example in case asset markets or market interest rates decline.

Insurance and finance come closer in the case of life insurance products with financial guarantees, but the nature of the relationship between the policyholder and the company remains of an insurance-type, and it is the company that is exposed to, and has to manage, the financial risk—through pooling, diversification, hedging, or cession.

1.2.2 *Are CDS 'Insurance' Contracts?*

Among the many financial products that are most confused with insurance contracts are those accepting credit risk such as credit insurance, financial guarantees, and credit default swaps (CDS), because they are often regarded as an insurance against the possible default of an issuer. CDS are mostly issued by banks[10] and sold to a very large range of investors. Investors can and do buy these contracts independent of whether they have an exposure to the issuer concerned or not. CDS are issued separately from the bonds by the issuer concerned and buyers receive a payout in case of default (or wider adverse 'credit events'), independently of whether they experience a loss from default on the underlying asset or not.

Are CDS insurance contracts? No, they are not, for two main reasons: first, because the default of a counterparty is an inherent feature in a market economy[11] and second, because CDS payouts are not damage-driven but event-driven. There are several further attributes that show how far such contracts are from being insurance: CDS contracts are created and sold independently of whether buyers would actually suffer a damage in case of default; they can be produced in unbound numbers and their value can far exceed the value of the underlying assets outstanding; they are determined by a market committee assessing debtor behaviour rather than by an insurance expert assessing creditor impact;[12] they are freely tradable and they can generate profits. It is for all these reasons that large-scale naked CDS selling creates systemic risk in the financial system.

[10] In practical terms, five large banking (not insurance) corporations dominate the CDS space and issue over 90% of contracts worldwide: Morgan Stanley, Bank of America Merrill Lynch, Goldman Sachs, BNP Paribas, and Deutsche Bank. The total value outstanding is estimated at $20 trillion as of end June 2014 (BIS 2014).

[11] The financial sector even created rating agencies to estimate this 'normal feature' of default as part of market functioning.

[12] The decision whether or not a default occurred and CDS payments need to be made is usually determined by the Determinations Committee of the International Swaps and Derivatives Association, comprising a predetermined set of financial market participants (usually dealers) as members.

In sum, these considerations illustrate that insurance companies serve to absorb risk,[13] whereas financial products spread risk: in insurance, for a given risk, there is a finite number of contracts with a given upper value that can be sold (for example, the number and value of cars in a region) and, assuming full coverage, the population is no longer exposed to the financial consequences of the risk materializing. In contrast, there is no limit to the number or value of CDS contracts that can be sold for a given risk and the population can be more exposed (positively in case of gain or negatively in case of loss) than before.[14] Finally, financial contracts are generally tradable and allow profit-making, whereas insurance contracts do not.

1.2.3 *Why and How Insurance is Regulated*

Even though insurance functionally differs from finance, the insurance industry is regulated and supervised as part of the financial system. This has not always been the case. Until the 1980s, the insurance industry was part of business services and at a 'safe distance' from banking; however, in the United Nation's reform of the national accounts at the time, a new 'financial sector' was created, including banking, insurance, and other financial institutions.

The insurance business is regulated and supervised essentially for three reasons: first, there is an overarching public interest in the smooth provision of insurance services to the economy and society at large because insurance contributes to the economic security and protection of households, firms, and communities.[15] Insurance also allows individuals and firms to develop their talents and business despite the presence of risk, which is an essential condition for economic development and growth.

Second, insurance contracts are typically long-term relationships, providing the desired protection only when the long-term survival of the insurance company is ensured. So regulation should ensure the long-term existence of

[13] Parametric insurance contracts are an interesting example of sophistication in insurance, which nonetheless respect its main features. Contracts continue to make explicit the precise conditions that will lead to compensations—as a car insurance contract would state under which conditions (its nature, intensity, and cause) a material damage will be (partly or fully) paid by the insurance company. Parametric insurance contracts are innovative in the sense that they relate to situations where damage is not directly observable, and estimated *ex ante* by a number of proxies taking the form of observable external parameters (not market conditions and not 'events' defined by an external commission as in the case of CDS). No profits are possible for policyholders and compensation is designed to increase according to the intensity of the damage. Examples include insurance against low snow levels for ski resort companies; or against droughts in specific regions for farmers.

[14] When Lehman Brothers defaulted in September 2008, it had $155 billion in outstanding debt, yet $440 billion of CDS referencing this debt had been sold (Geneva Association 2010).

[15] As many parts of life and health insurance are closely related to the public social security systems, there is an additional proximity between public systems and private insurance providers. Changes in one of these two sectors can have direct implications for the other.

insurance companies. This also relates to the fact that insurance companies are typically paid long before they deliver. In many insurance segments, the time lag between payment and delivery can extend to decades.[16] This means that insurance companies have to be credible in being able to honour their commitments far after they take them on.

And third, even though insurance is established through bilateral contacts with individual policyholders, the soundness of any single contractual relationship can only be assessed jointly with the management of other contracts. As risks are pooled and mutualized, a collective assessment needs to be undertaken. By the same token, to oversee the soundness of individual contracts, the regulator cannot act merely on the basis of individual contract law, but needs powers to address the collective management of risk.

Hence, both the time dimension and the cross-section of insurance services are crucial for regulation. Policyholders cannot assess by themselves the quality of management at any specific point in time nor over a period of time due to lack of information or disproportionate information costs, or lack of expertise and authority over the insurance provider. It is to incorporate such considerations that oversight is bestowed on the public regulatory authority (Stigler 1971; Peltzman 1976).

1.3 Further Defining Insurance

As part of the approach to control for systemic risk in finance, global regulators are also reviewing insurance activities. They stated that, while insurance activities do not generally give rise to systemic risk, some activities might do so, and they labelled the latter 'non-traditional' and 'non-insurance activities'. Variable annuities or derivatives are often put in the latter category.

Most industry experts would concede that the AIG debacle was caused by non-insurance activities, when the company engaged in large-scale sale of CDS protection on financial assets. However, while a distinction between 'insurance' and 'non-insurance' activities can be drawn—and very much along the lines outlined in this chapter, a distinction between 'traditional' and 'non-traditional' insurance activities is not meaningful. This is the topic of this section.

[16] The time lag also gives insurance a peculiar economic feature between services, where production and consumption necessarily coincide (for example, provision of advisory services), and goods, where production and consumption can be disconnected over time. This may be one of the reasons that insurance until some decades ago was not classified within the financial sector but within industry, and it is only in the System of National Accounts of 1993 that insurance companies were put in a new major sector of financial corporations (see the System of National Accounts 1993–1993 SNA from the United Nations Statistics Division).

1.3.1 *Tautological Definition*

Inspired by the well-known tautological definition of money—'money is what money does' (Spindt 1985)—it might be tempting to say 'insurance is what insurers do'. But for obvious reasons, such a definition is entirely unsatisfactory; it is also utterly inappropriate as all regulatory texts specify insurance activities in great detail. For example, the EU Directive on Solvency II of December 2009 defines the various activities of life and non-life insurance activities. They refer to provision of assurance on survival to a stipulated age, death, annuities, supplementary insurance, and insurance against personal injury, incapacity for employment, accident, or sickness as well as a two-page list of non-life activities.[17]

Hence, nobody self-declares as an insurer or self-declares an insurance product; such approval takes place by public authorities. An appropriate rephrasing of the above definition might therefore be 'insurance is what regulators allow insurers to do'.

1.3.2 *Chronological Definition*

GENERAL INSURANCE ACTIVITIES

Insurance is as old as mankind, and there are reports about insurance against transport losses among traders in China 3000 BC (Vaughan 1997); about commercial insurance through conditional loans in Babylon 2000 BC (Trennery 1926); and about health and life insurance through organized guilds in ancient Greece and the Roman empire (Holdsworth 1917).

Modern insurance is usually traced back to the period of enlightenment in the seventeenth century.

Property insurance as we know it today is usually traced to the Great Fire of London in 1666, after which the first fire insurance company was established.[18]

Commercial insurance in its modern form was developed around the same time. In 1688,[19] Edward Lloyd opened a meeting facility for parties seeking insurance of ships and cargoes and those willing to underwrite such risks. These informal beginnings led to the establishment of the insurance market 'Lloyd's of London', which eventually became the Society of Lloyd's.

[17] Annex I of the Directive provides under §14 also 'Credit insurance' against 'insolvency (general), export credit, instalment credit, mortgages, agricultural credit' (to be seen against what was said on financial insurance).

[18] But there were proofs of mutual fire insurance of houses in Hamburg already from 1591 (Evans 1987).

[19] http://www.lloyds.com/lloyds/about-us/history.

Life insurance developed in London around the same time. The first company to offer life insurance was the Amicable Society for a Perpetual Assurance Office, founded in London in 1706 and starting with 2,000 members. Half a century later, the necessary mathematical and statistical tools were in place for the development of life insurance as it is known today. In 1762, the world's first mutual insurer that used age-based premiums and estimated mortality rates was established: Equitable Life laid the framework on which virtually all life insurance schemes were subsequently based.[20]

DERIVATIVES

Derivatives are intensively used by modern insurance companies to manage their balance sheets and be able to be protected against external risks. Those who conjecture that *derivatives* are new may be reminded of the Old Testament, where in Genesis (29: 15–20), usually dated 1700 BC, Jacob acquired through seven years of labour an option to marry Laban's daughter Rachel. But his prospective father-in-law reneged (an early default) and Jacob had to purchase another option, requiring more labour, finally to marry Rachel.

Closer to modern times and closer to the formal finance definition of a derivative as a 'security the price of which is dependent on one or more underlying assets', derivatives started playing an increasingly important role from the seventeenth century onwards. They were an important driver of the famous Dutch tulip mania of 1637, when they allowed traders to conduct trade in tulips all year round, and at the same time the first 'futures' contracts were established in the rice market in Osaka around 1650, where they enabled rice traders to purchase rice for resale or future consumption at a pre-arranged price without having to worry about storing the rice in the meantime (Moss and Kintgen 2010).

It was during the same period when research on derivatives began. The ground-breaking analysis of 'modern' financial markets by the Spaniard José Penso de la Vega of 1688, which is still regarded as among the best finance books of all time,[21] discusses stock market functioning, including options, futures, and speculation, and bears the revelatory title 'Confusion de Confusiones'(Levine 1996).

Markets for derivatives were institutionalized through the creation of the Chicago Board of Trade in 1848 and the Chicago Mercantile Exchange in 1919. In 1922, the U.S. federal government made its first effort to regulate the futures market; and in 1955, the Supreme Court ruled that profits from

[20] Cf. Archive of the Equitable Life Insurance Society.

[21] The *Financial Times* classified this book among the ten best books of finance and investment ever written.

hedging were to be treated as ordinary income. In 1972, the Chicago Mercantile Exchange allowed trading in currency futures, responding to the floating of currencies; in 1975, the first pure interest rate future based on Treasury bills followed; and in 1982, the Eurodollar contract was created, which is now the most actively traded of all futures contracts. Stock index futures were created around the same time.

Again, in view of this continuous historic development since at least the seventeenth century, modern use of derivatives cannot be considered as formally 'non-traditional' (Chance 1995).

VARIABLE ANNUITIES

The most prominent items often seen as non-traditional insurance are so-called *variable annuities*. Variable annuities were invented in the United States in 1950. Until then, insurance companies only sold fixed-income annuities. To provide an appealing value proposition at a time of higher inflation rates, William C. Greenough of the Teachers Insurance and Annuity Association (TIAA), developed the idea to invest in 'units' of common equity, rather than 'dollars' of fixed income, and thereby to receive a pension with a variable payment stream, depending on market developments. The revolutionary idea underlying this proposition was that variable annuities are valued in terms of their underlying assets rather than their liabilities, as in a variable annuity, by definition, the assets always equal the liabilities.

These variable annuity contracts were provided by the newly founded College Retirement Equities Fund (CREF), which is now the world's largest issuer of variable annuities in a gigantic market amounting to almost 10 per cent of U.S. GDP. The fact that the world's largest issuer of variable annuities, TIAA-CREF, is not designated as systemically important by either U.S. or global insurance regulators proves that variable annuities as such should give no cause for concern.

The concern only refers to variable annuities with so-called secondary guarantees. Such guarantees started being offered in the 1990s and provide policyholders with minimum guaranteed benefits. This structure implies that in rising market conditions, policyholders benefit from market upswings, and in market downswings can draw on the guarantees. In economic terms, this means that policyholders have a put option that they can exercise when the market declines. The strike price of this put option equals the maximum value reached of the underlying asset, in this case the value of the guarantee. Obviously, the exercise of such options exposes the insurance provider to substantial risk in a market downswing.

To hedge itself against such risk as much as possible, the insurance company purchases swaps and forwards so that it makes no losses if policyholders exercise their options. More specifically, the insurance company is exposed to two types of risks: market risk and policyholder behaviour.[22]

This is why the variable annuity business with secondary guarantee is seen as risky within the financial system and why it is associated with a heavy use of derivatives, which in turn are seen as either risky or a source of (worrisome) interconnectedness. This is the heart of the matter of variable annuities with regard to systemic risk.

As we see from these considerations, a chronological definition of insurance activities or tools does not carry the discussion much further.

1.3.3 *Risk Transfer as a Definition of Insurance?*

The third definition of insurance that is often discussed is that insurance occurs whenever a risk transfer takes place. Most economists agree that 'AIG was not insurance' (Baranoff 2012, and Henderson 2009), but some consider that AIG was insurance 'because a risk transfer took place' through the products AIG sold.

We have already provided a substantive explanation of why the AIG debacle is not insurance, as these activities are beyond the scope of insurance properly defined and because CDS are a financial contract and not an insurance contract. In general, a 'risk transfer' does occur in insurance contracts, but not all that is a risk transfer is insurance; a risk transfer is a necessary element in insurance but it is not sufficient to define insurance as such. First, the nature of risk being transferred must be of insurance type, not of financial type, as defined above. The risk transferred in the AIG business violates all of the insurability assumptions: AIG was assuming risks that policyholders were not actually exposed to; it could not be pooled and mutualized subject to the law of large numbers; and it was not unrelated to the economic and financial cycle (Sorkin).

Interestingly, many risk transfers are undertaken in a context where no one would claim this is insurance in the sense that regulators understand it. In addition to the range of insurance products available—liability, property, business interruption—some large firms do, for example, run their own 'captive insurance' companies to distribute risks across their own different operations and subsidiaries (WEF 2014). They are not regulated as insurance companies when doing so, as the risk is seen as staying in the same group and as mutualization and pooling are only partial and without consequences for external actors. More widely, new non-insurance, risk-transfer markets are

[22] More precisely, market risk can arise in (only) three cases: basis risk, i.e. divergence between the asset and the hedging instrument; high volatility, which raises the cost of hedging above the price of the guarantee; and market disruption, which makes hedging temporarily impossible.

being created on some specific types of risks ('Alternative Risk Transfer' may, for example, refer to CatBonds, intellectual property insurance, etc.

1.3.4 *A Business Model Approach*

A business model approach would start from defining insurance activities through their economic function. As mentioned, insurance exists to provide protection against adverse events by linking the misfortune of the few to the fortune of the many. The object of protection may change over time; well-established objects such as property, health, old-age income, and life may remain, and new objects such as cyber-safety or reputation may be added.

The way in which protection is provided may also change over time because policyholder demands evolve and the macroeconomic and policy environment changes. Innovation in information technologies may allow for more tailor-made solutions and more refined pricing. Changes in the policy environment, such as macroeconomic developments or changes in social security systems and taxation, may also contribute to the evolution of the way insurance is provided.

Finally, the way in which insurance contracts are managed may evolve over time as new financial products that can serve insurance companies are developed and as regulation changes. The introduction of regulation based on economic risks, mark-to-market accounting, and quarterly market reporting may well affect the way in which insurance contracts are managed.

1.4 Conclusion

Insurance is seen as notoriously difficult to understand. A YouGov survey, conducted on behalf of the U.S. insurer Unum in 2011,[23] concluded that insurance was the most difficult to understand sector. Surveyed customers found it around twice as difficult to understand as banking and almost five times as difficult to understand as the food market. This survey was a customer study and related to insurance products, their terminology, technical language, and intricate product information, but a similar conclusion can be drawn for the general challenge to understand insurance. Even among economists and finance experts, insurance is a specialized field that is not easily understood and is often confused with general finance.

This chapter has argued that, as far as financial economics are concerned, part of the confusion surrounding insurance is caused by the fact that its

[23] The summary of the results of the survey can be found here: http://www.covermagazine.co.uk/cover/news/2146627/insurance-industry-difficult-understand-research.

terms—risk, value, loss—were taken up by the finance literature and used in financial risk and financial risks management, which is not the purpose of insurance that should be linked to exogenous events of risk materialization rather than to endogenous notions of risk as value fluctuations.

With the proper notions at hand, the specific role of insurance can be identified, and for the sake of diversity and stability in the financial system, its specific role should be highlighted.

Acknowledgements

The chapter resulted from initial discussions with Robert B. Zoellick and benefited from substantive comments by Henri de Castries, Nacim Dardour, Denis Duverne, Alban de Mailly Nesle, Amélie de Montchalin, Quentin Gisserot, Fabrice Lorillon and Pierre-Charles Pradier, which are gratefully acknowledged. Views expressed are those of the author.

References

Baranoff, Etti (2012): 'An Analysis of the AIG Case: Understanding Systemic Risk and Its Relation to Insurance', *Journal of Insurance Regulation*, Vol. 31, pp. 243–70.

BIS—Bank for International Settlements (2014): 'Buoyant Yet Fragile?', *Quarterly Review*, 7 December 2014.

Chance Don M. (1995): 'A Chronology of Derivatives', *Derivatives Quarterly 2*, Winter 1995, pp. 53–60.

Evans, Robert (1987): 'The Early History of Fire Insurance', *Journal of Legal History*, Vol. 8, Issue 1.

Fama, Eugène (1965): 'The Behavior of Stock-Market Prices', *Journal of Business*, Vol. 38, pp. 34–105.

FCIC—Financial Crisis Inquiry Commission (2011): The Financial Crisis Inquiry Report, 27-1-2011.

Federal Reserve Bulletin (2014): 'Changes in U.S. Family Finances: Evidence from the Survey of Consumer Finances', Board's Division of Research and Statistics, September, Vol. 100, No 4.

Geneva Association (2010): 'Systemic Risk in Insurance, An analysis of insurance and financial stability', Special Report of the Geneva Association Systemic Risk Working Group, March.

Henderson, M. Todd (2009): 'Credit Derivatives Are Not Insurance', *University of Chicago Law & Economics*, Olin Working Paper No. 476, 22 July 2009.

Holdsworth, W.S. (1917): 'The Early History of the Contract of Insurance', *Columbia Law Review*, Vol. 17, No. 2, pp. 85–113.

IAIS—International Association of Insurance Supervisors (2011): Insurance and Financial Stability: Report, 15 November 2011.

IAIS—International Association of Insurance Supervisors (2013): Global Systemically Important Insurers: Initial Assessment Methodology, 18 July 2013.
Knight, Frank H. (1921): *Risk, Uncertainty and Profit*. Hart, Schaffner, and Marx Prize Essays, No. 31. Houghton Mifflin, Boston and New York.
Leland, H. and Rubinstein, M. (1976): 'The Evolution of Portfolio Insurance', in Luskin, D.L., *Portfolio Insurance: A guide to Dynamic Hedging*. John Wiley & Sons, Hoboken, NJ.
Leland, Hayne E. (1980): 'Who should buy Portfolio Insurance', *Journal of Finance*, Vol. 35, pp. 581–94.
Levine, Ross (1996): 'Financial Development and Economic Growth: Views and Agenda', Policy Research Working Paper Series 1678, The World Bank.
Lintner, John (1965): 'The Valuation of Risk Assets and the Selection of Risky Investments in Stock Portfolios and Capital Budgets', *Review of Economics and Statistics*, Vol. 47, No. 1, pp. 13–37.
Lo, A. and C. MacKinlay (1999): *A Non-Random Walk Down Wall Street*. Princeton University Press.
Malkiel, Burton G. (1973): *A Random Walk Down Wall Street. The Time-tested Strategy for Successful Investing*. W.W. Norton.
Markowitz, Harry M. (1952): 'Portfolio Selection', *The Journal of Finance*, Vol. 7, pp. 77–91.
Markowitz, Harry M. (1957): 'A Simplex Method for the Portfolio Selection Problem', *Cowles Foundation Discussion Papers 27*, Cowles Foundation, Yale University.
Merna, Tony and F. Al-Thani (2008): *Corporate Risk Management*, 2nd Edition. John Wiley & Sons, Hoboken NJ.
Moss, D. and E. Kintgen (2010): 'The Dojima Rice Market and the Origins of Futures Trading', Harvard Business School, 10 November 2010.
Peltzman, Sam (1976): 'Toward a More General Theory of Regulation', *Journal of Law and Economics*, University of Chicago Press, Vol. 19(2), pp. 211–40, August.
Sharpe, W.F. (1963): 'A Simplified Model for Portfolio Analysis', *Management Science*, INFORMS, Vol. 9(2), pp. 277–93.
Sharpe, W.F. (1964). 'Capital Asset Prices: A Theory of Market Equilibrium under Conditions of Risk', *Journal of Finance*, Vol. 19, No. 3, pp. 425–42.
Sorkin, Andrew R. (2009): 'The Case for Saving AIG, by AIG', New York Times, 2 March 2009.
Spindt, Paul (1985): 'Money Is What Money Does: Monetary Aggregation and the Equation of Exchange', *Journal of Political Economy*, Vol. 93, No. 1, pp. 175–204.
Stigler, George J. (1971): 'The Theory of Economic Regulation', *Bell Journal of Economics*, RAND Corporation, Vol. 2(1), pp. 3–21, Spring.
Trennery, Charles F. (1926): *The Origin and Early History of Insurance: Including the Contract of Bottomry*. P.S. King & Son, Ltd, London.
Vaughan, Emmett J. (1997): *Risk Management*. University of Iowa.
World Economic Forum (2014): *Global Risks 2014*, 9th Edition, 16 January 2014.

2

The Macroeconomic Role of Insurance

Denis Kessler, Amélie de Montchalin, and Christian Thimann

2.1 Introduction

Insurance is largely invisible in our economies, as it mainly provides conditional financial promises for the future. The only material dimension is the paperwork that describes those promises. Compared with other financial services, it is even less on people's minds because insurance customers have rare encounters with their insurance company, agent, or broker. In financial markets, too, insurance companies generally attract less attention than commercial banks, investment banks, or investment funds—because insurers act as long-term investors, mostly with 'buy-and-hold' strategies and very limited trading.

Nonetheless, insurance is everywhere in developed economies and societies. A vast number of actions and interactions are covered by an insurance contract: people's health, their movements, purchases, homes, and even their lives. Without any form of insurance, it would be difficult to take risks to invest, to innovate, and to create companies: because modern insurance manages risks, it allows individuals, companies, and societies to take them.

From a more anthropological and historical perspective, the concept of insurance has existed in many ways since Antiquity and the Middle Ages. It has been a 'mirror' of the evolution of social and economic values and priorities, as well as our relationship with risk and its consequences.[1] In that sense,

[1] From the glorification of noble death (Achilles, Roland) or honour (the 'Bushidô' code of samurai warriors) carried through ages by warrior societies to the virtues of stability and transmission of heritage, but also of accumulation of capital and financial risk-taking emphasized by the bourgeois society, one can assume that the perception of risk is influenced by economic and social structures and values. The formalization and systematic use of insurance goes hand in hand with this evolution.

insurance as we know it today is a formalized, monetized, and sophisticated form of what many traditional and pre-industrial societies had developed as tools for creating 'confidence' among people, private organizations, and public authorities. Indeed, in many languages, the words insurance and confidence have the same roots or overlapping meanings. These more traditional 'self-insurance' tools for collectively transferring, managing, and compensating for risks often took the form of community savings supervised by a 'wise' person or more complex family, hierarchical, and social norms and relationships.

The genuine way to gauge the importance of insurance and its externalities in industrialized, capitalist, and liberal societies would be to imagine our modern economies without any formal insurance products. One can easily envisage how many economic activities would be discontinued or reduced, and how the behaviour of firms and individuals would change. The whole range of activities or projects would be affected that represent a physical risk (for example, driving), technological risk (air travel), legal risk (launching and selling new products), natural risk (farming, dwelling close to river banks and sea shores) or economic risk (signing a commercial contract as a supplier).

Another way to measure the importance of formal insurance would be to assess the impact of the introduction of simple insurance products in less developed economies where social and economic relationships rely on informal confidence-creating tools. Micro-insurance experiments undertaken in recent years are relevant here.

More generally, without any forms of insurance, the unpredictability of future conditions of living would become a major concern, with individuals afraid of being sick and unable to pay for treatment, or leaving their families in dire straits were they to pass away prematurely. In such a world, economic opportunities and outcomes would be highly volatile and highly unequal: those able to invest and take risks with sufficient financial margins versus those affected by the materialization of risk and without financial cover to cope with it.

For a long time, because of its perceived invisibility, the macroeconomic role of insurance has not been a major topic of interest. Traditionally, it has been reported in national accounts through two proxies: premiums collected and number of people employed. This approach maintains the image of a sector with a relatively low value-added and a limited contribution to economic growth and development. Indeed, as collected premiums in aggregate broadly match the losses and claims that insurance companies compensate,[2]

[2] Combined ratios (which compute a ratio of claims paid over premiums collected) have been superior to 100 for many years in developed countries, signalling that insurance companies were

insurance is seen mostly as a means for 'redistributing' funds across individuals and organizations, at any point in time and over time. Its positive externalities remain therefore to be further studied and assessed.

Recently, insurance has generated renewed interest because of the conjunction of at least three factors: first, the debate about systemic risk in insurance that emerged in the wake of AIG's failure in 2008; second, the identification of insurance companies as vital providers of long-term funding for infrastructure projects and investment in securitized loans to small and medium-sized enterprises (SMEs); and third, the ultra-low interest-rate environment, which is modifying and, in some markets, jeopardizing the functioning of life insurance and retirement management, shedding light on the social role of insurance for retirement savings.

Yet, conceptual and empirical research on the macroeconomic role of insurance has remained to date relatively limited,[3] even if some core insights on the need for insurance are widely shared. The United Nations Conference on Trade and Development (UNCTAD) declared as early as 1964 that '*a sound national insurance and reinsurance market is an essential characteristic of economic growth*'. More recently, it was noted (Skipper 1997) that insurance is not merely a characteristic of economic growth, but a *necessity* for such growth,[4] and the development literature highlights insurance as a key component of broader financial inclusion and entrepreneurship, including through micro-insurance (Brainard 2008).

One reason for the limited research on the specific macroeconomic role of insurance is that the sector has long been subsumed in financial intermediation in general, which presents financial institutions as natural enablers of economic growth and activity (Rajan and Zingales 1998). But it would be mistaken to amalgamate the insurance business model with that of banks; and even life insurance activities are closer to asset management than banking. As a signal of the peculiarity of insurance in the financial sector, insurance was treated in national accounts globally as part of the industry sector until 1993, when it was then reclassified as industrial service. In addition, the prudential frameworks developed for banks and insurance companies are

mostly profitable because of the financial revenues generated by the investment of premiums in financial markets. The recent trends of cost reduction and optimization lead to improved combined ratios of 96% to 98% for the largest European players.

[3] While numerous and diverse research has been conducted more specifically over the conceptual and econometric role of the banking sector in economic growth (see the work of Levine and colleagues), the role of insurance has been much less studied in part because of the lack of available data.

[4] He presented a framework where he envisaged insurance as contributing to economic growth in seven different aspects: '(1) Promotes financial stability and reduces anxiety; (2) Can substitute for government security programs; (3) Facilitates trade and commerce; (4) Mobilizes savings; (5) Enables risk to be managed more efficiently; (6) Encourages loss mitigation; (7) Fosters a more efficient capital allocation.'

known to be extremely different, for example, as far as Basel III and Solvency II in Europe are concerned (Gatzer and Wesker 2012).

This chapter presents a framework for understanding the macroeconomic role of insurance, based on its economic contribution to the functioning of the economy and society, beyond the traditional role of financial intermediary and long-term investor. More specifically, the chapter provides a conceptual framework for analysing insurance interactions with the wider economic functioning by looking at three main functions: economic growth; stabilization; and distribution. In addition, it sheds some light on the relationships between insurance and innovation, and the potential future development of insurance activities in view of major changes in technology ('Big Data'), the nature of risk (notably climate risk) and social expectations around risk (the lower acceptance of risk itself, and the primacy given to prevention over compensation). It also includes reflections on the weaknesses and potential downsides of insurance for the functioning of the economy—including the risk of failure in insurance, the consequences of 'over-insurance', and involvement in pure financial activities.

The fact that the framework we develop resembles Musgrave's (1959) view of the role of the state in providing allocation, stabilization, and redistribution functions is not a coincidence. Many states provide key insurance functions through public schemes (social security, social, and unemployment benefits, etc.), the provision of public goods, and redistributive taxation. In turn, many modern and now privately owned insurance companies were often initially public agencies and companies, their function being seen as totally aligned with the objectives of the public and the state.

2.2 Insurance and Economic Growth

> *New York City has only been made possible by insurers. They are the ones who really built this city. Without insurers, there would be no sky-scrapers. No investor would finance buildings that one cigarette butt could burn to the ground.*[5]
>
> *Henry Ford (1863–1947)*

2.2.1 *Risk-Taking and Economic Growth*

Economic growth is typically defined as the combined effect of two major factors: growth in the quantity and efficiency of labour (a product of advances in technology on the one hand and improvements in economic and social

[5] The first two skyscrapers, the New York's Equitable Life Assurance Building built in 1870 and the Chicago's Home Insurance Building built in 1885 were, as their names display it, funded by and built for insurance companies.

organization on the other) and the economy's capital intensity. With this frame in mind, policies that accelerate innovation or improve institutions and so boost the efficiency of labour accelerate economic growth and create prosperity, as do policies that boost investment and raise the economy's capital intensity to a higher level. The neoclassical model refines this approach and proposes a growth model where a balanced growth path is determined by the economy's ratio of savings to investment, the growth rate of labour and productivity, and the capital stock depreciation rate.

Statistically, economic growth is a stochastic process and many different equilibria are possible at a given moment. As outlined by Robert Solow (1956):

> *No credible theory of investment can be built on the assumption of perfect foresight and arbitrage over time. There are only too many reasons why net investment should be at times insensitive to current changes in the real return to capital, at other times oversensitive.*

This approach highlights the uncertain or unpredictable nature of economic development, based on a sum of individual decisions, which all carry an intrinsic form of unpredictability, linked in particular to the risk-taking they involve. This unpredictability naturally leads to the need to create mitigation factors—such as insurance—which enable decision-taking. Keynes, in his General Theory (1936) hinted at such mitigation factors:

> *We should not conclude from this that everything depends on waves of irrational psychology. [...] We are merely reminding ourselves that human decisions affecting the future, whether personal or political or economic, cannot depend on strict mathematical expectation, since the basis for making such calculations does not exist [...]. There are, however, certain important factors which mitigate in practice the effects of our ignorance of the future.*

In the context of the inherent uncertainty surrounding the individual and collective decisions on which economic growth is based, the development of insurance becomes an interesting dimension to study as part of the theory of economic growth.

CORRELATION AND CAUSATION BETWEEN THE GROWTH OF INSURANCE AND MACROECONOMIC GROWTH

Insurance has historically developed closely in parallel with economic development and growth, and in particular in parallel with the development of manufacturing industry as shown in the U.K. during the nineteenth century (see Figure 2.1).

There is ample evidence of a general correlation between formal insurance penetration and GDP growth. Ranges of impact are different depending on methodologies and scope of surveys. Empirical evidence (Lee et al. 2013) suggests that for OECD countries, a 1 per cent increase in life insurance premiums raises real GDP by 0.06 per cent per year. On a larger set of

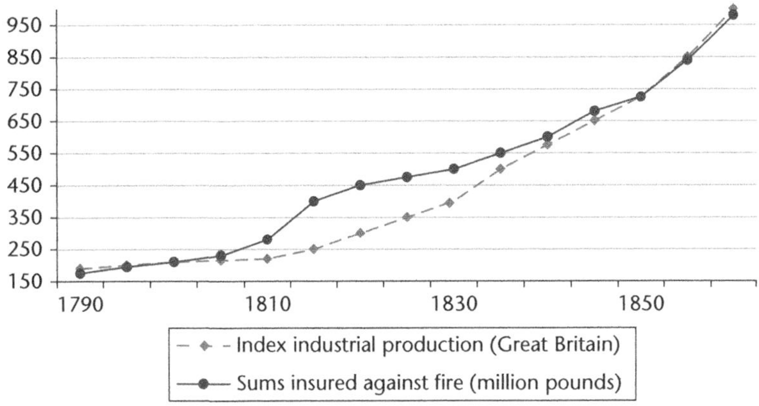

Figure 2.1. Correlation between fire insurance and growth in the U.K.
Source: L.T. Little (1937) and USAID (2006)

seventy-seven advanced and emerging economies for the period 1994–2005, Han et al. (2010) find that a 1 per cent increase in total insurance penetration led to a 4.8 per cent increase in economic growth per year (versus a 1.7 per cent increase in economic growth per year when only considering life insurance). For the purposes of comparison, the positive impact of banking activities on economic growth is no more than 1.8 per cent per year given a 1 per cent increase in bank credit (Beck and Levine 2004).

Part of the difference in the estimated impact of insurance on growth can be explained by the non-linear nature of insurance development relative to GDP. Cross-country data (USAID 2006) show that over the last forty years, formal insurance penetration is not linearly correlated with economic growth but follows an 'S'-curve (Enz 2000). Low levels of economic development are typically associated with low insurance penetration, while informal and traditional self-insurance mechanisms are operating and not easily quantifiable. Then, at levels of around U.S.$3,000–5,000 GDP per capita, insurance penetration rises faster than GDP until the maturity of the market sets in to reach a form of 'plateau' (see Figure 2.2).

Some refinement of this S-curve shows differences between life and non-life insurance. While life insurance is causally linked to growth only in higher income economies, non-life insurance makes a positive contribution in both developing and higher income economies, as Figure 2.2 highlights (Arena 2006 and Brainard 2008).

A number of empirical studies have also been able to demonstrate the causal relationship between formalized insurance, growth, and productivity:

- Granger causality tests with disaggregated measures of specific clusters of life and non-life insurance in the U.K. find that eight out of nine clusters

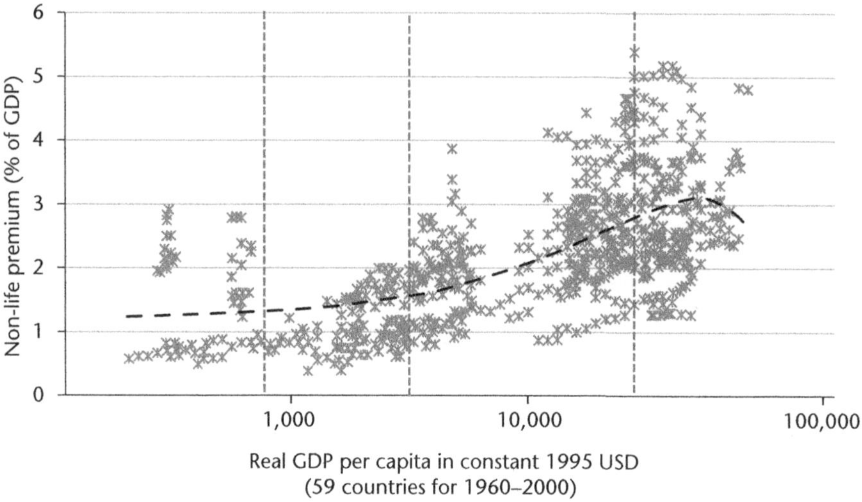

Figure 2.2. Increasing insurance penetration versus economic growth
Source: Swiss Re, WorldBank and USAID (2006)

of insurance show evidence of causing economic growth (Kugler and Ofoghi 2005).

- Life insurance has contributed to the productivity and economic growth of the United States over a thirty-year period (Soo 1996).
- The macroeconomic contribution of insurance is fundamentally linked to the general impact of greater financial market development and inclusion: insurance and banking system deepening appear to play complementary roles in the growth process. Although insurance and banking separately each make positive contributions to growth, their individual contributions are greater when both are present (Brainard 2008).[6]

Reflecting all these interactions, including causalities, between insurance and economic growth, insurance became a major economic sector in virtually all mature economies: there are 5,000 insurance companies in the European Union (Insurance Europe 2014), with close to one million direct employees and around the same number of indirect employees in insurance distribution.

[6] There is some contrary evidence on this point. Thus, for example, Adams et al. (2005) find that banking sector growth but not insurance market growth preceded economic growth in Sweden during the nineteenth century and more broadly that the insurance sector appears to be more economic development driven than leading, though still important for it. While in some specifications life and non-life insurance do not appear to be significant contributors to growth in the presence of an interaction term with banking, subsequent research such as Webb et al. (2002), suggests the independent contribution of insurance is robust to the inclusion of banking sector variables, and higher levels of insurance and banking penetration jointly produce a greater effect on growth than their individual contributions combined.

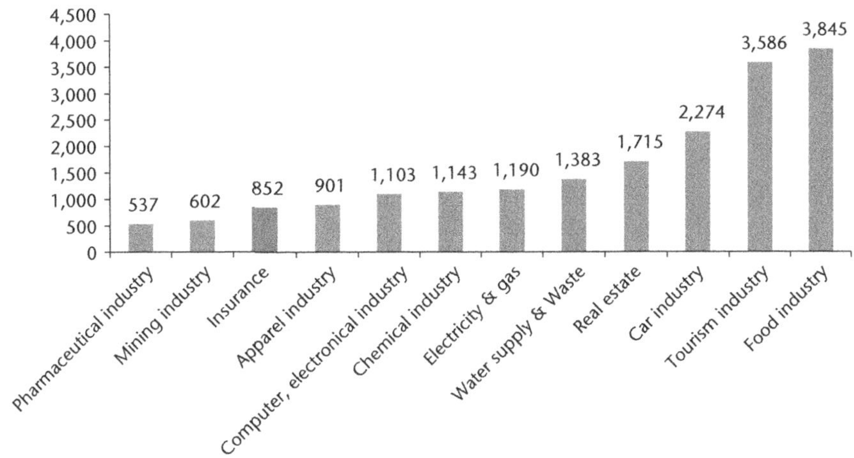

Figure 2.3. Employees by economic sector (European Union, in thousands)
Source: Eurostat

In terms of direct employment, insurance is larger in Europe than the pharmaceutical and mining industries and comparable to the apparel industry (see Figure 2.3). In the United States, there are 6,000 insurance companies and 2.6 million jobs, of which 1.4 million people are working directly for insurance companies (III 2015).

MICROECONOMIC RISK-TAKING AND GROWTH

To understand the close relationship between insurance and economic growth, one has to go back to the microeconomic foundations and decision-making processes that underlie economic growth. Unlike banking activities—which can support growth through the provision of credit, coupled with the creation of money, leverage, and maturity transformation, and which are thus reflected directly in the economic cycle—insurance contributes to economic growth at a microeconomic level.

Most human activities are coupled with uncertainty—starting from life itself, health, economic opportunity, future standards of living, and others. Individuals therefore develop complex decision-making routines to cope with uncertainty and continuous risk-taking in decisions. The ability to cope with perpetual uncertainty is so essential that psychiatrists find that 'intolerance to uncertainty' is a source of major mental disorders (Paulus and Yu 2012).

Economic growth, as most other 'man-made' processes, is rooted in decisions that involve taking risks, be it financial, human, reputational, or other. In industrialized and capitalist societies, the scope of risks goes beyond individuals' capacities to bear them. This calls for the advanced forms of personal and collective risk-management mechanisms that are the essence of insurance activities.

It is not surprising therefore that insurance has historically grown exponentially, in line with the Industrial Revolution, when the technological, technical, and social risks to be taken became larger than individuals could bear. With the development of factories and modern capitalism, entrepreneurs[7] became exposed to uncertainties that could destroy their business and reputation, leaving them unable to restart their activities using their own means (Ewald 1999).

Beyond the first steps of the Industrial Revolution, all industrial activities, even those that are not seen as particularly innovative, embed uncertainty, mostly in the form of technical and technological risks. Such risks can come from a lack of scientific knowledge about technical developments, from unequal understanding of the nature of the risks and vulnerabilities, and from a lack of awareness of actual conditions of use of a product or from natural risks.

INSURANCE AS A COLLECTIVE RISK-MANAGEMENT TOOL FOR A FRACTION OF THE RISKS

To manage this general uncertainty and the risks it creates for individuals, companies, and societies, insurance systems based on pooling and mutualization emerged early in human history. Their sophistication increased alongside the growing complexity of risk arising.

Accordingly, since modern insurance companies came into existence in the late eighteenth century, the nature of the protection that they were able to provide evolved over time. This created a moving definition of the risks that insurance companies would accept holding, often described as those being 'insurable' (Thimann 2016). Specifically, insurance can be described as the business of accepting insurable risks, managing them, and providing compensation for possible losses.

Insurable risks are traditionally understood as those that are, at a given moment:

- faced by individuals or firms, but beyond their control;
- not systematic but subject to a defined and observed law of large numbers, or at least to a known maximal loss[8]—this latter condition making it possible to insure relatively new products or activities;

[7] The first formal theory of entrepreneurship by Cantillon (1755) described entrepreneurs as the self-employed who 'adjust themselves to risk' where the returns are uncertain. Although theorists disagree over exact definitions, entrepreneurs are widely considered to be attracted to risky ventures that promise above-average profit and growth (d'Amboise and Muldowney 1988).

[8] The maximum losses can be unknown for many reasons: by nature (systemic risk), because of state intervention (which, for example, may forbid caps on maximum indemnities), because of moral hazard (when insurees have no incentive for prevention) or anti-selection (when a lack

- non-financial—that is, not directly related to the economic and financial cycle.

The management of these different insurable risks then takes place through pooling—that is, the aggregation of a large number of similar risks; through mutualization—that is, linking the misfortune of the few to the fortune of the many, with insurers using reinsurance or hedging to eliminate the tail risk. Finally, it is important that in insurance, compensation takes place for losses that have actually occurred, not for hypothetical losses or for events that may have potentially caused losses.

Parametric insurance contracts are an interesting example of sophistication in insurance, which nonetheless respect its main features. Such contracts continue to make explicit the precise conditions that will lead to compensation, but are innovative in the sense that they relate to situations where the damage is not directly observable and is instead estimated *ex ante* by a number of proxies taking the form of observable external parameters (not market conditions and not 'events' as defined by an external committees as in the case of CDS.[9]) No profits are possible for policyholders and compensation is designed to increase according to the intensity of the damage. Examples include insurance against low snow levels for ski resort companies; or against droughts in specific regions for farmers.

At the level of the individual, insurance covers many of the risks involved in decision-making underlying growth: protection, health, and life insurance contracts typically allow people to engage in potentially riskier activities and environments. In turn, insurance has clear limits: mostly because of moral hazard and asymmetry of information, no contract exists to protect individuals for example from lower-than-expected wage increases or the impact of major technological changes in their professional sector that would make their skills obsolete.

At the corporate level, insurance is decisive to allow for trade and contract agreements (as included in typical counterparty risk and credit risk insurance contracts). Insurance also provides companies with protection against future consequences or outcomes of their actions, which were not measurable at the time of the contract, such as those included in civil, criminal, and administrative professional liability insurance products. Finally, insurance contracts provide means to enable continuity of service—and therefore sales and revenues—by protecting production tools—for example, protecting a factory

of information leads insurance companies to raise premiums and to cover only the higher-risk profiles).

[9] In the case of Credit Derivatives (typically CDS), Credit Derivatives Determinations Committees are established to make 'determinations' in connection with Credit Derivative Transactions, and in particular to decide if an 'event of default' has occurred to trigger the CDS payments.

against flood and fire, or a service company against the theft of its intellectual property or its client data.

Hence, insurance can be described as an enabler for people and companies to take risks and as a way to allow individuals' minds and assets to be productively and confidently invested in the economy. In the reverse sense, higher economic growth usually leads to larger risk-taking and greater financial inclusion and sophistication supporting insurance development.

2.2.2 *Insurance and Interest Rates*

A key channel to explain the positive impact of insurance on economic growth is the role it plays in reducing risk aversion (Gollier and Pratt 1996), thereby reducing the market risk premium and equity premium (while admittedly reducing in parallel individual precautionary savings and theoretically raising the risk free rate). Insurance also lowers term premiums, thereby easing credit conditions, facilitating investment, and increasing financial returns. The impact of insurance on the general level of interest rates has therefore to be seen as the result of the interaction of various simultaneous factors. The impact of insurance on the yield curve can be summarized as being that it allows 'lower interest rates and a longer maturity curve'.

INSURANCE AND ALLOCATION OF CAPITAL

A major driver of impact is the fact that the ability of an economy to allocate resources efficiently is highly determined by the level of development of its financial sector and the degree of financial intermediation. Therefore, in markets with low penetration of banks and insurance companies, adverse selection for formal insurance contracts or bank loans tends to arise, and lead to a combination of high interest rates and low growth, leading to a sub-optimal equilibrium.

In turn, the risk management provided by a complete insurance market allows the economy to allocate resources more effectively and reach a more efficient mix of activities, as higher risk-taking usually means higher returns, productivity, and growth.

This allocation process is based on the identification and standardization of risks and contracts, as well as the pricing of risk generated by insurance companies and then disclosed and shared with the entire economy. This pricing and signalling of risk is a key tool for helping resources to be allocated more productively. The allocation signal provided by insurers reduces the transaction costs of investors and borrowers by enabling them to identify underlying risks carried by specific projects.[10]

[10] As USAID (2006) points it out: 'It is not surprising that insurance is generally a necessary precondition in many mortgage finance markets and large-scale industrial investments.'

In doing so, insurance increases expected investment returns by reducing the costs of risk financing (Webb et al. 2002). Life insurance can increase productivity by reducing the demand for liquidity in the whole economy as hinted by Skipper et al. (2000),[11] and by shifting resources from unproductive to more productive uses, thereby easing the funding conditions for a wider range of activities. This is similar to the impact of banking on investment quality (Pagano 1993).

INSURANCE AND CREDIT RISK

By providing a range of insurance services to firms and households against property losses, damages, and negative events affecting loan repayment abilities, insurers effectively help lower credit risk and therefore contribute to the development of credit markets.

Non-life insurance directly helps to reduce the likelihood of households or firms not being able to meet payments on the loans they contracted. Indeed, by covering households and companies from major losses provoked by hazards (such as fire, accidents, sickness), non-life insurance helps to smooth available income profiles, allowing them to meet regular interest payments on their loans, thereby reducing the share of non-performing loans at the macroeconomic level and reducing funding costs and interest rates offered by banks (Garmaise and Moskowitz 2009).

In 2013, higher non-life insurance premiums, which also reveal a greater general economic development, were associated with lower aggregated value of non-performing loans in OECD countries. Figure 2.4 illustrates an empirical correlation between repayment ability through the ratio of non-performing loans to total loans and the penetration rate of non-life insurance in the main OECD countries in 2013. Further research and analysis could be performed to test these observations over time and geographies.

Insurance development can also be specifically targeted at increasing loan repayment abilities and confidence, through trade and credit insurance. Credit insurance protects companies against the failure of their customers to pay their trade credit debts: credit insurance helps in managing account receivables and mitigates losses in the event of non-payment. Such contracts naturally improve banking relationships and access to finance, and ultimately access to credit at lower interest rates.

[11] 'Insurers create liquidity. Insurers invest the funds entrusted to them by their customers to make long-term loans and other investments. Policyholders, however, have immediate access to loss payments and savings while borrowers need not repay their loans immediately. If all individuals instead undertook equivalent direct lending, the proportion of their personal wealth held in long-term, illiquid assets would be unacceptably high. Insurers and other financial intermediaries thereby reduce the illiquidity inherent in direct lending.'

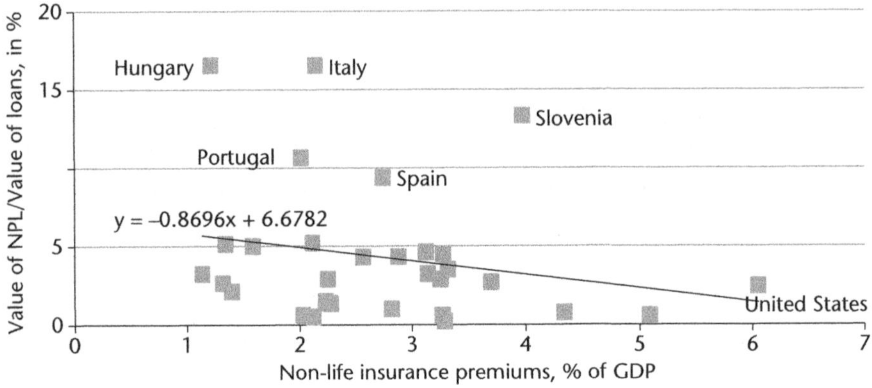

Figure 2.4. Correlation between NPL value and non-life insurance penetration in 2013[1]

[1] For all the studies included in the section on insurance and interest rates, insurance penetration data are those of OECD's main database, covering the period 2004–2013 for 34 OECD countries.

Source: World Bank, OECD, NPLvalue/Lvalue = -0.8696 Non-life premiums + 6.6782

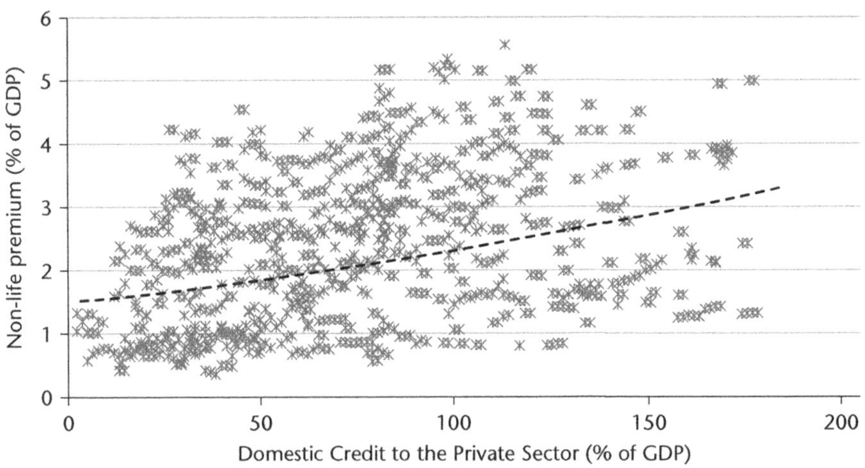

Figure 2.5. Correlation between non-life insurance and credit

Source: USAID (2006)

As a consequence, insurance provision helps to improve the overall efficiency of the financial sector, notably by facilitating the provision of credit to the private sector. There was a strong correlation between the latter and the amount of non-life premiums in fifty-nine developed and developing countries between 1960 and 2000 (see Figure 2.5).

Through this angle, insurance development is a necessary condition for banks and financial markets to develop. The development of life insurance companies and pension funds is specifically associated with more efficient banking systems (Impavido et al. 2001) and the development of securities markets (Vittas 1998).

INSURERS' INVESTMENT STRATEGIES AND LONG-TERM PREMIUMS

As institutional investors, insurers also reduce long-term premiums through their purchase of long-term assets and by raising the time horizon of savings that they allow through the collective and durable nature of life insurance. Without life insurance, households may well also purchase long-term assets directly, but life insurance also organizes the intergenerational risk-sharing that the individuals' strong preference for liquidity (Skipper et al. 2000) does not allow and, by acting as a perpetual investor, systematically extends the investment horizon beyond a single generation.

This 'perpetual investor' is responsible for honouring its commitments to its policyholders over several decades and the profile of its investments must therefore reflect it. This is achieved through the Assets and Liabilities Management strategy, which aims to match duration on both sides of the balance sheet and which explains in particular the strong demand for long-term assets, be they government bonds or infrastructure.

By increasing the demand for long-term assets with stable income flows, insurers reduce the term premium on the fixed income market as illustrated by the observations presented below, on the observed negative relationship between life insurance penetration and ten- and thirty-year bond yields. For OECD countries over the period 2004–2013, our basic estimates with simple linear regressions show that a one GDP-point increase in life-insurance premiums is associated to a 0.21 percentage point decrease in ten-year sovereign bond yields and a 0.20 percentage point decrease in thirty-year sovereign bond yields. These first illustrative results (see Figures 2.6 and 2.7) need to be further investigated over time and geographics.

This long-term bias can also lead insurers to favour long-term holding of assets such as infrastructure investments, particularly in the context of overall low interest rates in bond markets. For developing countries, the greater development of insurance and opening to investments from international insurance companies are consequently often seen as a welcome step for having large infrastructure projects being funded,[12] and contributing to greater growth potential and economic activities, with a large economic multiplier.

[12] 'Contractual savings institutions, such as pension funds and life insurance companies, are particularly suited to making long-term investments. These institutions levy fixed premiums, have steady and predictable cash inflows, and incur long-term liabilities, making them ideal suppliers of term finance for infrastructure projects' (World Bank 1994).

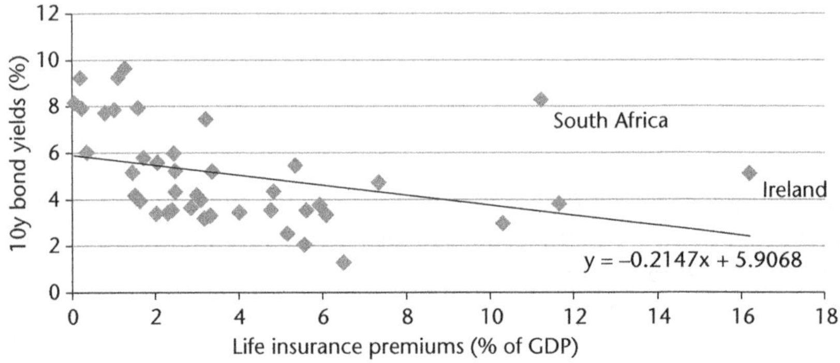

Figure 2.6. Average 10-year sovereign bond yields and life insurance penetration, 2004–2013[1]

[1] Simple averages over the available data periods, in most cases 2004–2013, but most observations are missing, especially for non-OECD countries; in this case the average is made over available years of observation.

Estimated impact: Av10YByields = –0.2147 AvLifepene + 5.9068

Source: Reuters, OECD, A one GDP-point increase in life insurance premiums is associated with a decrease in 10 year sovereign bond yields of 0.21 percentage point (impact estimated with simple linear regression)

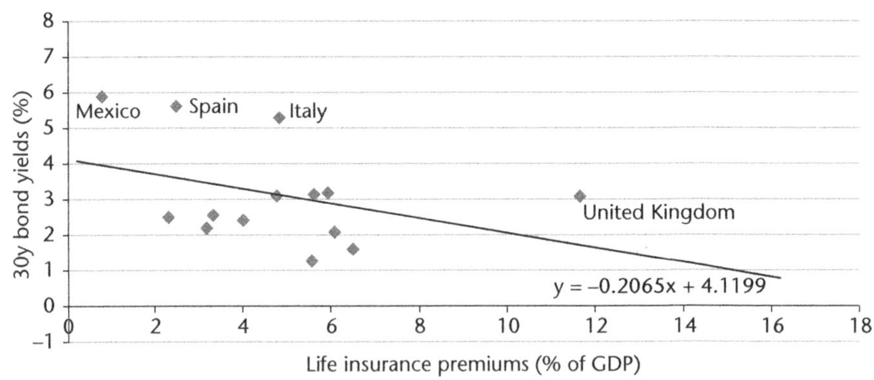

Figure 2.7. Average 30-year bond yields and life insurance penetration in OECD countries emitting at this horizon, 2004–2013

Estimated impact: Av30YByields = –0.2065 AvLifepene + 4.1199

Source: Reuters, OECD

2.2.3 *Insurance and Savings*

By easing decision-making in the face of risks and uncertainty, a direct role of insurance is to optimize savings at the individual level by reducing its precautionary component and therefore optimizing capital allocation at the collective level thanks to pooling mechanisms (Guiso et al. 1992).

Insurance also enhances savings behaviour by providing incentives for long-term savings objectives and gives customers access to more competitive and long-term contractual savings vehicles than those offered by other financial institutions (USAID 2006).

INSURANCE AND PRECAUTIONARY SAVINGS

By providing a sense of safety and protection against risk, insurance contributes to reducing precautionary savings at the individual level and may therefore have potential negative consequences on growth. In fact, the impact of insurance is to lower sub-optimal precautionary savings at the individual level (typically small amounts of cash to face future shocks) and increase the collective optimization of savings to enhance investment. Individuals covered by a formal insurance contract use their remaining available income to invest and the insurance company also invests the collected premiums in the economy.

The provision of liquidity at the macro level is therefore optimized, enhanced, and stabilized over the long term, allowing investment to be larger and less volatile. These links between savings, insurance, and investments enhancing economic growth are particularly emphasized through the development of micro-insurance.

In the absence of risk-pooling mechanisms, plunges in incomes due to death, disability, and adverse agricultural outcomes often translate into substantial decreases in consumption and investment, which can permanently set back a poor family's livelihoods and prospects (Brainard 2008). When drought or floods lead to low agricultural yields, critical health interventions may be delayed, education of younger members of a household put on hold indefinitely, and land, livestock, or equipment sold to regain liquidity quickly.

There is evidence that micro-insurance can help prevent the adverse consequences of such disasters for households' human capital investments and their future productivity by enabling them not to give up their assets or reduce their consumption during crises (Janzen and Carter 2013).

Should there be no formal insurance, there is also extensive evidence that due to the expected catastrophic consequence of such losses, poor households and communities attempt to 'self-insure' through a combination of building assets, diversifying sources of income, implementing basic pooling schemes at the community level, or simply short-term hoarding. This all leads to sub-optimal allocation of capital in the economy and a lower level of investment due to lack of visibility on the actual nature and efficiency of the risk-mitigation strategy in place. In turn, formal insurance and the broader development of financial services create economic opportunities:

- by enabling people to manage their assets in a way that generates income and decisions options (Sutton and Jenkins 2007);

- by increasing investment, especially to enhance productivity in agriculture (Karlan et al. 2014).

EMPIRICAL RESULTS PRESENTED IN THE MICRO-INSURANCE LITERATURE

While the term 'micro-insurance' was first published around 1999, it is a part of micro-finance that has existed for a long time. Micro-insurance is designed to manage the risks faced by low-income people, through products tailored to their needs, income, and risk profile, and managed according to insurance principles. Operationally, the distinction between micro-insurance and typical insurance schemes is often made by regulatory authorities through placing a cap on the sum assured and/or premium, as an empirical means of ensuring that these products benefit low-income people (Churchill 2012).

The micro-insurance market is a particularly important and fast growing one, estimated at more than four billion people and a potential premium volume of U.S.$40 billion with Asia-Pacific being the largest regional market (Swiss Re 2010).

As hinted above, evidence has been widely provided that the development of micro-insurance induces economic benefits at both the micro- and macro-economic levels. This positive impact can first be linked to the very provision of formal insurance schemes instead of the informal ones prevailing in traditional or village societies.[13] Platteau (2000) stresses the imperfections carried by informal insurance mechanisms developed by small communities: restricted scope of risks and population covered, fragile (opportunistic entry or exit, low resistance to frequent shocks), unreliable in protecting the poorest households (and implicit or explicit denial of income redistribution through risk sharing), and susceptible to retarding capital accumulation and economic growth.

But even if formal insurance schemes may offer enhanced protection, which would in turn favour riskier and productivity-enhancing investments, such an impact is strongly linked to the very design of the insurance products and services, as shown by Munro (2015) in the case of farmers in rural India.

By providing external financial protection to poor households, micro-insurance can enable the beginning of specialization, as households do not need to resort to substitute and ineffective coping mechanisms.[14] Last but not

[13] In the case of an Indian village, Townsend (1994) provides a list of potential risk-bearing institutions in the absence of a formal insurance market: (i) diversification of a given farmer's landholding into various spatially separated plots and various crops; (ii) storage of grain from one year to the next; (iii) purchases and sales of assets such as bullocks and land; (iv) borrowing from village lenders or itinerant merchants and borrowing/lending more generally; (v) gifts and transfers from family networks.

[14] Such mechanisms can include depleting savings and additional supplies of goods like food and livestock, selling valuable and income-generating assets, borrowing at high interest rates,

least, insurance can also increase people's productivity by inducing healthier habits, as in the case of health insurance: there have been solid findings that health micro-insurance helps to reduce out-of-pocket health expenditure and increase the use of healthcare services (Radermacher et al. 2012). Polonsky et al. (2009) find that members of nine Oxfam operated Armenian micro health-insurance schemes visited health facilities three and a half times more often than uninsured persons.

2.3 Insurance and Stabilization of the Economic and Financial Cycle

> *If it was possible for me, I would write the word 'insurance' in each home and on each man's forehead, since I am so convinced that insurance can, at a moderate price, liberate families of irreparable catastrophes.*
>
> *Winston Churchill*

2.3.1 *Stabilization of the Economic Cycle Through the Insurance Products' Core Features*

Insurance has a key function of economic stabilizer in times of individual shocks, smoothing the consumption of individuals facing idiosyncratic shocks or aggregated shocks, such as natural catastrophes.

INSURANCE AND RESILIENCE IN CASE OF NATURAL CATASTROPHES
This stabilization role is visible when natural catastrophes hit lower income countries, where there is a lack of funding and prioritization of disaster preparedness activities.[15] As these countries may not have the funds or borrowing capacity to recover expeditiously from natural disasters, risk transfer to insurance markets can be particularly effective for these countries to avoid drastic disruptions to economic growth (Brassard and Raffin 2011). In addition, the international risk-sharing made possible by internationally active insurance companies allows for reduced premiums in countries with high risks of natural catastrophes, adding to the economic benefits of formal insurance in these countries and the smoothing effect that insurance has on national GDP growth (OECD 2000).

adjusting labour supply, altering purchases and consumption patterns or withdrawing children from school (Radermacher et al. 2012).

[15] In general, disasters are exacerbated by poverty, badly planned and badly managed urbanization, environmental degradation, and weak institutions for managing risk at local and national levels. These effects were exemplified by the Thailand and Cambodia floods of 2011.

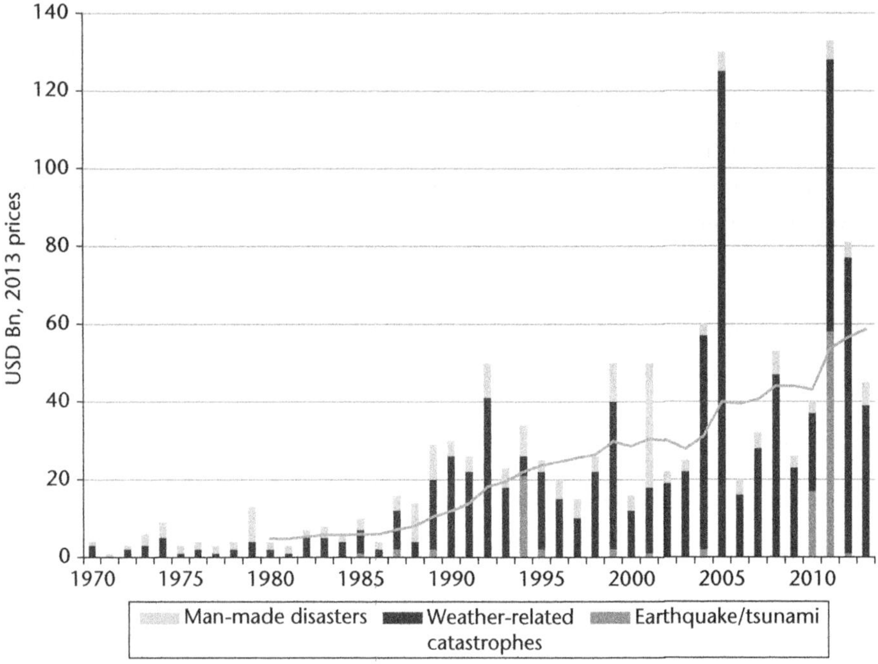

Figure 2.8. Insured catastrophe losses, 1970–2013 (in US$ billion)
Source: Swiss Re, Economic Research and Consulting

A positive trend in the insured losses due to natural catastrophes highlights the growing implicit resilience capacity of economies with increasing exposures to extreme and destructive events without having to suffer their full-blown economic consequences. According to Swiss Re (2014), it is estimated that almost one-third, or U.S.$45 billion, of the U.S.$140 billion in total economic losses from natural and man-made disasters in 2013 were covered by the insurance industry. Natural catastrophes generated claims of U.S.$37 billion and large man-made disasters generated insurance claims of U.S.$8 billion in 2013 (see Figure 2.8).

INSURANCE AND STABILIZATION OF LONG-TERM INCOMES

A second function of insurance is to protect savings and retirement income thanks to modern and innovative products. Various insurance products and services enable people to undertake actions that require projection into the future and where choices therefore rely on estimated permanent income (Friedman 1957).

Variable annuities are a good example of individuals' incomes stabilization at the individual level provided by insurers. Such contracts enable policyholders to diversify their savings allocation towards a wider and potentially more profitable range of investment products while benefiting from future minimum guaranteed incomes.[16] These guarantees prevent households from withdrawing their investment in the event of a market fall and thus from experiencing losses as they are insured that their future annuities will be based on high points. In that sense, insurance can stabilize incomes when it continues to rely on pooling and mutualization of individual, non-financial risks.

A second example is unemployment insurance attached to mortgages, which enables people facing unemployment to maintain the needed level of income to meet their payments. When an economic downturn occurs and the unemployment rate increases, without any insurance to allow for mortgage payments for home owners who lost their jobs—at least for a temporary period—one would see severe and immediate real estate price adjustments, banks affected by higher non-performing mortgages, and families losing shelter—three outcomes that would make an economic recession deeper.

2.3.2 *Stabilization of the Financial Cycle Through Long-Term Orientation*

As mentioned earlier, insurance is a key source of stable funding, and therefore stabilization, for the global financial markets and economy, as it fosters lending and investment with long-term perspective. Looking at the U.S. economy, the insurance sector has been historically substantially more stable than the banking sector. Insurance is five times less volatile than aggregate GDP, while investment banking is almost twice as volatile as aggregate GDP (Gollier et al. 2014).

Behind this stability is the business model of insurance, which is different from banks in its timing and functioning. Insurers can be seen as 'future-oriented': they collect the current liquidity of individuals and organizations to fund their future lifestyles and projects. In contrast, banks can be seen as 'present-oriented': through credit, they fund today's projects and lifestyles by pre-funding future liquidity. This difference in relationship with time is visible in the nature and importance of liquidity for insurers and banks: banks are extremely and permanently dependent on the market liquidity to stay solvent; while insurers are liquidity-rich and can well be temporarily lacking capital while not failing.

Insurers have long-term, stable liabilities which they match with their assets profile. The result is that insurers are net suppliers of stable capital in the

[16] Depending on contractual terms, the initial guaranteed investment (and future payments to the policyholder) can be revised upward on a minimum regular growth rate basis or benefit from a 'ratchet effect' based on the underlying assets' performance.

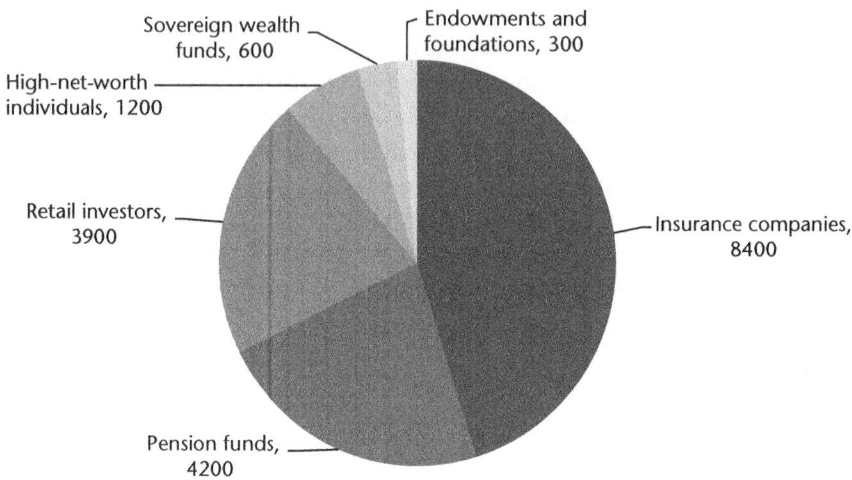

Figure 2.9. European institutional assets under management, 2012 (in EURO billion)
Source: Insurance Europe

economy. Life insurers are large players in financial markets. In 2010, they managed U.S.$18.7 trillion of assets, or 11 per cent of the world's total financial assets (Geneva Association 2010). The insurance sector is also the largest institutional investor in the European Union, with over €8.4 trillion of assets under management invested in the economy in end 2012, which represent 60 per cent of the GDP (see Figure 2.9).

Finally, insurers have a natural attraction for financial assets that can deliver stable returns and income flows over the long run. In 2013, the largest component of insurance companies' portfolio in four major markets (France, Germany, the U.K. and the United States) were public and private bonds (63 per cent) followed by listed equities (12 per cent), according to the OECD (see Figure 2.10).

2.3.3 *The Role and Use of Derivatives and Alternative Risk Transfer Schemes*

To offer credible protection to policyholders and reinforce the positive impact of insurance on growth, insurers need to be able to withstand external shocks while honouring commitments to policyholders. To achieve this self-reinforcement, insurance companies rely on derivatives for limiting financial risk, 'Alternative Risk Transfer' schemes, and reinsurance treaties to limit peak exposure to catastrophes (storms, earthquakes, pandemics, large losses).

Derivatives are unfunded instruments essentially allowing the transfer of financial risk to another investor. As diversification is the essential foundation

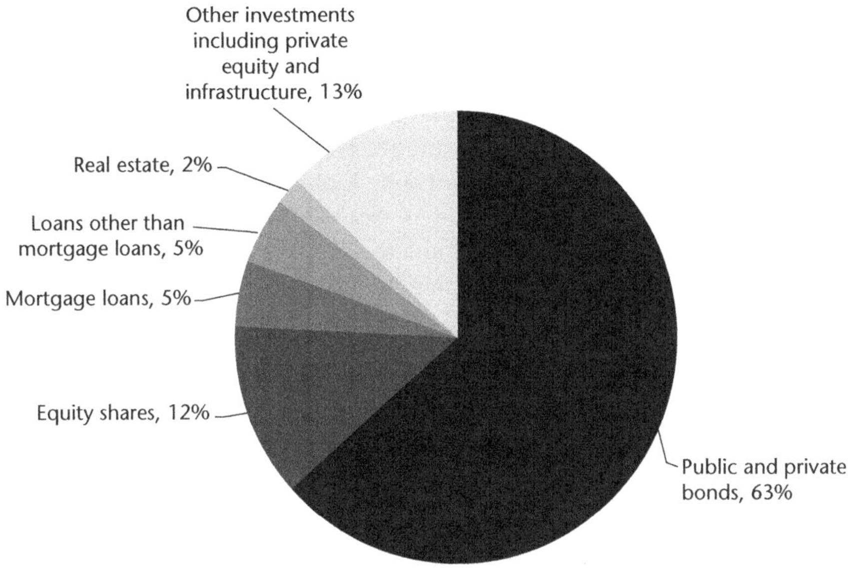

Figure 2.10. Portfolio allocation of insurance companies in France, Germany, U.K. and U.S., 2013 (in % of total assets on balance sheet)
Source: OECD Insurance Statistics, 2014

of the modern portfolio management (Markowitz 1952, Sharpe 1964), financial risk is not increased but transferred to willing investors.

Derivatives are essential to buffer potential shocks affecting the insurance balance sheet and make credible the provision of guarantees over time. As insurance companies invest premiums received from policyholders into financial markets and, as a result, get a pure long exposure to financial markets, they need to 'hedge' against this undiversified risk and therefore resort to financial risk-transfer instruments—derivatives—to limit their exposure to large capital markets variance. From an operational perspective, derivatives allow an insurer to smooth the income stemming from its investment decisions, and to be less exposed to financial cycles and corporate insolvency risks.

Without derivatives, insurance companies would be completely exposed to financial shocks and the result would be a weakening of the whole financial system.

2.3.4 *The Impact of Recent Regulations on the Stabilizing Role of Insurance*

There is evidence that the development of insurance markets contributes to the health and stability of securities markets (Impavido et al. 2001). Insurers are indeed active, directly or indirectly, in many financial markets, and help to provide liquidity through various techniques and tools such as securities lending, as hinted by the Bank of England (2011).

At the same time, some questions have emerged about the riskier and more pro-cyclical investment biases of insurance companies in recent years. Such behaviour cannot be understood without looking at the evolution of the regulatory environment. For example, Solvency II calibration and IFRS accounting standards had counterproductive effects on behaviour in financial markets even before their actual implementation.

Intrinsic incentives were perceived as twisted towards: more short-termism; stronger investment biases towards government bonds; and transition to a uniform balance sheet composition and maturity across the insurance sector given the single benchmarks provided by regulators (typically with a volatility adjuster in Solvency II being industry-wide and based on a single investment benchmark portfolio for each country, defined as the average portfolio in the country the previous year).

Moreover, in a period of durably low interest rates environment, insurers suffer from regulatory developments to increase their exposure to asset classes generating higher returns (equity, alternative investments such as real estate or infrastructure, Della Croce 2013). Frameworks such as Solvency 2—which indeed require higher capital charges for riskier asset classes (typically listed equity shares, see Table 2.1)—are having a massive impact on insurers' portfolio allocation and ultimately on their capacity to contribute to the long-term, stable financing of the economy, as highlighted by changes in investment allocation since the early 2000s (see Figure 2.11). In this regard, short-term biases, such as mark-to-market valuations and risk-based solvency standards, have hindered the ability of pension funds and insurers to invest in infrastructure and other alternative asset classes (Della Croce and Yermo 2013).

Table 2.1. Solvency II calibration of capital requirements, current standard formula[17]

Listed equity in an OECD country	39% (+/−10%)
Non-listed equity and capital investment, and listed equity outside OECD countries	49% (+/−10%)
BBB corporate bonds or loan	12.5% (for 5 years)
BBB securitization	15% (for 5 years)
Infrastructure	Treated like corporate risk*
Sovereign bonds	0%

* Currently under revision

[17] Reading explanation: for 100 euros of investment in a listed equity, insurance companies applying Solvency II standard formula must hold 39 euros in capital.

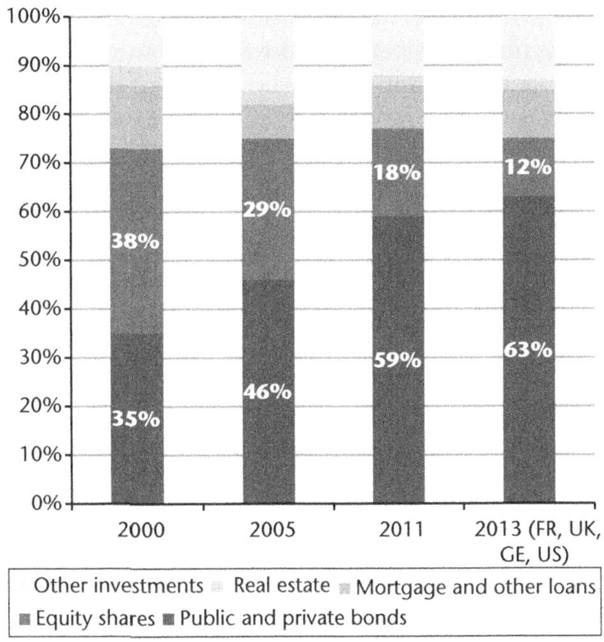

Figure 2.11. Direct domestic life insurers' asset allocation in broad Europe 2000, 2005, and 2011 (as % of total assets)

[1] Based on available data among the 27 European countries (including Turkey and Russia) referred in OECD insurance indicators database.

Source: OECD Insurance Statistics[1]

2.4 Insurance and Distribution

2.4.1 *The Unequal Nature of Risk*

Insurance creates an invisible net of solidarity between economic agents, interconnecting them in time and place, around shared preferences and priorities. Insurance gives economic materiality to the concept of solidarity (Ewald 1999), and organizes it financially through its fundamental principles of pooling—that is, aggregating risks—and mutualizing—that is, pricing them depending on their statistical occurrence for the larger pool and not for the individual.

As is often said, insurance is about connecting 'the misfortunes of the few to the fortunes of the many' (Thimann 2015), which naturally operates a form of distribution. This distribution of income happens *ex post* and is linked to an accident—which is fundamentally different from the one allowed by public redistribution, which happens based on the comparison of *ex ante* and desired *ex post* income levels. Risks are indeed not equally shared among individuals in society and in time for a given individual (Ewald 1999), and this inequality has little to do with initial income levels.

There is also a genuinely social dimension of risk, and technology contributes to increasing inequality between those who control and understand the industrial cycle—and risk—and those who are affected by it. Multiplicity of risk is a new given in modern societies, and how to share the burden of its consequences has become central to the social and economic decisions of public authorities and states, local professional communities, and companies, and over time.

2.4.2 *Intergenerational Distribution*

The mechanism of risk pooling and the strategy of long-term investment and holding of securities enable insurers and pension funds to deliver income redistribution between generations. This intergenerational sharing of financial risk by life insurers has an impact on intergenerational welfare that has been deemed equivalent to an increase in asset returns by as much as a full 1 per cent every year (Gollier 2008). This social benefit is obtained by an anticyclical retention of the return of the general account, as well as the guarantees provided by the insurer over time.

In addition, 'there exist intergenerational cross-subsidization effects in guaranteed interest rate life and pension contracts as the different generations partially share the same reserves. Early generations build up bonus reserves, which are left with the company at expiry of the contract' (Døskeland and Nordahl 2006) and then benefit later generations.

2.4.3 *'Inter-Individuals' Distribution*

Insurance is also a redistributive force among individuals at any given point in time—theoretically independent from the level of their income.

Insurers appear to be actively recycling and redistributing liquidity (claims and payments) among economic agents towards those having faced some risks. This is different from the redistribution operated by public authorities, which looks at economic needs and means to transfer income from the 'richer' to the 'poorer'. As highlighted earlier, mutualization and pooling of risks are the natural engines for this redistribution to happen—typically for P&C markets.

In addition, mechanisms such as participating contracts (designed so that the pool of policyholders retains a part of the financial risks linked to the investments of their savings and premiums) create redistribution between individuals, as some would have entered in respective high/low market environments and then exited in low/high ones, which offsets other individuals with opposite decisions.

To illustrate the scale of the redistribution coming from these pooling mechanisms, U.S.$2.6 trillion and U.S.$2 trillion of respectively life and non-life insurance premiums were collected in 2012 around the world, representing 6.5 per cent of world GDP (Swiss Re 2013). At the European level, premiums collected amounted to €1.4 trillion in 2012 (7.7 per cent of EU GDP), which equals an average of €1887 per capita in premiums (10 per cent of EU average income). See Figures 2.12 and 2.13.

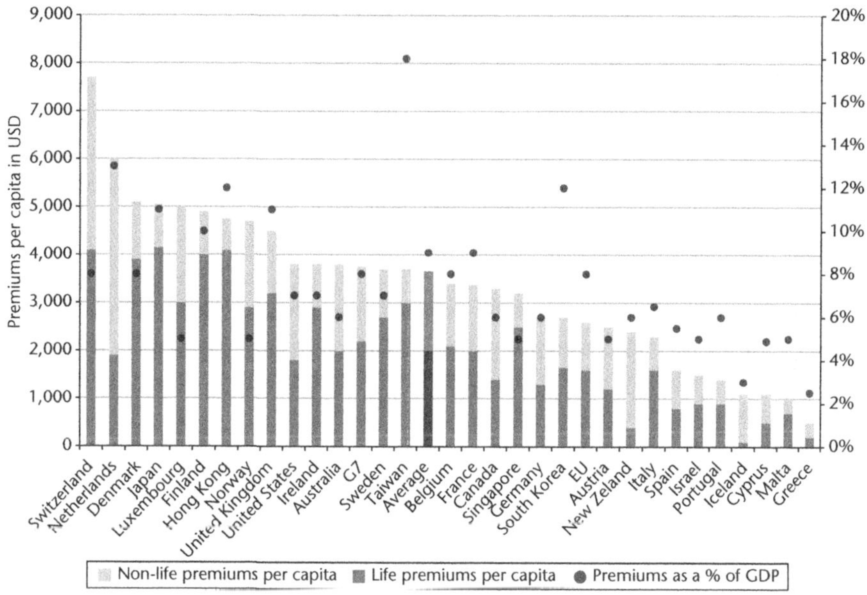

Figure 2.12. Insurance density and penetration in advanced markets, 2012 (in US$ per capita and % of GDP)

Source: Swiss Re, Economic Research and Consulting

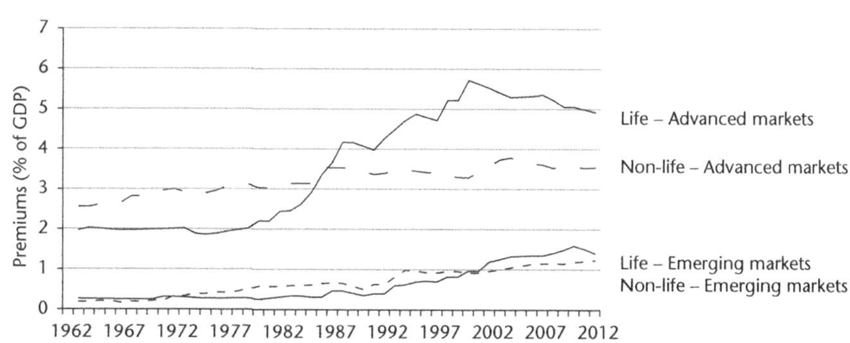

Figure 2.13. Life and non-life insurance penetration, 1962–2012 (in % of GDP)

Source: Swiss Re, Economic Research and Consulting

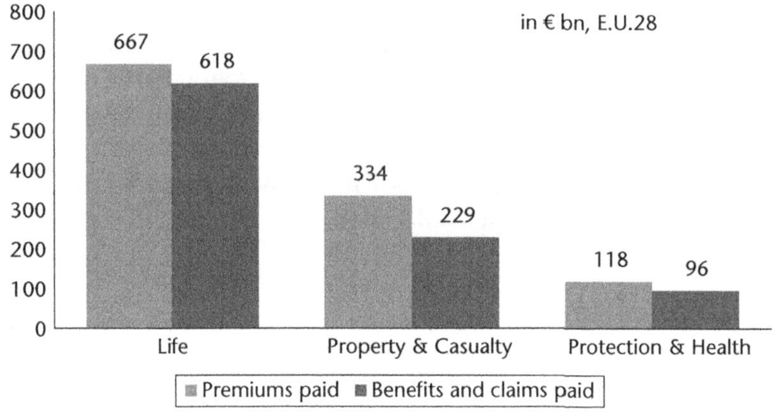

Figure 2.14. Premiums collected and claims paid, European Union, 2011 (in EURO billion)
Source: Insurance Europe

These collected premiums have to be put in perspective of the benefits and claims paid. At the European scale, €0.9 trillion benefits and claims were paid in the EU28 in 2011, which represents the equivalent of Spain's GDP (see Figure 2.14).

2.5 Insurance: Innovation, Limits and the Future

2.5.1 *Insurance and Innovation*

> *The UK insurance industry is known for its innovation and entrepreneurialism, typified through the modest beginnings of Edward Lloyd's coffee house. The role played by the insurance sector in future will be contingent upon maintaining that tradition of competition and innovation.*
>
> *Paul Fischer*

By creating confidence and reducing uncertainty, insurance is an enabler of human and technical endeavours, through its economic function, its long-term investments, as well as the diversified nature and size of insurers' balance sheets.

The nature of risk has followed economic progress, and insurance has been created as a tool to address new risks and limit their potential consequences. In the eighteenth century, the new risks were those taken by entrepreneurs during the Industrial Revolution; in the nineteenth century, those relating to work accidents; and in the twentieth century, those linked to work contracts and more widely the overall environment of economic development (health, technology, and the environment). Over time, society went from a perception of risk to one of catastrophes, given the increasing power of industrial activities (wider effect and more lasting effect). This mechanically leads insurance companies to follow, understand, and price innovation and new risks.

2.5.2 *Insurance and the Paradox of Innovation*

More widely, insurance entertains a paradoxical relationship with innovation, as it allows innovation in particular by protecting the innovator from external shocks and protecting its wealth, while insurance simultaneously limits innovation by being rather slow in covering new types of risks or adapting its own functioning to technological changes.

Facing the unknown, insurance is what makes the risk acceptable, or at least bearable, but insurers are not ready to insure immediately everything that is new (Biener et al. 2015), as currently for instance cyber risk or driverless cars. In turn, as soon as insurability and the fact that insurance companies, regulators, and society accept a new risk to be collectively covered is granted, scaling up of a technology beyond the initial circles of pioneers and entrepreneurs can be very fast. In that sense, insurance is a signal of the 'technological and technical' frontiers of a given time.

Insurance and innovation in insurance mechanisms have therefore quite naturally been closely linked to many great human projects, by taking risks and allowing others to take some by strategically mobilizing savings previously pooled. History is filled with such examples:

- 1400 years BC, stonemasons in Lower Egypt were among the first to establish an aid fund in case of accidents on very large projects such as tombstones and pyramids.
- The U.K., which is commonly seen as the birthplace of the Industrial Revolution, turned to various forms of insurance early on its economic development, thereby contributing to the development of modern insurance market know-how and practices (USAID 2006).
- The first two skyscrapers—the New York's Equitable Life Assurance Building built in 1870 and Chicago's Home Insurance Building built in 1885—were, as their names indicate, funded by and built for insurance companies.
- If not for life insurance, major entrepreneurial successes such as Disneyland or McDonald's would not exist. Stanford University might have been a short-lived tribute to a son who died young.
- As materialized after the 9/11 attack, airline activities, even if not considered as extremely innovative anymore by the public, were immediately interrupted when there was a lack of insurance coverage. In this case, (re)

insurers suspended their liability cover in case of terrorist attacks as they estimated these attacks had changed the nature of the risk. The suspension ended only when governments accepted a private–public partnership with the Terrorism Risk Insurance Act for instance in the United States. This illustrates that no economic activity can be pursued without a sufficient insurance cover, especially for liability risks.

INSURANCE AND INNOVATION: THE EXAMPLE OF THE HEALTHCARE MARKET

The healthcare market is traditionally characterized by a tension between the social need for affordable medication and the need for permanent innovation (new drugs, etc.). This tension can be seen as a potential time trade-off between rewarding today's patients with lower prices or rewarding tomorrow's patients by inducing more innovation. Such a difficult choice is a one that insurance can help to solve.

Lakdawalla and Sood (2005) show that in the particular case of medical care innovation, society may be able to achieve efficiency for both today's and tomorrow's patients thanks to the existence of a health insurance market that allows for a two-part pricing strategy for innovators. Such a strategy consists of charging consumers with an upfront fee equal to net consumer surplus to reward innovation in exchange for the possibility of buying as much of the innovation as they like at marginal cost. As the authors explain, health insurance works in the same way: policyholders pay *ex ante* premiums in exchange for lower prices *ex post* in case of illness.

2.5.3 *The Limits of Insurance in the Economy*

INSURANCE DEVELOPMENT IS NOT INFINITE, NOR ARE ITS IMPACTS

Insurance can surely not be an end in itself (Radermacher et al. 2012) and the limits to its further development in mature markets clearly proves it. The 'S-curve' relationship between the penetration rate of insurance and economic growth reminds us that at a certain stage the former can no longer outpace the latter.[18] The reason is that increasing risks and product complexity makes insurance more expensive to potential buyers (mainly companies), which prefer to retain greater amounts of risks. The recent development of self-insurance subsidiaries, so-called captives, within large manufacturing or services companies is a good example of this trend.

[18] When no 'insurance gap' prevails, i.e. when financial institutions and economic activity no longer outpace insurance supply, no potential economic benefit from an insurance market intervention can therefore be expected by private companies (USAID 2006).

THE 'UNINSURABILITY' OF CERTAIN RISKS

As described earlier, insurability follows a certain number of criteria. Some risks appear to be outside the scope of 'insurability', such as cyber risk at the moment. The debate about insurability is complex. First, there are the technical barriers, both statistical and linked to the understanding of the nature of the risk itself: does the risk obey the law of large numbers and do we have a sense of the potential maximum loss? This is a difficult question with few historical views on the nature of the risk (see paragraph on Insurance as a Collective Risk-Management Tool).

Second, there are the social and political questions: is the risk one wants to insure a public good and therefore should it be covered by the state or can private sector companies manage it introducing selective pricing methods?

And third, there are the more cultural questions: is this a risk we can let exist and for which one should invent compensation mechanisms—or should it be totally prevented by forbidding any activity leading to it? This last question is typically at play in debates on the primacy to be given to prevention over compensation (as in the 'precaution principle' introduced in the French Constitution). It highlights a shift in social preferences and tolerance to the very idea of risk, even before considering its consequences.

Biener et al. (2015) specifically question the adequacy of insurance for managing cyber risks by extracting 994 cases of cyber losses from an operational risk database and analysing their statistical properties. Their findings suggest the development of a sustainable cyber insurance market may be hindered by problems such as highly interrelated losses and severe information asymmetries. They also highlight the need for a discussion on the potential public good characteristic of privacy, data protection and more broadly cyber security.

THE RISK OF OVER-INSURANCE

A potential downside of insurance occurs if people and companies 'over-insure' themselves or duplicate coverage for a same type of risk. In such a world, excessive caution and premiums collection would lead to a sub-optimal allocation of resources, lower liquidity for investments, and riskier projects, as well as lower consumption and demand for goods and services. Insurance would in this case clearly act as a disincentive to take useful risks or to adapt one's behaviour or organization.[19]

Too high levels of insurance are also not optimal as they might deter useful actions to prevent the risk or protect oneself against its consequences. Insurance indeed functions based on the assumption that insurees have natural

[19] One could also argue that over-insurance could induce excessive risk-taking but such possibility is balanced by insurers' pricing practices through bonus-malus mechanisms. We consider downsides with regard to ineffective allocation of resources.

incentives to manage the risk and implement expected preventive actions. In that sense, a traditional result of insurance economics is that an insurance deductible is optimal to create this minimal level of incentives towards basic risk management. A good counter-example is given by Annan and Schlenker (2014) who show that U.S. federal crop insurance may, in some cases, give farmers a disincentive from engaging in possible adaptation strategies to cope with extreme heat, thereby exacerbating potential losses.

INSURANCE COMPANIES CAN FAIL

Just like any other business, insurance companies can fail (Gollier 2014). Their specific economic and social role within society has justified the long existence of a stringent regulatory framework as insurers' liabilities to their policyholders often extend to decades. But the Asset and Liability Management implemented by insurers makes their risk of failure not only less likely to happen but also much more manageable than failures from other types of financial institutions.

First, insurance companies operate a thorough selection of risks they cover among their policyholders and cover themselves through diversification, hedging, and reinsurance.

Second, in case of financial distress, 'insurance runs' are less likely to occur as the termination of a life insurance contract generally leads to financial penalties for policyholders, therefore ensuring a form of bail-in capacity for insurance companies. For non-life insurance, such 'runs' are actually impossible unless there is massive and coordinated fraud, as the payment is triggered by an external event, and not controlled by the policyholder (a car accident, a natural catastrophe, etc.)

Third, insurance companies are, within the scope of their traditional activities, much less exposed to financial risks as they are much less indebted and leveraged than other financial institutions.

2.5.4 *The Future of Insurance*

Insurance as we know it today is the result of the conjunction of many different inputs: social preferences around risk management; appetite for monetized and financial tools; a capitalist economic model; and subtle division of roles between private and public agents around large social risk (health, longevity, and climate).

The degree of financial sophistication we have reached today will therefore undoubtedly be put under pressure by many changes and challenges created by our economic, financial, and social evolutions. The role that insurance plays today in our economic functioning is likely to evolve, because of major changes in: (1) technology and Big Data capabilities, in particular opening new understanding or risks and inter-individual financial interdependencies (crowd-funding, peer-insurance, etc.); (2) the very nature of risk as highlighted by the highly correlated, unpredictable, and interdependent nature of the global climate risk; and (3) renewed social expectations around risk, with a much lower acceptance of risk itself, and the primacy given to prevention over compensation and reparation.

2.6 Conclusion

This chapter has presented a framework for describing the variety of contributions that modern insurance makes to macroeconomic performance. There are three main levers: the role of insurance in the mechanisms of economic growth; the role of insurance in stabilizing individual incomes and the economic cycle; and the role of insurance in redistributing risk and misfortunes among people and over time.

The role of modern insurance is multilayered. By managing risks, insurance allows individuals and companies to take risks and innovate. Insurance also reduces the level of interest rates, by lowering default probabilities and investing with long-term horizons. Finally, insurance modifies the level and allocation of individual and aggregated savings, leading to a more optimal allocation of capital. By doing so, it has an impact on the economic cycle and on the distribution of income and shocks across economic agents.

Interestingly, some of these observations rely on the long established methods of pooling and mutualizing risk, while others are linked to the financial, statistical, and sophisticated form that insurance has taken since the late nineteenth century.

Given the major changes in the risks created by technology and social evolutions, the new tools and capabilities emerging as well as the social acceptance of risk and the growing importance given to prevention, one cannot predict how the macroeconomic role of insurance will evolve. But as all human societies organized themselves over time to reduce uncertainty by collectively managing risks, we can trust that insurance mechanisms will continue to exist in some form.

Acknowledgements

Excellent research assistance by Nacim Dardour is gratefully acknowledged. Many ideas and concepts in this chapter benefited from discussions with Denis Duverne, François Ewald, Christian Gollier, Charles Moussier, Laura Munro, Romain Rancière, Jean-Marc Tallon, Philippe Trainar, and Robert B. Zoellick. Views expressed are those of the authors.

References

Adams, M.J., Andersson, L.F., and Lindmark, M. (2005): 'The Historical Relation between Banking, Insurance and Economic Growth in Sweden: 1830 to 1998', *Department of Economic Discussion Paper*, SAM, 26.

Annan, Francis and Wolfram Schlenker (2014): 'Federal Crop Insurance and the Disincentives to Adapt to Extreme Heat', NBER Working Papers.

Arena, Marco (2006): 'Does Insurance Market Activity Promote Economic Growth? A Cross-Country Study for Industrialized and Developing Countries', *World Bank Policy Research Working Paper*, No. 4098.

Bank of England (2011): 'Developments in the Global Securities Lending Market', *Quarterly Bulletin* Q3.

Beck, T. and Levine, R. (2004): 'Stock Markets, Banks, and Growth: Panel evidence', *Journal of Banking and Finance*, 28(3): 423–42.

Biener, Christian et al. (2015): 'Insurability of Cyber Risk: An Empirical Analysis', *Working Papers on Finance No.2015/3*, University of St.Gallen, School of Finance.

Brainard, L. (2008): 'What is the Role of Insurance in Economic Development?', Zurich Government Industry Affairs Thought Leadership series. Zurich.

Brassard, C. and A. Raffin (2011): 'Resilience in Post Disaster Societies: From Crisis to Development', *Asian Journal of Social Science*, 39(4): 417–24.

Cantillon, Richard (1755): *Essai sur la nature du commerce en général.*

Churchill, Craig and Michal Matul (2012): *Protecting the Poor: A microinsurance compendium Vol II.* International Labour Organization.

D'Amboise, G. and M. Muldowney (1988): 'Management Theory for Small Business: Attempts and Requirements', *The Academy of Management Review*, 13(2): 226–40.

Della Croce, R. and Yermo, J. (2013): 'Institutional investors and infrastructure financing', *OECD Working Papers on Finance, Insurance and Private Pensions*, No.36, OECD Publishing.

Døskeland, Trond and A. Helge Nordahl (2006): 'Intergenerational Effects of Guaranteed Pension Contracts', *The Geneva Risk and Insurance Review 06/2008*, 33(1):19–46.

Enz, R. (2000): 'The S-Curve Relation between Per-Capital Income and Insurance Penetration', *Geneva Papers on Risk and Insurance*, 25 (3): 396–406.

Ewald, F. (1999): 'Le risque dans la société contemporaine'. In Tubiana M., Vrousos C., Carde C. and Pages J.-P., *Risque et Société*. Nucléon, Paris, pp. 41–54.

Fisher, Paul (2015): 'Regulation and the Future of the Insurance Industry', Speech given at the Westminster Business Forum Conference, Bank of England, 22 January.

Friedman, Milton (1957): *A Theory of the Consumption Function*, National Bureau of Economic Research, Princeton, NJ.

Garmaise, Mark and Tobias Moskowitz (2009): 'Catastrophic Risk and Credit Markets', *Journal of Finance*, 64 (2): April.

Gatzer, N. and H. Wesker (2012): 'A Comparative Assessment of Basel II/III and Solvency II', *Geneva Papers on Risk and Insurance* 37: 539–70.

Geneva Association (2010): 'Systemic Risk in Insurance: An Analysis of Insurance and Financial Stability', *A Special Report of the Geneva Association Systemic Risk Working Group.*

Gollier, Christian (2008): 'Intergenerational risk-sharing and risk-taking of a pension fund', *Journal of Public Economics*, 92, 1463–85.

Gollier, Christian and John W. Pratt (1996): 'Risk Vulnerability and the Tempering Effect of Background Risk', *Econometrica*, Econometric Society, 64(5): 1109–23, September.

Gollier, Christian et al. (2014): 'Analysis of Systemic Risk in the Insurance Industry', Toulouse School of Economics.

Guiso, Luigi, Tullio Jappelli, and Daniele Terlizzese (1992): 'Earnings Uncertainty and Precautionary Saving', *Journal of Monetary Economics, Elsevier*, 30(2): 307–37, November.

Han Liyan, Li Donghui, Fariborz Moshirian, and Yanhui Tian (2010): 'Insurance Development and Economic Growth', *Geneva Papers on Risk and Insurance*, 35: 183–99.

Impavido, Gregorio, Alberto R. Musalem, and Thierry Tressel (2001): 'Contractual Savings Institutions and Banks' Stability and Efficiency', World Bank, Washington, DC.

Insurance Europe (2014): *European Insurance—Key Facts.*

III Insurance Information Institute (2015): *A Firm Foundation – How Insurance Supports the Economy.*

Janzen, Sarah A. and Michael R. Carter (2013): 'The Impact of Micro Insurance on Consumption Smoothing and Asset Protection : Evidence from a Drought in Kenya', NBER Working Papers.

Karlan, Dean et al. (2014): 'Agricultural Decisions after Relaxing Credit and Risk Constraints', *The Quarterly Journal of Economics*. Oxford University Press, 129(2): 597–652.

Keynes, John Maynard (1936): Chapter 12 'The State of Long-Term Expectations' in *The General Theory of Employment, Interest and Money*. Macmillan, London.

Kugler, Maurice and Reza Ofoghi (2005): 'Does Insurance Promote Economic Growth?: Evidence from the UK', Working Paper, University of Southampton.

Lakdawalla, Darius and Neeraj Sood (2005): 'Insurance and Innovation in Health Care Markets', Working Paper No. 11602, NBER.

Lee, C.C., C.C. Lee, and Y.B. Chiu (2013): 'The Link between Life Insurance Activities and Economic Growth: Some New Evidence', *Journal of International Money and Finance*, 32: 405–27.

Markowitz, Harry M. (1952): 'Portfolio Selection', *The Journal of Finance*, 7: 77–91.

Munro, L. (2015): 'Risk Sharing, Networks and Investment Choices in Rural India', PhD research at the London School of Economics and Political Science.

Musgrave, R. (1959): *The Theory of Public Finance. A Study in Public Economy*. McGraw Hill, New York.

OECD (2000): 'Developing Life Insurance in Economies in Transition', OECD Workshop on Insurance in the Baltic States, Riga, Latvia, 14–15 December 2000.

Pagano, M. (1993): 'Financial markets and growth: An overview', *European Economic Review* 37: 613–22.

Paulus, Martin P. and Angela J. Yu (2012): 'Emotion and Decision-making: Affect-driven Belief Systems in Anxiety and Depression', *Trends in Cognitive Sciences September 2012*, 16 (9).

Platteau, Jean-Philippe (2000): 'Community Imperfections as an Obstacle to Participatory Development', Annual World Bank Conference on Development Economics, Washington, DC.

Polonsky, Jonny et al. (2009): 'Equity in Community Health Insurance Schemes: Evidence and Lessons from Armenia', *Health Policy Plan* 24 (3): 209–16.

Radermacher, R., H. McGowan, and S. Dercon (2012): What is the impact of microinsurance? Chapter 3 in *Microinsurance Compendium* Vol II.

Rajan, R. and Zingales, L. (1998): 'Financial Dependence and Growth', *American Economic Review* 88: 559–86.

Sharpe, W.F. (1964): 'A Simplified Model for Portfolio Analysis', *Management Science*, INFORMS, 9 (2): 211–40, August.

Skipper, Harold D. (1997): 'Foreign Insurers in Emerging Markets: Issues and Concerns', Occasional Paper 97–2, Center for Risk Management and Insurance.

Skipper, Harold D. Jr, C.V. Starr, and J. Mack Robinson (2000): 'Liberalization of Insurance Markets: Issues and Concerns', *Report as a part of the OECD Insurance and Private Pensions Compendium*, Book 1 Part 1:6.

Solow, Robert M. (1956): 'A Contribution to the Theory of Economic Growth', *The Quarterly Journal of Economics*, 70 (1): 65–94, February.

Sutton, Christopher N. and Beth Jenkins (2007): 'The Role of the Financial Services Sector in Expanding Economic Opportunity', CSR Initiative Report No. 19. Kennedy School of Government, Harvard University, Cambridge MA.

Swiss Re (2010): *Microinsurance: Risk Protection for 4 billion People,* Sigma Studies.

Swiss Re (2013): *World Insurance in 2012: Progressing on the Long and Winding Road to Recovery,* Sigma 3/2013, Sigma Studies.

Swiss Re (2014): *Natural Catastrophes and Man-made Disasters in 2013: Large Losses from Floods and Hail; Haiyan Hits the Philippines*. Sigma Studies.

Soo, Hak Hong (1996): 'Life Insurance and Economic Growth: Theoretical and Empirical Investigation', University of Nebraska: Dissertation.

Thimann, Christian (2016): 'What Is Insurance and How Does it Differ from General Finance?' in F. Hufeld et al. *The Economics, Regulation and Systemic Risk of Insurance Markets*, Oxford University Press.

Townsend, Robert M. (1994): 'Risk and Insurance in Village India', *Econometrica*, Econometric Society, 62 (3), pp 539–91, May.

USAID (2006): 'Assessment on How Strengthening the Insurance Industry in Developing Countries Contributes to Economic Growth'.

Vittas, Dimitri (1998): 'Institutional Investors and Securities Markets: Which Comes First?', *Policy Research Working Papers,* World Bank.

Webb, I., M.F. Grace, and H.D. Skipper (2002): 'The Effect of Banking and Insurance on the Growth of Capital and Output', Working Paper No. 2, Center for Risk Management and Insurance.

World Bank (1994): *World Development Report 1994: infrastructure for development—executive summary*, World Development Report; World Bank Group.

3

How the Insurance Industry Manages Risk

Denis Duverne and John Hele

The insurance industry is a market mechanism for the sharing of risk. Without it, risks would be borne solely by individuals, businesses, governments and other societal entities.[1]

3.1 Introduction

Consumers face many risks in their daily lives, such as health, property, and casualty risks. Examples include loss of income upon death or disability, large expenses for health care, damage to homes or automobiles, and liability for losses suffered by others. Consumers are also exposed to the risk of loss of capital as they accumulate wealth, due to market fluctuations or credit risk. Examples include losses due to equity market declines, changes in prevailing market interest rates or currency exchange rates, or default by the issuers of securities. Finally, consumers are exposed to the risk of outliving their assets.

The insurance industry exists to protect consumers against these types of risks, selling contracts that transfer the risk from the consumer to the insurer's broad-based and diversified risk pool in exchange for the payment of premiums or fees. Insurers underwrite the risk, deciding which risks they want to take and avoid; pool the risks from many consumers onto their balance sheets; and employ a wide range of techniques to manage these pools of aggregated risks. The ability of consumers to transfer risk to others provides a wide range of economic and social benefits. For instance, consumers have more flexibility

[1] 'The global state of sustainable insurance: understanding and integrating environmental, social and governance factors in insurance', UNEP Finance Initiative, 2009.

Table 3.1. Key protection, savings and income risks, and insurance solutions

Consumer need	Risks faced by consumers	Examples of insurance solutions
Protection	Premature death Illness Disability Liability to others	Life insurance Disability insurance Long-term care Medical expense Liability coverage
Savings	Market Credit	Fixed deferred annuities Variable annuities Endowments
Income	Longevity (outliving one's assets)	Income annuities Group payout annuities

because they do not need to self-insure, reliance on government safety nets is reduced, and insurers serve as stable, long-term investors supporting local economies. Millions of individuals, families, and businesses across the world benefit from insurance. For example, in 2013 European insurers paid out €952 billion in benefits and claims. That is equivalent to €2.6 billion being paid out to people and businesses every day (including weekends and holidays); see Table 3.1.

In an efficient insurance market, consumers have access to a wide range of products at competitive rates from a wide selection of insurers. The market serves as a risk transfer mechanism, allowing consumers to decide how much risk to keep and how much to pool. For example, at retirement, consumers may choose to use a portion of their retirement savings to buy an annuity and guarantee a certain level of income for life. They may keep and invest the rest in other vehicles, such as bank deposits, stocks, and bonds. To the extent they buy annuities, longevity risk is passed to an insurer; to the extent they hold investments such as stocks and bonds directly, longevity risk is retained.

The question arises how insurance companies, which assume risks from often hundreds of thousands or millions of individuals, manage such risk? How do they protect themselves from unforeseen shocks, be they from financial market developments or from the behaviour of policyholders?

These are the questions this chapter addresses. It explains how insurers absorb large risks on their balance sheet and how they manage them. It thereby focuses on what is usually called 'long tail'[2] insurance business, as this business has long dated assets and liabilities which are more sensitive to market fluctuation. For the sake of simplicity we will discuss mainly life insurance.

[2] This is composed mainly of the life insurance business and of some property and casualty lines such as workers compensation, liability, and construction insurance.

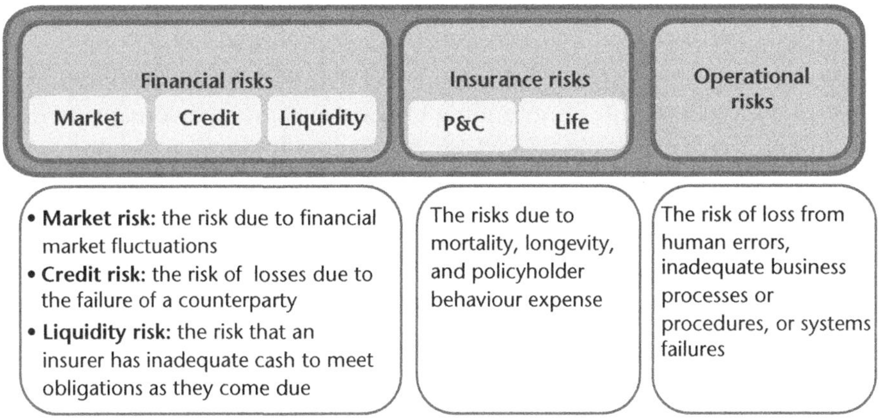

Figure 3.1. Aggregate risk

There are three main categories of risk faced by life insurance companies. These are insurance risks, financial risks, and operational risks. In the following sections, we break these down and explain how they are managed.

Financial risks: which include credit risk, market risk, and liquidity risk.

Market risk is the risk of loss due to changes in the level and the degree of fluctuations in the market price of securities, derivatives, or other financial instruments. Market risk includes the impact of changes in market prices on the cost of honouring investment guarantees. Market risk is comprised of interest rate risk, equity risk, and currency risk. Product features such as embedded policyholder options are key sources of market risk.

Credit risk is the risk of losses due to the failure of a counterparty. As insurers invest premiums in bonds and debt products to meet future obligations to policyholders, they are naturally exposed to credit risk; for example, on 30 June 2015 AXA had 83 per cent of its investment portfolio (€451 billion) in fixed income investments. All types of insurance products give rise to elements of credit risk, but more asset-intensive products are larger sources of credit risk. Credit risk can also arise from sources other than investments. For example, insurers can be exposed to credit risk from their interaction with other financial intermediaries such as reinsurers, derivative counterparties and banks.

Liquidity risk is the risk that an insurer has inadequate cash to meet obligations as they become due. Liquidity risk varies by product type. Many products are completely illiquid, where the policyholder has no ability to surrender or terminate the contract, and any payments to a policyholder are made only on fixed schedules or upon the occurrence of specified events. Some products may provide customers with more access to funds, and thus the potential for more liquidity risk.

Another aspect of liquidity risk is financing risk, which is the uncertainty of the ability to obtain sufficient funding in due time and on favourable terms.

Liquidity risk can be measured by a liquidity indicator—the difference between liquidity resources and net outflows under stress. The stressed conditions are calibrated so as to reflect extreme circumstances, and include:

- distressed financial markets (in terms of asset prices, liquidity and access to funding through capital markets);
- confidence crises (increase in lapses, decrease of premiums received, no new business).

Insurance risks: the risk that actual experience related to mortality, morbidity, longevity, claims, and policyholder behaviour (such as policy lapses or the rate at which policyholders use optional policy features) emerges differently than expected. Protection, Savings, and Retirement Income products will all involve insurance risks to varying degrees. For example, protection products expose the insurer to mortality and morbidity risks, retirement income products typically involve longevity risk, and many savings products generate policyholder behaviour risks and sometimes mortality risk as a result of minimum guaranteed death benefits.

Operational risks: the risk of loss from human errors, inadequate business processes or procedures, or systems failures, or due to external events such as natural catastrophes or political unrest. Undertaking any kind of business activity naturally gives rise to operational risk; it is not unique to insurance. All insurance products and operations involve operational risk, to varying degrees. Risk can vary with the market, the product type, the distribution channel, and the strength of the insurer's business procedures and process controls (see Figure 3.1).

3.2 Risk Management

The business of insurance companies is to accept risks from customers; the total amount of risk they absorb from customers, prior to consideration of the impact of their risk management practices, is much less significant than the residual risk that remains after the company has taken steps to manage and mitigate risk. Figure 3.2 below illustrates a typical breakdown of risk across the major categories and demonstrates that financial risks are the dominant risks for life insurance companies. So, how do insurers manage their risks?

The risks are managed both at the individual and aggregate levels.

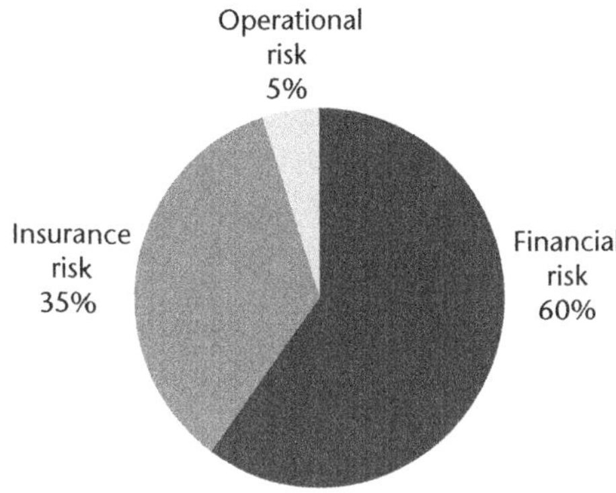

Figure 3.2. Risk contribution by category for a typical life insurance company

3.2.1 *Managing Individual Risks (Insurance Risk, Financial Risk, and Operational Risk)*

INSURANCE RISK

Product design, policy terms and underwriting are particularly powerful tools for managing insurance risk. Appropriate analysis, categorization, and pricing of insurance risks are important to an insurer's success. Basic policy features, such as maximum policy sizes, are fundamental controls on insurance risk. Controls include both an assessment of the probability and severity of claims, and also estimates and appropriate contractual controls of policyholder behaviour risks, such as the exercise of policyholder options and lapses. Underwriting protocols are designed to minimize adverse selection, which is the tendency of insureds to seek insurance if they are inordinately exposed to a particular risk or more likely to incur a claim than the average population. Underwriting and pricing to assess the appropriate premium for the risk being assumed are supported by experience studies.

Diversification among product offerings is another tool companies may use to manage insurance risk. A company may offer a diverse mix of coverages where exposures are uncorrelated or negatively correlated. An example would be a multi-line insurer offering both life insurance policies, which protect against dying earlier than expected, and annuities, which protect against living longer than expected. A life insurance company may be hesitant to retain $100 million of life insurance coverage on a single person; it is a much less risky proposition to write $1 million policies on each of one hundred individuals.

Insurance risks that are in excess of the company's risk appetite can be passed on to reinsurers, which in essence are insurers to the insurance companies. Insurance securitization such as catastrophe bonds, industry loss warranties, longevity swaps, etc., can be used to transfer insurance risks to the capital markets through the creation and issuance of financial securities.

FINANCIAL RISK

Credit Risk

Insurers use many practices to manage credit risk. Insurers typically retain trained, experienced professionals to analyse investment opportunities. Fundamental credit analysis of investment opportunities supplements available public credit analyses, such as those available from third party credit rating agencies. Insurers ensure diversification of counterparty risks by establishing investment guidelines for their portfolios, including limits such as restrictions by asset class, credit quality, and issuer.

These techniques allow insurers to substantially mitigate, but not entirely eliminate, counterparty default risk.

Counterparty default risk may have more impact on insurers in situations where it is correlated with other risks, or where there is increased correlation of risks across counterparties. For example, the risk of exposure to a reinsurer may be heightened in situations where reinsurers are stressed by other events, such as a catastrophe insurance shock. Likewise, the risk of counterparty defaults on bonds or derivatives will potentially have more impact in situations where there is increased correlation of each firm's default risk, which may occur in a broad and deep financial crisis. In situations such as these, tools such as diversification, hedging, and securing collateral are likely to provide substantial value, but the protection may not be complete. For these reasons, to provide an additional buffer to absorb losses in situations where risk mitigation techniques are less than fully effective, insurance companies hold capital against credit risk.

Finally, it is important that insurance companies understand their residual (post-mitigation) counterparty default risk. Stress testing provides valuable insights. For stress testing purposes, an insurer may assume, for example, that their credit default hedging is less than fully effective, or they may model an idiosyncratic credit shock, such as a reinsurer failure. The results of such stress tests allow insurers to identify potential residual risk exposures, model the impact of severe scenarios, and design further risk mitigation protocols.

Market Risk—Interest Rate Risk

A wide variety of risk management techniques are used to control and mitigate market risks. These techniques include:

- defining an optimal strategic asset allocation with respect to the liabilities' structure;
- a disciplined investment process, requiring for any sophisticated investment a formal thorough analysis by the Investment Department, and a second opinion by the Risk Management Department;
- hedging of market risks when they exceed the tolerance levels.

Product design is also a key element in controlling market risk, and interest rate risk in particular. Whether or not a product offers a guaranteed interest rate—and if so, the level and duration of that guarantee—will fundamentally impact the amount of interest rate risk the insurer assumes. Interest rate guarantees may be explicit in the design and communication of the product, or implicit in how the product is designed and priced. Options granted to the customer through product design also impact interest rate risk.

Market Risk—Equity Risk

Equity risk, including risk from public equities, private equities, and real estate, will commonly arise when insurers hold these investments in their general account portfolios and the investment experience is not passed directly to policyholders. In many cases, insurers invest in equities but policyholders bear the investment risk. Good examples include unit-linked policies (without guarantees) and non-guaranteed group policies, such as separate account pension products.

Insurers can also share risk with policyholders, as with participating or with-profits products. In these arrangements adverse experience is passed along to policyholders but may be smoothed over time, or customer losses may be capped. Other contractual features also share equity risk with customers. For example, variable annuities may provide a guarantee on equity market performance, but only if the policy is paid out over time as an annuity. If policyholders lapse early, they may only receive the current market value of the underlying investments, thus passing the equity risk, upon lapse, back to the customer.

Where insurers do take equity risk, they commonly manage it in the derivative markets, using hedges to protect themselves from adverse movements in equity markets. The insurer's liabilities (reserves) will fluctuate with both the level of the equity markets and with equity volatility levels. The reserves themselves may be established based upon the results of stochastic modelling. Insurers can purchase hedges to fully or partially offset the movement in reserves as equity markets move. The anticipated cost of these hedges is typically included in the pricing of the underlying insurance products sold to customers.

Market Risk—Foreign Exchange Risk

A common practice is to currency-match assets and liabilities, thus reducing or eliminating foreign exchange risk. There are cases where an insurer may invest assets backing reserves in a different currency. This can arise, for example, when an insurer seeks additional diversification, or when the customer has some control over the allocation of policy funds, including the ability to select foreign currency denominated investments. In these

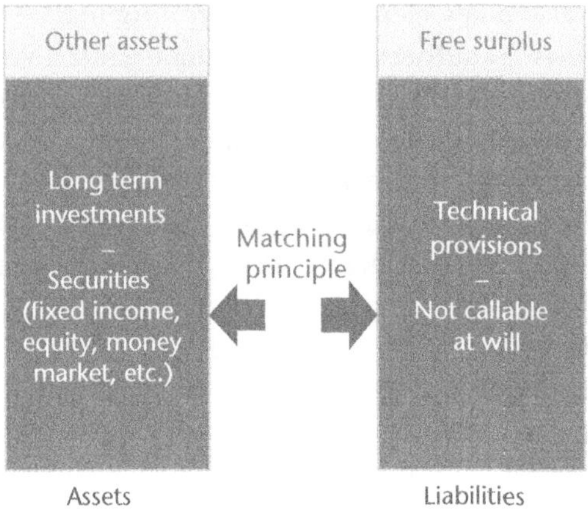

Figure 3.3. Balance sheet of a typical life insurance company showing the liquidity profile

cases, derivative instruments may be used to hedge the risk introduced to the carrier's balance sheet.

Liquidity Risk

Liquidity risk is managed using a combination of product features and investment management strategies. Unlike in banking, maturity transformation is not a significant element of the insurance business model (See Figure 3.3). In many cases an insurer's promise to its policyholder may be for a very long duration and illiquid, unlike the 'on demand' nature of bank deposits. In some markets, including the United States, it is also common for insurance products to have contract features allowing the insurer to delay payment of cash value for some period of time (for example, six months). These features provide substantial protection in stressed market conditions.

OPERATIONAL RISK

Operational risk is a broad category including many different types of risk. Operational risk is most commonly addressed using specific control systems to minimize residual risk. Within their own frameworks, insurers will identify and document operational risks, establish and enact controls, monitor progress, and validate control effectiveness. They will also report on any operational loss events and use that information to help redesign or modify controls as necessary. A wide range of policies, procedures, systems, and training will comprise the overall operational risk framework.

PRODUCT FOCUS: VARIABLE ANNUITIES 'VAs'

Annuities are contracts sold by insurance companies that are designed to provide regular payments to the contract holder (also known as the annuitant) and his or her annuity partner.

An annuity generally has two stages: the accumulation stage and the payout stage. During the accumulation stage the funds are invested in fixed or variable accounts. Any growth on the investment is tax deferred and the annuitant may have the ability to access all or part of the funds. Investments in variable accounts have risks associated with them including loss of principal and may be subject to early withdrawal tax penalties, depending on local tax rules.

The two primary types of annuities are 'fixed' (or guaranteed) and 'variable.' In fixed or guaranteed annuities, the funds are invested in the insurance company's general account, which typically contains fixed income securities like bonds. The issuer, not the contract owner, assumes all investment risk. Fixed annuities offer a guaranteed payment, with the payout amount based on the assumed future returns of the investments and the annuitant's life expectancy. The payment can be fixed for life, or can allow for future increases. For many people, this guarantee of lifetime income is the annuity's major advantage when compared with other retirement income options.

Variable annuities (VAs) provide the contract owner with the ability to invest in both fixed income and stock-based accounts whose values change depending on the performance of these underlying investments. While variable annuities offer the potential for higher long-term returns than fixed annuities, generally their payouts will fluctuate (sometimes dramatically) from year to year. Unlike owners of fixed annuities, owners of variable annuities assume all investment risk.[3]

In the late 1990s, as competition for customers increased, companies began offering different options, including secondary guarantees. These guarantees are benefit riders that have been added to the base annuity policy and provide policyholders with guaranteed minimum benefits based on option(s) chosen. These guarantees put some of the investment risk back onto the insurance company's balance sheet.

These guarantees are embedded in the annuity contracts and are managed by the insurer with derivatives, either with fixed hedges at inception for structured products, or with dynamic hedging (i.e. hedging which varies with the evolution of the insurer's exposure and the financial markets). Between 1996 and 2002 insurance companies were able to take out reinsurance on embedded guarantees. However, the VA market grew much faster than the reinsurance market and by the end of 2002 insurance companies had exhausted all the available reinsurance capacity.

Over the years, the complexity of the products has grown, increasing the number and level of risks borne by the insurance companies.

The risks to insurance companies writing VAs comes from movements in the equity markets, long-and short-term interest rates, mark-to-market losses from imperfect hedges, and the deviation of policyholder behaviour from the models. These risks were illustrated during the 2008 global financial crisis. Insurance companies had taken a lot of basis risk, and when actively managed investment portfolios significantly underperformed the markets, rebalancing the hedges became more costly than anticipated. Furthermore, policyholders did not lapse to the extent predicted by the models.

Since the global financial crisis, there have been some changes in the features of the products to improve their risk profile such as better management of the in force books, offering lower guarantees, and a transition to passively managed investments.

[3] 'Dismantling The Myths of Annuities', TIAA-CREF.

3.2.2 *Managing Aggregate Company Risk*

As we have seen, insurers use a wide variety of techniques to mitigate risk, tackling each type of risk individually. There are also several tools they use to manage risk in a comprehensive fashion to supplement their product-level or risk-by-risk efforts.

RISK APPETITE

Setting the risk appetite is usually the starting point of risk management. Insurers typically employ a structure of formal risk appetites, whereby they define the aggregate amount of risk they are willing to accept to achieve their strategic objectives. Firms will generally define their appetite for each major risk category (insurance, financial, and operational), as well as other key elements, such as capital adequacy and earnings stability.

Risk appetites can be guided by the relevant regulatory framework, for example, in the European Union, Solvency II requires insurance companies to be able to withstand shocks in a 1 in 200 scenario over a one-year horizon, i.e. an insurance company should be solvent in 99.5 per cent of the modelled scenarios.

The modelled scenarios include adverse scenarios such as a financial market crash, deflation, spikes in mortality, major natural catastrophes, and combined scenarios where extreme financial and insurance events happen simultaneously. The results of the modelled scenarios are reviewed against actual losses in historical market stress scenarios.

Risk appetite frameworks help management understand a company's risk profile, find an optimal balance between risk and return, and nurture a healthy risk culture in the organization. They explain the risk tolerance of the company both qualitatively and quantitatively. The term risk appetite encompasses: (i) the quantitative and qualitative measurement of risk; (ii) the setting of limits and budgets around chosen risk measures; and (iii) the allocation of risk budget and limits across sources of return in the business.

By covering all risks borne by an insurance company (from financial risks to insurance and operational risks), a strong risk management framework ensures a challenging second opinion is provided on all business decisions. These risk appetites are typically cascaded down to the business unit level to set operating boundaries and control aggregate business-unit risks within corporate limits.

CONTINGENCY PLANNING

Contingency planning is another important tool insurers use to manage their risk. Companies will generally develop contingency plans regarding both liquidity and capital, laying out how they will respond to pressure on cash and capital positions in the event of severe stress. Business continuity plans may be developed to minimize operational risk in the event of natural disasters or systems failures. Developing the plan challenges firms to recognize, analyse, and confront potential threats before a crisis environment develops. The planning process may motivate immediate action, such as the implementation of committed credit facilities, as well as define specific actions that will be undertaken if and when the need arises.

'MACRO-HEDGING'

Hedging programmes are useful in managing different types of risk at the portfolio or block-of-business level. Firms often employ macro-hedging programmes at the group level as well to provide additional protection against low frequency, high severity tail risk events. Macro-hedging programmes can be particularly helpful in situations where the risks across different portfolios are partially dependent, and thus looking at each portfolio individually can understate the aggregate risk. Macro-hedges can take the form of derivative securities, such as interest rate or equity hedges.

They can also take the form of less traditional securities, including catastrophe bonds, longevity bonds, and mortality bonds. With these instruments the carrier essentially shares some of its risk with lenders, particularly for types of risk that are of particular concern to the company. In turn they pay a higher cost to carry the debt, but if the particular stress event rises, they have additional protection in place.

3.3 Asset/Liability Management

Life insurance companies have long dated assets and liabilities. Both the assets and liabilities are sensitive to the level of interest rates (interest rate duration) and generally, due to the impact of discounting, the longer the duration of the assets or liabilities, the greater the sensitivity to changes in interest rates. The impact of changes in interest on the assets and liabilities should be matched very closely to minimize volatility in the level of solvency.

Therefore, insurance companies are liability driven investors; that is to say, they invest premiums in assets with cash flow characteristics similar to their liabilities. This is referred to as Asset/Liability Management, or ALM. Insurers commonly manage their interest rate risk by closely managing (or matching) these asset and liability cash flows. Companies use models to project the liability cash flows arising from the policies they have written and invest accordingly. To the extent that cash flows are perfectly matched, a company will have no interest rate risk. However, perfectly matching cash flows is not possible in practice. Cash flows for some products will extend beyond the point at which deep and liquid fixed income security markets exist. In addition, liability cash flows may diverge from projections. Liability cash flows can also change fundamentally as market conditions change, so interest rate risk can change as rates themselves change. For example, a product with a fixed, guaranteed interest rate is likely to experience low lapses when market rates are well below the guaranteed level and high lapses if market rates significantly exceed the guaranteed level. Changes to the market level of rates will impact lapses, which in turn changes liability cash flows, and thus changes the level of interest rate risk.

While it is possible to purchase assets with cash flows of twenty or thirty years, these are not available in all markets. This is particularly true in less developed economies and in countries with low or no government deficits, where long duration assets may be completely unavailable. However, as insurers provide a market for long-term protection to their customers, liability cash flows for some insurance products extend even beyond thirty years. In many cases, where the customer has no option to demand early payment, these liability cash flows may be illiquid—good examples include fixed annuities and payout pension products, where payments can continue well beyond thirty years and the customer cannot surrender the policy. Some insurers may choose to purchase assets other than fixed income securities to back these types of liabilities. Such assets may include public or private equities, equity real estate, and infrastructure investments. As the present value of liabilities is sensitive to rate movements, but equity assets generally are not, backing very long liabilities with equity investments introduces interest rate risk. However, since insurers have a very long investment horizon for long duration, illiquid liabilities, they have decades over which to manage the investment without threat of the liabilities being called early. The key factor for an insurer is to have access to the necessary funds when obligations to policyholders come due.

3.4 Derivatives

Derivatives are a fundamental element of any insurer's risk management toolbox. For the most part, insurers use derivatives for hedging. They hedge various risks stemming from both the asset and liability sides of the balance sheet: interest rate, foreign exchange, credit, equity, inflation, volatility, and longevity.

Derivatives are primarily used for:

- managing interest rate exposures on fixed maturity investments, long-term debt and guaranteed interest rates on insurance contracts;
- reducing foreign-currency exposures on foreign-currency denominated investments and liabilities;
- managing liquidity positions (including the ability to pay benefits and claims when due) in connection with Asset Liability Management and local regulatory requirements
- limiting equity risk; and
- limiting credit risk with regard to certain investments in corporate debt instruments.

Interest rate derivatives, notably swaptions and forward options, can be used by an insurance company to secure its future reinvestment interest rate when the universe of investable assets has a shorter maturity than its insurance policies. They are also used to protect an insurance company's investment portfolio against a rise in interest rates which could trigger an acceleration of surrenders.

Equity derivatives can be used to protect an insurance company against a fall in the equity markets by limiting its loss exposure to a fixed amount.

Credit default swaps can allow a protection against the default of a single corporate issuer of credit. They can also be used, in combination with an investment in a sovereign bond, to replicate an investment in a single corporate name.

Derivatives are either traded on a regulated market, in which case the counterparty risk is extremely limited, or underwritten by a bank. In the latter case derivatives are fully collateralized on a daily or weekly basis and require rigorous liquidity management. For example, as of 31 December 2014, AXA had a notional value of off balance sheet derivatives of €433 billion. These derivatives had a mark-to-market value of €17 billion of which €16 billion was fully collateralized, leaving only €1 billion of outstanding counterparty risk.

This demonstrates that at any point in time, the exposure of an insurance company to credit risk is not the full notional value of the derivative contract (e.g. €433 billion above). Instead, the exposure is the mark-to-market value of the derivative contract (e.g. €17 billion above, if this is favourable to the insurer). There is no credit risk on exchange-traded derivatives as the clearing house stands between insurer and counterparty. For Over-The-Counter (OTC) derivatives, contracts can require collateral based on daily or weekly mark-to-market values. In the case of our example, as illustrated above, if €16 billion collateral is provided, residual outstanding exposure is only €1 billion of credit risk.

HOW DOES AXA MANAGE RISKS IN DERIVATIVES?

Derivative exposure, 31 December 2014

Derivative instrument	Notional amount € billion
Interest rates derivatives	262
Equity derivatives	23
Currencies derivatives	101
Credit derivatives	22
Other derivatives	26
TOTAL	**433**

The European Union (European Market Infrastructure Regulation—EMIR) and the United States (principally through the Dodd-Frank Act) set several prescriptive guidelines for derivatives which impact operations, liquidity, and credit risk management for derivatives.

In terms of **governance** at AXA, derivative strategies are systematically reviewed and validated by local Investment and Asset Liability Management 'ALM' committees in the same way as any other ALM or investment strategies.

The **market risk** arising from derivatives is regularly monitored in multiple processes: (i) risk appetite process, in which the market risk position is continuously monitored, separating the impact of physical investments and derivatives; (ii) Solvency II process, in which the sensitivity of AXA to financial risk factors is monitored, also separating the impact of physical investments and derivatives; (iii) this monitoring ensures that there is **no leverage** arising from derivatives.

Legal risk is addressed by defining a standardized master agreement. AXA business units may trade derivatives only if they are covered by legal documentation which complies with the requirements set out in the Group standard. Any change to certain mandatory provisions defined in the Group standard must be approved by Group Risk Management.

There is a centralized **counterparty risk** policy. Group Risk Management has established Group-wide rules on authorized counterparties, minimum requirements regarding collateral, and counterparty exposure limits. In particular, AXAs **collateral process** allows reducing the credit risk arising from OTC derivatives at a limited level compared to the total value of derivatives in position.

The **operational risk** related to derivatives is measured and managed in the context of AXA's global operational risk framework.

Furthermore, four centres of expertise have been selected to centralize execution of derivatives and reduce operational risk.

The **valuations** are also a key element of the Derivatives Management. AXA entities rely on the Derivatives Platforms of the Group (located in the internal asset managers, AXA Investment Managers and Alliance Bernstein) to independently counter-valuate the derivatives positions so as to get comfort on the accounting but as well on the prices proposed by counterparties in case the AXA entity wished to early terminate or restructure the derivatives. This pricing capability requires deep technical knowledge which has to stay updated and must follow market developments for new derivatives instruments usage.

Furthermore, since derivatives are mainly used for hedging a mark-to-market gain or loss in an underlying asset or liability, the derivative position will have an offsetting loss or gain, resulting in an insignificant net gain or loss.

Regulatory trends toward market consistent valuation will most likely continue to increase derivative hedging activities. Indeed, in a regime where the capital requirements are based on the value at risk over a one-year horizon of the mark-to-market balance sheet, the extensive use of derivatives is a major way to decrease the risk of the options and guarantees that are implicit in most life insurance and savings products.

3.5 Stress Testing and Scenario Analysis

Stress and scenario testing is an important tool that underlies many, if not all, of the other risk mitigation techniques. Scenarios can be defined by the firm or stochastically generated. Viewing the company's resilience under stress provides critical information to better understand, manage, and mitigate risk. Stress testing is generally performed on the balance sheet and income statement under the various accounting frameworks to which the insurer is subject. An insurer may also wish to stress test its economic balance sheet and other internal measures.

Reactions to troublesome stress test results can include reductions to risk appetite and risk limits, adding elements to the contingency plans to make sure specific stresses are addressed, and the addition of additional macro-hedges. Stress tests can also point to risk issues at the portfolio and block-of-business level that warrant action. While they are not a risk mitigation tool directly, stress tests are an important diagnostic device that helps the firm bring other risk management techniques to bear.

3.6 Three Lines of Defence

Many companies employ a 'three lines of defence' model,[4] which helps to organize the efforts of a wide array of resources in different departments, all designed to better manage risk.

[4] The Institute of Internal Auditors Position Paper: The Three Lines of Defense in Effective Risk Management and Control, January 2013.

- First line: business or corporate area is responsible for and directly manages risk (e.g. sales, underwriting, claims, business leadership, finance, operations, human resources);
- Second line: oversees risk (e.g. risk management, compliance, system security, financial controls);
- Third line: provides independent review and validation (e.g. internal audit).

A three lines of defence model helps ensure that all risks are covered, roles are clear, and redundancy is reduced. The first line establishes policies and sound business procedures around business-as-usual activities and also puts basic monitoring and measurement in place to control risk. The second line can assist the first line in establishing and enacting controls, and also monitors those controls. The third line validates controls and is critical because it brings independence and objectivity that may not exist in either the first or second line of defence.

3.7 Risk Culture

Finally, an important element of risk management is a company's risk culture.[5] A sound risk culture supports effective governance of risk within an organization, and helps ensure that business decisions are made with the appropriate risk controls in place. When a strong risk culture is in place, awareness of risk will permeate the company, further strengthening all of the other risk management tools and activities. Strong risk governance practices, an effective risk appetite framework, and an alignment between risk and compensation are all considered foundational elements of a sound risk culture. Company practices that are indicators of risk culture include:

- The Tone from the Top—does senior management and the board set the appropriate values and expectations when it comes to risk, and do their actions match their words?
- Accountability—do employees understand and embrace their roles as they pertain to risk, and are they held accountable?
- Communication and Challenge—does the company foster an environment that promotes open and constructive engagement around risk?

[5] Financial Stability Board, Guidance on Supervisory Interaction with Financial Institutions on Risk Culture: A Framework for Assessing Risk Culture, April 2014.

- Compensation and Incentives—are the financial and non-financial incentives for employees aligned with the desired risk behaviour? Do compensation plans encourage excessive risk-taking?

3.7.1 *Impact of Shocks on Insurers*

Throughout this chapter we have covered the risks that consumers face, how those risks are transferred to insurance companies, and how insurers manage those risks on both a micro and macro level. Next, let us consider how an insurance company is impacted by external shocks such as liquidity, insurance risk events, and a sharp decline in the financial markets.

3.8 Liquidity in Insurance Companies

A common concern regarding banks is a 'run on the bank' scenario, where a real or perceived weakness at the bank motivates customers to rapidly withdraw their funds. Banks rely on maturity transformation as part of their model, taking in cash through short-term deposits and other short-term funding (liabilities) and investing in longer-term assets, such as loans. This maturity transformation makes a 'run on the bank' a very real risk. Of course, this risk can be reduced or eliminated, particularly at the retail level, with the introduction of government-backed deposit insurance schemes.

Insurers do not rely on maturity transformation as part of their core business model, and they also have many tools for managing liquidity risk. In general, insurers are liability driven investors. They raise funds by issuing long-term promises to pay, in the form of products such as insurance policies and annuities, and invest the premiums in matching, long-term assets.

While the overwhelming majority of an insurer's liabilities may be long-term in nature, some will have features that allow them to be surrendered prior to their contractual term. These features typically include specified terms, conditions, and time periods. A number of characteristics of insurance policies mitigate the likelihood that an insurance policy will be surrendered. At the most basic level, holders of insurance policies typically do not purchase their policies to provide a source of funds for short-term liquidity needs, and the historical experience of insurers confirms that insurance policyholders do not act like bank depositors. Moreover, the majority of policies with surrender provisions are sold to retail customers, who historically have reacted less rapidly, and in smaller numbers, to adverse market events. Policy surrenders are also subject to certain administrative requirements, typically requiring a week or longer—a significant difference from the immediate availability of demand deposits.

Many policies that do permit surrender under prescribed circumstances contain a number of contractual provisions. For example, customers who surrender their policies may face a variety of economic disincentives, including:

- receiving only the surrender value of their policy, which is less than the amount that a customer ultimately would receive on a policy claim;
- forfeiting the benefit of any contractual guarantees (such as guaranteed income benefits);
- paying a surrender charge;
- being subject to adverse tax consequences upon surrender;
- being subject to additional underwriting and potentially paying higher premiums to obtain equivalent coverage from another insurer to take into account changes in age or health status; and
- a provision permitting the insurer to delay payment for some period (for example, up to six months) following a surrender.

Historical data demonstrate that these factors produce low surrender rates. Very few policyholders ever exercise surrender rights—even in times of widespread economic distress. In fact, certain products may actually experience a decline in surrenders during market stress, as the value of their embedded guarantees may increase. So, a run on an insurance company is a highly unlikely event, impeded by many elements of insurance products.

This does not mean that insurers are immune to liquidity concerns. While a traditional run on an insurer is unlikely, insurers still must be disciplined and vigilant with respect to managing their liquidity risks. Certain activities frequently undertaken by insurers can introduce liquidity risk when not appropriately managed or controlled. For example, funding agreements where the insurer's counterparties can demand immediate repayment, or where such repayment is triggered by events such as a downgrade, can pose liquidity risk. This is particularly true when the funds raised under the funding agreement are reinvested in less liquid assets. Careful risk analysis, control of contract features, and tools such as liquidity stress testing, are important for managing this risk.

Some insurers engage in securities lending activities where collateral is held and invested while securities are on loan. The term structure of these loans is generally very short, and therefore the insurer will typically invest the collateral in short-term, highly liquid securities to ensure sufficient liquidity under stress conditions. Risks posed by such programmes are specific to how the insurer manages the risk; liquidity stress testing plays an important role in managing the liquidity risk exposure arising from this activity.

3.9 Insurance Risk Events

Depending on the type of business they write, insurers may be exposed to a range of insurance risk events. Of course most insurance claim experience is relatively stable and predictable, and insurance risks can often be well diversified. But significant shocks can happen. A significant mortality event, like a global pandemic, could challenge an insurer with a large life insurance portfolio. A catastrophic natural disaster, such as a hurricane or earthquake, could stress a property and casualty insurer. And there can even be events that have adverse impact across multiple insurance lines simultaneously. The Japanese earthquake, tsunami, and nuclear disaster of March 2011 are examples.

While such extreme events are rare, given their potential importance, insurers spend significant resources preparing for them. Stress testing and contingency planning are commonplace. Basic insurance risk controls are also important. Insurers will set risk appetite constraints and other limits on the total amount of insurance risk and the risk concentrations that they will accept. Appropriate diversification is a key element of an insurer's defence against insurance risk events, as they diversify across geographies and product lines. Tools such as reinsurance, including catastrophic risk reinsurance, are used to reduce total risk exposure and to help improve diversification. We also discussed securities such as catastrophe bonds, longevity bonds, and mortality bonds that insurers may use to add protection.

Even when insurance risk shocks do take place, they typically play out over an extended period of time. Pandemics may play out over many months or years. Some product shocks, like asbestos-related liabilities, are realized over decades. Even in cases like hurricanes it can take eighteen months to two years for claims to be fully assessed and paid. This timing of insurance claims is a key benefit to insurance companies, as it avoids turning insurance events into liquidity crunches, and lets carriers sell appropriate assets to pay claims in an orderly fashion, over an extended period of time.

3.10 Financial Market Decline

A broad financial market decline is likely to impact insurance companies in many different ways, manifesting through the different types of risk. A broad decline may be characterized by falling equity markets, increased market volatility, reduction in risk-free rates as investors search for safe haven assets, turbulence in foreign exchange rates, and increases in credit spreads and credit defaults. These environmental changes will impact insurers through market and credit risk exposures. There can also be an impact on elements of insurance risk, such as through policyholder behaviour changes. For example, as market interest rates decline, policy lapses may decrease. Still, liquidity can be a concern for firms that have not adequately managed their liquidity risk, as a broad market decline is likely to have an impact on cash demands for certain types of products and funding arrangements (see Section 3.8 Liquidity in Insurance Companies).

Essentially, the heightened risk from a broad financial market decline arises from increased correlation among risks that are normally less correlated during normal market conditions. The actual risks—market, credit, insurance, operational, and liquidity—are no different, but they may now act in concert to exert stress on insurance companies. Insurers generally use stress testing to

IMPACT OF SOLVENCY II IN EUROPE

Solvency II introduces risk-based capital charges for insurance companies across Europe. Capital must be held to support all the risks to which the balance sheet is exposed. This includes non-life, life, and health insurance as well as other balance sheet risks such as market, or counterparty risk and operational risk.

Solvency II reflects the European Commission's (EC) desire to link solvency capital more directly to the actual risks faced by individual insurance companies, and it contains specific incentives to encourage insurance companies to improve their risk management function. In short, insurers will be able to directly influence their solvency capital requirements in a number of ways under Solvency II.

More specifically, Solvency II has been a catalyst for a substantial amount of work on a risk-based approach to solvency including through internal modelling. Under this regime, an internal model can be used to derive regulatory capital requirements (versus the 'Standard Formula' which is proposed by default to all European insurers). Insurers are encouraged to develop internal models that can be integrated within an Enterprise Risk Management (ERM) framework and used to support business decisions. Achieving an internal model architecture not only complying with the new regulatory standards but reflecting as closely as possible the risks borne by the company at short and long term is not a simple process. Significant work needs to be done to convince regulators to accept the results of the internal model as a alternative for the standard Solvency II Pillar I capital requirements (the 'standard formula') and a broad range of risks is scrutinized in this context.

An internal model, as required within the Solvency II framework, that is implemented, validated and understood by management and the Board is at the heart of helping an organization manage its risk exposures. More than just a device to measure the risk, validation goes beyond the theoretical soundness of the calculation kernel. It is a process built on firm foundations that comprehensively reflect the characteristics of the business and is understood and accepted in decision making.

Over the last six years, regular on-site reviews have been organized to challenge assumptions and ensure that the internal model accurately reflects risks, is complete, well implemented and used throughout the insurance value chain. These reviews have also served to deepen the Supervisory Authority's (both group-wide and local for international groups) and insurance management's appreciation of each other's concerns.

model and understand the impact of such market environments. Insurers hold capital to absorb losses in such times. Stress testing helps determine whether capital buffers are sufficient or need to be raised, and whether other risk controls need to be deployed. Techniques described in the section 'Managing Aggregate Company Risks' are also helpful in addressing the risks posed by broad financial market disruption. A well-defined risk appetite will help make sure the company is appropriately limiting its risk, particularly in times of stress. Macro-hedging can provide added protection against 'tail-event' scenarios. Contingency planning can help companies analyse and define how they will respond should difficult situations arise.

3.11 Conclusion

In this chapter we have seen how insurance companies assume risks from their customers and how they manage that risk. They use sophisticated techniques to analyse, measure, and manage individual risks, such as specific insurance, financial, and operational risks. They also employ many tools to manage risks at the aggregate level, across their entire balance sheet. Diversification, Asset/ Liability Management, hedging with derivatives and stress testing are but a few of the many ways that insurers manage their risks. The result of these risk management practices is a manageable level of residual risk within insurers and the insurance industry, and a broad range of benefits for consumers and society as a whole.

Part 2

Financial Stability and the Possibilities of Systemic Risk

4

Risk of Life Insurers

Recent Trends and Transmission Mechanisms

Ralph S. J. Koijen and Motohiro Yogo

4.1 Introduction

The traditional sources of risk for life insurers are uncertainty in interest rates, aggregate longevity or mortality, and policyholder behaviour. Life insurers manage interest-rate risk by investing a significant share of their assets in long-term bonds. They manage longevity or mortality risk by offsetting annuities with life insurance. Uncertainty in policyholder behaviour may be more difficult to hedge, but life insurers have decades of experience to assess the policyholder risk of traditional annuities and life insurance. Finally, life insurers diversify these risks through unaffiliated (i.e. third-party) reinsurance.

Although modern life insurers are exposed to the traditional sources of risk, their risk profile has become increasingly complex and opaque over the last decade because of two developments. First, variable annuities with minimum-return guarantees, which are more difficult to value and hedge than traditional products, have grown to be a significant share of liabilities. Second, life insurers are now using sophisticated capital management tools such as shadow insurance, securities lending, and derivatives.[1]

[1] Shadow insurance is affiliated reinsurance (within the same financial group) between an operating company (i.e. a regulated and rated company that sells policies) and a shadow reinsurer (i.e. a less regulated and unrated off-balance-sheet entity).

Evidence from the 2008 financial crisis suggests that variable annuities and securities lending could cause significant risk mismatch. For example, the failure of AIG was not only due to their credit default swaps, but also due to securities lending in their insurance subsidiaries (McDonald and Paulson 2014; Peirce 2014). Like AIG, Hartford also received government support through the Troubled Asset Relief Program (TARP) because of significant losses on their variable annuity business. Other companies that were involved in variable annuities or securities lending (e.g. Allstate, Genworth Financial, and Prudential Financial) also applied for TARP but were ultimately rejected or withdrew their application. These examples refute the conventional wisdom that the insurance industry is immune from macroeconomic shocks.

Building on these examples, Section 4.2 of this chapter summarizes recent trends in risk exposure from variable annuities, shadow insurance, securities lending, and derivatives. Our analysis is based on public financial statements for U.S. life insurers from 2002 to 2013 and captives domiciled in Iowa for 2014.[2] We see our analysis as a first step in identifying risks that are potentially important to guide the next generation of insurance regulation. A common theme that emerges from our analysis is *risk concentration*. That is, the aggregate size of a given activity (e.g. shadow insurance) is dominated by a few large players, although the composition of these players varies somewhat across activities. Another theme is that while it is possible to identify exposure to individual risks, it is difficult to assess how they aggregate to overall risk mismatch because of insufficient data.

Shadow insurance has grown from $11 billion in 2002 to $370 billion in 2013 (Koijen and Yogo 2016). Shadow reinsurers usually report their liabilities under more favourable accounting standards than operating companies from which they assume reinsurance, and moreover, they are not subject to risk-based capital regulation. Thus, shadow insurance potentially allows life insurers to reduce risk-based capital and increase leverage, which is an important amplification mechanism for any risk mismatch. In general, we cannot quantify the capital reduction that may arise from shadow insurance because the financial statements of captives are not publicly available. However, the Iowa Insurance Division (2014) recently released financial statements for captives in their domicile, and we find that they have significantly negative equity when valued under the same accounting standards as the operating companies.

Life insurers use derivatives to hedge risk mismatch between their investment assets and insurance liabilities, including that which arises from minimum-return guarantees in variable annuities. However, the use of derivatives could expose life insurers to basis risk because of imperfect hedging and

[2] See Appendix A of this chapter for a description of the data.

counterparty risk. Overall, we find that derivatives have consistently reduced the volatility of accounting equity over the last decade. However, additional data are necessary to fully assess the economic effectiveness of the hedging programmes.

Section 4.3 discusses how risks in the insurance industry could be amplified and transmitted to the rest of the financial sector and the real economy. Banks are important counterparties in shadow insurance, securities lending, and derivatives transactions. In addition, risks in the insurance industry could be amplified and transmitted to other institutional investors through the corporate bond market. Finally, insurance demand and precautionary saving could endogenously respond to risks in the insurance industry, which has important implications for household welfare.

Section 4.4 suggests ways to improve financial disclosure on variable annuities, interest-rate risk, captive reinsurance, derivatives, and international activity. We also draw some tentative conclusions for insurance regulation.

4.2 Recent Trends in Risk Exposure

Informational frictions, agency problems, and regulatory frictions could create incentives for life insurers to increase leverage, pay higher dividends, and take more risks. For example, the presence of state guaranty funds could lead to a moral hazard problem (Lee, Mayers, and, Smith 1997). Shareholders may prefer dividends to retained earnings because portfolio decisions outside the insurance industry (e.g. in mutual funds) are not subject to risk-based capital regulation. These frictions could lead to a higher cost of external finance and introduce a role for capital management tools such as shadow insurance, securities lending, and derivatives (Froot 2007).

4.2.1 *Variable Annuities*

Variable annuities are long-term savings products whose underlying assets are invested in traditional mutual funds. In exchange for additional fees, life insurers guarantee a minimum rate of return on the mutual funds.[3] Partly because of the shift from defined-benefit to defined-contribution plans, there has been a growing demand for minimum-return guarantees. The total account value of U.S. variable annuities associated with guaranteed benefits grew from $875 billion in 2003 to $1.726 trillion in 2013.

[3] See Bauer, Kling, and Russ (2008) and Credit Suisse (2012, Appendix B) for an overview of the various types of variable annuity guarantees.

Table 4.1. Operating gain in 2008 for top ten life insurers by variable annuity account value

Financial group	Account value (billion $)	Operating gain (share of capital and surplus)
MetLife	143	−0.05
AXA Financial	139	−0.18
Hartford Life	119	−0.52
AIG Life	105	0.00
ING USA Life	98	−0.14
Lincoln Financial	97	−0.01
Manulife Financial	94	−0.46
Prudential of America	79	−0.28
Aegon USA	61	−0.26
Ameriprise Financial	57	−0.44
Total for life insurers		
with VA guarantees	1,460	−0.09
without VA guarantees	0	0.01

A.M. Best financial groups are ranked by variable annuity (VA) account value associated with guaranteed benefits in 2007. Net operating gain from individual annuities in 2008 is reported as a share of capital and surplus in 2007. The last two rows report the total for the insurance industry, separately for life insurers with and without VA guarantees in 2007.

The variable annuity market is highly concentrated. Table 4.1 reports the top ten life insurers by variable annuity account value associated with guaranteed benefits in 2007. These life insurers accounted for $991 billion of variables annuities in 2007, which is a significant share of $1.460 trillion for the industry.

The long-term nature of these guarantees presents significant challenges for both valuation and risk management. During the financial crisis, the variable annuity business experienced significant losses because of falling stock prices, high volatility, and low interest rates. The last column of Table 4.1 reports the net operating gain from individual annuities in 2008 as a share of capital and surplus (i.e. accounting equity) in 2007.[4] Hartford Life and Manulife Financial suffered the largest losses on the order of half of their capital and surplus. When aggregated over the industry, life insurers with variable annuity guarantees lost 9 per cent of their capital and surplus from the individual annuity business, while those without guarantees gained 1 per cent.

To put the 2008 losses into historical perspective, Figure 4.1 reports the time series of net operating gain from individual annuities, aggregated over life insurers with positive variable annuity account value associated with guaranteed benefits in the previous year. We report the net operating gain in total dollars and as a share of capital and surplus in the previous year. The −$24 billion loss in 2008 is certainly extraordinary in historical perspective. Although the profitability of individual annuities recovered after 2008, the experience illustrates the sensitivity of variable annuity guarantees to stock

[4] Prior to the change in reporting requirements in 2010, life insurers reported the net operating gain for fixed and variable annuities combined, rather than separately.

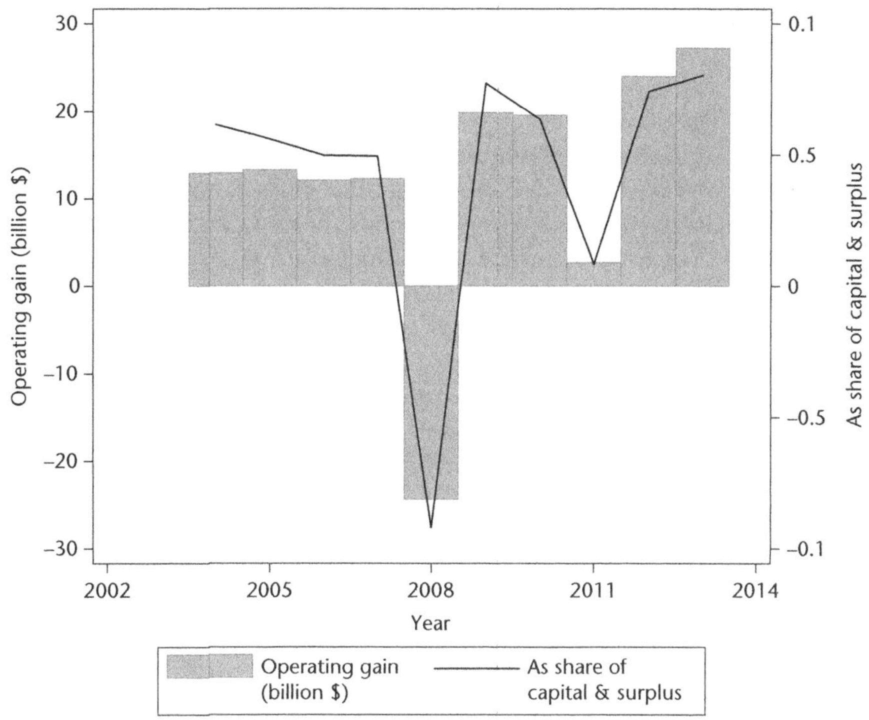

Figure 4.1. Operating gain from annuities for life insurers with variable annuity guarantees

Net operating gain from individual annuities is reported in total dollars and as a share of capital and surplus in the previous year. The sample consists of A.M. Best financial groups with positive annuity account value with guaranteed benefits in the previous year.

prices and volatility. An ongoing concern is whether further losses could yet occur, especially if interest rates remain low. An additional concern is that losses are not immediately transparent because variable annuity guarantees are not marked to market.

As discussed in A.M. Best Company (2015), life insurers have responded to the 2008 experience by reducing the riskiness of variable annuity guarantees in various ways. Many companies have raised fees, reduced the generosity of guarantees (e.g. by limiting the investment options), or closed existing accounts to new investment. In particular, MetLife and Prudential Financial have reduced sales, while Hartford and John Hancock have exited from the market entirely.

In addition to financial market risks, variable annuities are exposed to uncertainty in policyholder behaviour because of the various surrender and conversion options. Relative to traditional annuities, life insurers have less experience with policyholder behaviour, especially since the product design of variable annuities has changed over the last decade. Furthermore, the risks associated with financial markets and policyholder behaviour could interact in important ways. For example, lapse rates have fallen significantly since the financial crisis in a low interest-rate environment (Credit Suisse 2012).

The risks associated with minimum-return guarantees are not limited to the United States. For example, Equitable Life in the United Kingdom failed partly because of guarantees that were too generous (Roberts 2012). Perhaps more relevant to the current interest-rate environment, many Japanese life insurers experienced significant losses because of overly generous guarantees in the early 2000s (Kashyap 2002). The European Systemic Risk Board (2015) reports that guaranteed products represent a significant share of insurance liabilities in Austria, Germany, the Netherlands, and Sweden. In these countries, the average duration of liabilities exceed that of assets by five to ten years, which implies significant losses if interest rates remain unexpectedly low (European Insurance and Occupational Pensions Authority 2014b; Domanski, Shin, and Sushko 2015).

The economics of minimum-return guarantees for life insurers are similar to those of defined-benefit pension guarantees, which have a longer history. Therefore, the widespread underfunding of both public and private pensions is a cautionary lesson for life insurers (Novy-Marx and Rauh 2011).

4.2.2 *Shadow Insurance*

Regulation XXX in 2000 and AXXX in 2003 forced life insurers to hold more capital on newly issued term life insurance and universal life insurance with secondary guarantees. These regulations are part of National Association of Insurance Commissioners' (NAIC) statutory accounting principles that apply to operating companies.

In response to the new capital requirements, twenty-six states have now passed a version of captive laws, starting with South Carolina in 2002 and Vermont in 2007 (Captives and Special Purpose Vehicle Use Subgroup 2013). These laws allow life insurers to establish captives for the exclusive purpose of assuming reinsurance from affiliated companies. Captives are not subject to Regulation XXX and AXXX and may record lower reserves for term life insurance and universal life insurance with secondary guarantees under generally accepted accounting principles (GAAP). Therefore, a life insurer could reduce accounting liabilities, and thereby increase accounting equity, by moving liabilities from operating companies to captives.

Because captives are subject to lower capital requirements than operating companies, the additional accounting equity that captive reinsurance generates could be paid back to the parent company (and eventually to shareholders). Because the financial statements of captives are not publicly available, we cannot generally tell how much equity they have. However, as we discuss later in this Section, two case studies suggest that captives have much less equity than operating companies.

The potential risk of affiliated reinsurance depends on whether the reinsurer is subject to oversight by either state regulators or rating agencies. An authorized reinsurer is subject to the same reporting and capital requirements as an operating company in its state of domicile, whereas an unauthorized reinsurer is not. Even if an affiliated reinsurer is unauthorized, rating agencies could request financial statements and ensure that it has enough capital. Therefore, affiliated reinsurers with the least oversight are those that are unauthorized and unrated by A.M. Best Company, which we refer to as *shadow reinsurers*. Our definition of shadow reinsurers is more restrictive than 'captives' because some captives are actually authorized.

Like variable annuities, shadow insurance is highly concentrated. Life insurers using shadow insurance are on average larger and are mostly stock instead of mutual companies (Koijen and Yogo 2016). Table 4.2 reports the top ten life insurers by life and annuity reinsurance ceded to shadow reinsurers in 2013. These life insurers ceded $331 billion of liabilities in 2013, which is a significant share of $370 billion for the industry.

To summarize the recent trends in reinsurance, Figure 4.2 reports the time series of reinsurance ceded to affiliated, shadow, and unaffiliated reinsurers. Affiliated reinsurance grew from $90 billion in 2002 to $617 billion in 2013. The part of affiliated reinsurance that was ceded to shadow reinsurers grew from $11 billion to $370 billion during the same period. The growth of shadow insurance accelerated during the financial crisis from 2006 to 2009. Since shadow insurance effectively lowers capital requirements, this timing is consistent with the evidence that some life insurers were financially constrained during the financial crisis (Koijen and Yogo 2015).

Table 4.2. Top ten life insurers by shadow insurance

Financial group	Reinsurance ceded (billion $)
John Hancock Life Insurance	118
MetLife	45
Athene USA	40
Hartford Life	40
Aegon USA	30
Great-West Life	14
Voya Financial	13
AIG Life and Retirement	12
Global Atlantic	11
Lincoln Financial	7

A.M. Best financial groups are ranked by life and annuity reinsurance ceded to shadow reinsurers in 2013. Reinsurance ceded is the sum of reserve credit taken and modified coinsurance reserve ceded. Shadow reinsurers are a subset of affiliated reinsurers that are unauthorized and do not have an A.M. Best rating.

The growth of shadow insurance has slowed since 2009, partly because of more regulatory scrutiny in states like California and New York. Interestingly, unaffiliated reinsurance grew from $270 billion in 2012 to $331 billion in 2013 after a long period of essentially no growth. Although it is premature to extrapolate these trends, there could be substitution from shadow insurance to other types of reinsurance due to changes in the regulatory environment.

Figure 4.3 decomposes the time series of shadow insurance in Figure 4.2 into life and annuity reinsurance. Since Regulation XXX and AXXX apply only to life insurance, the growth of annuity reinsurance implies that shadow insurance does not exist simply to circumvent these regulations. Curiously, annuity reinsurance grew from $134 billion in 2011 to $163 billion in 2013, while life reinsurance remained flat at $208 billion during the same period. In response, NAIC initiated a working group in 2015 to investigate why captive reinsurance is being used on variable annuities.

The usual reasons for captive reinsurance are more favourable capital regulation and tax laws. In addition, a possible reason for captive reinsurance of variable annuities in particular is the volatility of reserves under statutory accounting principles (i.e. under Actuarial Guideline 43). Statutory accounting

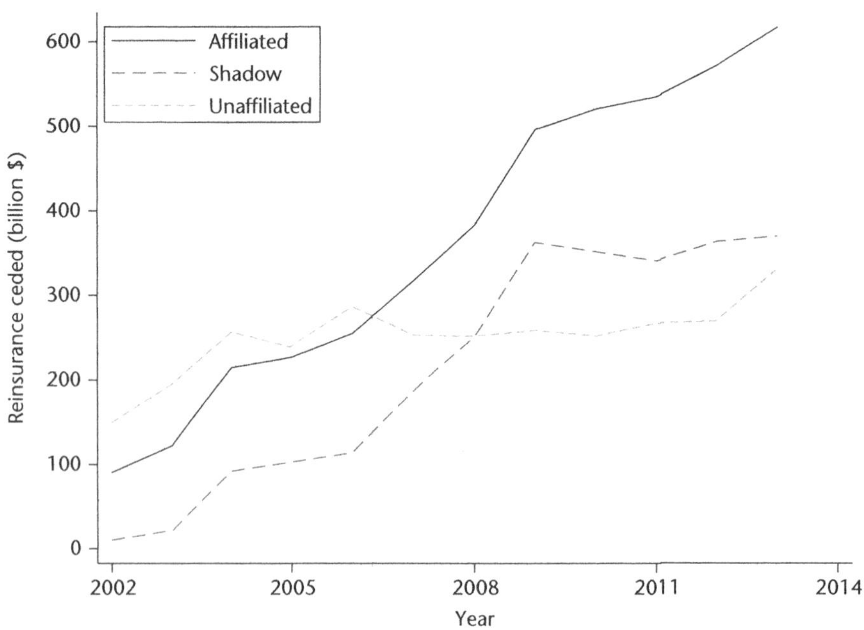

Figure 4.2. Reinsurance ceded to affiliated, shadow, and unaffiliated reinsurers

Life and annuity reinsurance ceded by U.S. life insurers to affiliated, shadow, and unaffiliated reinsurers is reported. Reinsurance ceded is the sum of reserve credit taken and modified coinsurance reserve ceded. Shadow reinsurers are a subset of affiliated reinsurers that are unauthorized and do not have an A.M. Best rating.

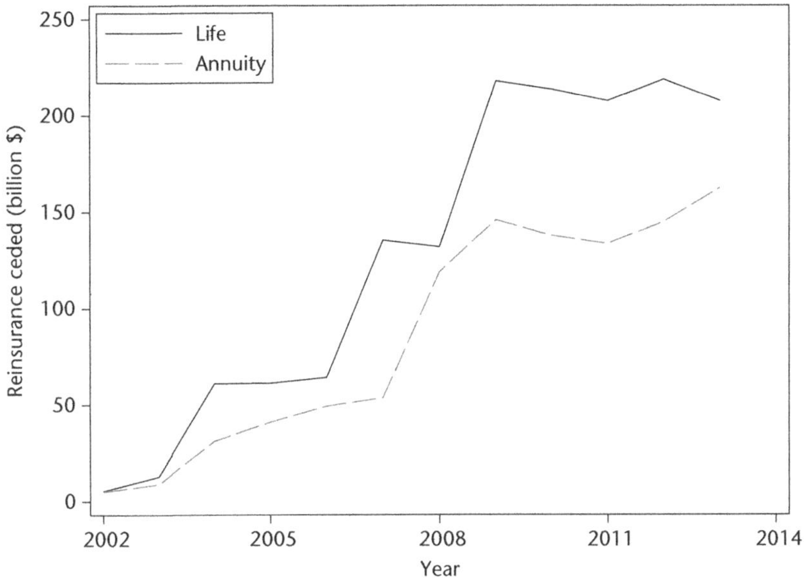

Figure 4.3. Life versus annuity reinsurance ceded to shadow reinsurers

Reinsurance ceded by U.S. life insurers to shadow reinsurers is reported separately for life and annuity reinsurance. Reinsurance ceded is the sum of reserve credit taken and modified coinsurance reserve ceded. Shadow reinsurers are a subset of affiliated reinsurers that are unauthorized and do not have an A.M. Best rating.

essentially forces life insurers to record variable annuity guarantees based on historical tail scenarios, while GAAP allows them to record reserves at market value. Therefore, the difference between statutory accounting and GAAP could increase after a period of high volatility. Related to this issue, a life insurer may not get proper credit for hedging variable annuity guarantees under statutory accounting, which provides an additional incentive to hedge these guarantees in a captive. Of course, the lack of transparency is a clear drawback of having variable annuity guarantees and corresponding hedging programmes in captives.

Shadow insurance is a potential source of risk for three reasons (Koijen and Yogo 2016; Schwarcz 2015). First, a significant share of shadow insurance is funded through letters of credit, which have shorter maturity than the insurance liabilities. Therefore, shadow insurance exposes life insurers to liquidity risk. Second, shadow reinsurers could take more investment risk than operating companies, which exposes the life insurer to more risk mismatch. Finally, shadow reinsurers could reduce risk-based capital and increase leverage within the financial group. Of course, higher leverage amplifies any risk mismatch in the overall balance sheet.

In fact, two case studies suggest that captives have much less equity than operating companies. First, Lawsky (2013) finds that captives that assume

Table 4.3. Surplus of Iowa captives based on Iowa versus statutory accounting

Captive	Iowa	Statutory
Cape Verity I	27	−432
Cape Verity II	140	−548
Cape Verity III	54	−169
MNL Reinsurance	118	118
Solberg Reinsurance	207	207
Symetra Reinsurance	20	−51
TLIC Riverwood Reinsurance	817	−1,113
TLIC Oakbrook Reinsurance	114	−675
Total	1,497	−2,663

Surplus of Iowa captives in 2014 are reported on the basis of permitted accounting practices of the Iowa Insurance Division and statutory accounting principles. All amounts are in millions of dollars.

reinsurance from operating companies in New York have less equity, especially in cases where letters of credit are conditional and are ultimately backed by the parent company instead of an unaffiliated bank. Moody's Investors Service shares a similar view that 'because many companies' captives are capitalized at lower levels compared to flagship companies, the use of captives tends to weaken capital adequacy' (Robinson and Son 2013, p. 3).

Second, the Iowa Insurance Division (2014) recently released financial statements for captives in their domicile for 2013 and 2014. These financial statements report surplus (i.e. accounting equity) under both the permitted accounting practices of Iowa and statutory accounting principles. Table 4.3 summarizes these statements. Six of the eight captives would have significantly negative surplus under statutory accounting, while two of the captives voluntarily report under statutory accounting. When aggregated over the eight captives, total surplus under statutory accounting would be −$2.663 billion.

4.2.3 *Securities Lending*

The two sources of risk that we have discussed so far, variable annuities and shadow insurance, relate to the liabilities side of the balance sheet. The conventional wisdom is that risk exposure on the asset side is well regulated by risk-based capital regulation. However, the experience of securities lending during the financial crisis shows that there could be important gaps in the regulation. Prior to 2010, the reporting requirements for securities lending was sufficiently lax that life insurers left important details about their activity unreported, particularly regarding how the collateral was reinvested (National Association of Insurance Commissioners 2011).

In a securities lending transaction, a life insurer lends bonds in exchange for cash collateral with an agreement to return the collateral back for the bonds at some future date. The life insurer could reinvest the cash collateral to earn higher returns by taking on additional credit, interest-rate, or liquidity risk. Liquidity risk arises from the fact that the reinvested collateral has longer duration than the maturity of the lending agreement. If borrowers are unwilling to roll over the lending agreement in bad times, the life insurer may be forced to liquidate the investment at fire-sale prices. This is precisely what happened to AIG during the financial crisis, as they had reinvested their cash collateral in mortgage- and asset-backed securities. AIG lost at least $21 billion through securities lending, which is a similar order of magnitude to the $34 billion that they lost through credit default swaps (McDonald and Paulson 2014).

Securities lending by life insurers grew significantly prior to the financial crisis. The amount of admitted assets subject to securities lending agreements grew from $49 billion in 2002 to $130 billion in 2007, then suddenly collapsed to $43 billion in 2008. After important changes to the reporting requirements in 2010, securities lending further dropped to $34 billion in 2011 and has remained low at $47 billion in 2013. Given the improved reporting requirements and the smaller scale of activity, securities lending no longer appears to be an important source of risk. However, the experience during the financial crisis is a cautionary lesson that gaps in risk-based capital regulation could have significant consequences.

Like variable annuities and shadow insurance, securities lending is highly concentrated. Table 4.4 reports the top ten life insurers by the amount of admitted assets subject to securities lending agreements in 2007. These life insurers accounted for $115 billion of securities lending in 2007, which is a significant share of $128 billion for the industry. AIG Life alone accounted for $54 billion in securities lending.

The last column of Table 4.4 reports the total capital gain from investment activity in 2008 as a share of capital and surplus in 2007.[5] The capital loss for AIG Life in 2008 was 169 per cent of its capital and surplus in 2007. When aggregated over the industry, life insurers with securities lending activity lost −39 per cent of their capital and surplus, while those without securities lending activity lost −18 per cent. To put the 2008 losses into historical perspective, Figure 4.4 reports the time series of capital gains, aggregated over life insurers with securities lending agreements in the previous year. The 2008 losses are extraordinary, both in total dollars and as a share of capital and surplus in the previous year.

An important question is whether other gaps remain in risk-based capital regulation that governs investment risk on the asset side of the balance sheet. This question is especially relevant in the current interest-rate environment as

[5] Our conclusions remain the same if we add investment income (i.e. coupon and dividend payments) to the total capital gain.

Table 4.4. Capital gain in 2008 for top ten life insurers by securities lending agreements

Financial group	Amount of assets (billion $)	Capital gain (share of capital and surplus)
AIG Life	54	−1.69
MetLife	38	−0.07
New York Life	6	−0.34
Prudential of America	5	−0.28
Northwestern Mutual	4	−0.52
Hartford Life	2	−0.07
Genworth Financial	2	0.12
Allstate Financial	2	−0.48
Manulife Financial	2	−0.07
Woodmen Life	1	−0.26
Total for life insurers		
with securities lending	128	−0.39
without securities lending	0	−0.18

A.M. Best financial groups are ranked by the amount of admitted assets subject to securities lending agreements in 2007. Total capital gain from investment activity in 2008 is reported as a share of capital and surplus in 2007. The last two rows report the total for the insurance industry, separately for life insurers with and without securities lending activity.

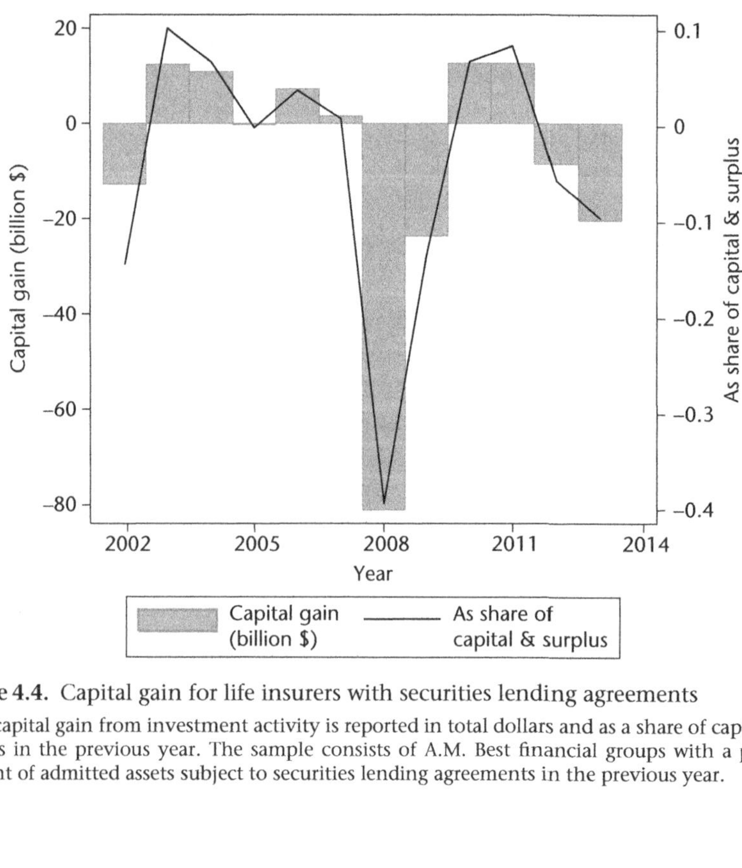

Figure 4.4. Capital gain for life insurers with securities lending agreements

Total capital gain from investment activity is reported in total dollars and as a share of capital and surplus in the previous year. The sample consists of A.M. Best financial groups with a positive amount of admitted assets subject to securities lending agreements in the previous year.

life insurers may reach for yield to earn higher returns. Three examples from the literature suggest that life insurers do take additional investment risk when risk-based capital regulation is not sufficiently sensitive to risk. Becker and Ivashina (2015) find that, within each of the NAIC bond classes defined by ratings, life insurers invest in corporate bonds with higher yields and risk as measured by credit default swap spreads. Becker and Opp (2013) find that life insurers increased the riskiness of their residential mortgage-backed securities portfolio in response to a reduction in capital requirements. Finally, life insurers invest in high yield assets through special purpose vehicles that are funded by funding agreement-backed securities, which are exposed to liquidity risk that is similar to securities lending (Foley-Fisher, Narajabad, and Verani 2015).

4.2.4 *Derivatives*

Life insurers use derivatives to hedge interest-rate risk on their investment assets and insurance liabilities, including minimum-return guarantees on variable annuities. Berends and King (2015) report that the total notional amount of over-the-counter derivatives held by U.S. life insurers was $1.1 trillion in 2014. Although this amount may be small relative to the size of international derivatives markets, it is still an important share of life insurer assets, especially given the concentration in derivatives activity.

The use of derivatives could expose life insurers to basis risk for two reasons. First, variable annuity guarantees have much longer duration than the maturity of derivatives that are readily available. Second, life insurers may not want to hedge economic capital because they report and are regulated based on statutory capital. A hedging programme that smoothes market equity may actually increase the volatility of accounting equity under statutory accounting principles or GAAP (Credit Suisse 2012). In addition to basis risk, derivatives could expose life insurers to counterparty risk. Although collateral could reduce counterparty risk, it potentially raises the cost of hedging programmes (Berends and King 2015).

A basic question in understanding the role of derivatives is whether they indeed hedge, rather than amplify, balance sheet fluctuations. The answer is not as obvious it may seem because Begenau, Piazzesi, and Schneider (2015) find that in the case of banks, interest-rate derivatives actually amplify fluctuations in the overall balance sheet. Figure 4.5 reports the growth rate of capital and surplus with and without derivatives, aggregated over life insurers with non-zero derivatives exposure. The Figure shows that derivatives have consistently reduced the volatility of capital and surplus over the last decade. In 2008, capital and surplus fell by 6 per cent, which would have been 15 per cent without offsetting gains on derivatives.

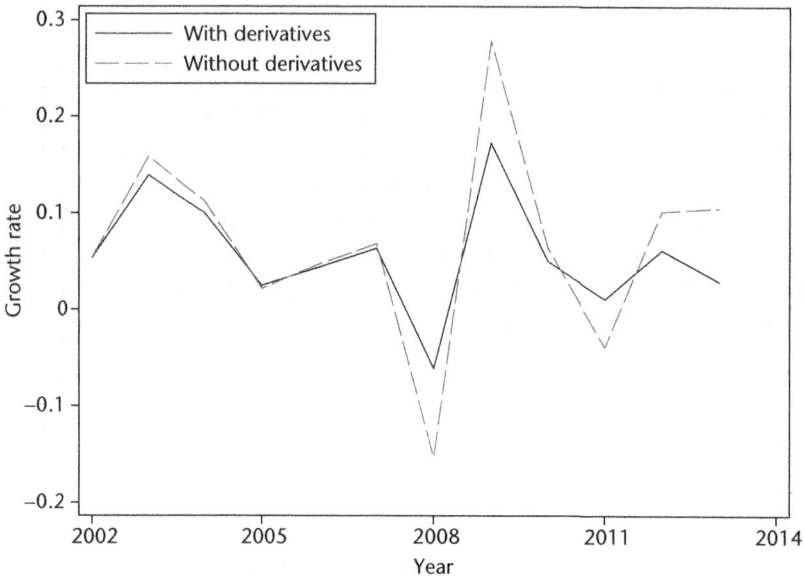

Figure 4.5. Growth rate of capital and surplus with and without derivatives

The growth rate of capital and surplus without derivatives is the growth rate of capital and surplus minus the sum of net investment income and total capital gain from derivatives. The sample consists of A.M. Best financial groups with non-zero derivatives exposure.

Our preliminary analysis suggests that derivatives reduce balance sheet fluctuations. However, additional data are necessary to fully assess the effectiveness of the hedging programmes. In Schedule DB, life insurers currently report how derivatives are used to hedge broad categories of risk (e.g. variable annuities instead of the type of guaranteed benefit). The same schedule also reports 'hedge effectiveness', which is difficult to interpret because it depends on statutory accounting principles for variable annuities. In Section 4.4, we suggest ways to improve financial disclosure on both variable annuities and derivatives.

4.3 Potential Transmission Mechanisms

We now discuss how risks in the insurance industry could be amplified and transmitted to the rest of the financial sector and the real economy. Our discussion will be qualitative because it is difficult to assess the quantitative importance of the transmission mechanisms, given the available data and our current state of knowledge. Based on the risks that we outline in this Section, one could make a case that life insurers are systemically important (Acharya and Richardson 2014). However, we also acknowledge the counterargument that the risks are still isolated and may not be sufficiently large (Harrington 2009; Cummins, and Weiss 2014).

4.3.1 *Transmission to Banks*

Life insurers are interconnected to banks through at least three channels. First, banks are counterparties in securities lending and derivatives transactions. The experience of AIG suggests that counterparty risk could be significant in bad times (McDonald and Paulson 2014; Peirce 2014). Second, life insurers provide an important source of funding for banks through the corporate bond market. Any reduction in funding could lead to liquidity problems for banks, at least in the short run. Finally, banks fund a significant share of captive reinsurance through letters of credit. Therefore, a systematic shock to insurance liabilities (e.g. from equity risk in variable annuity guarantees) could trigger drawdowns of letters of credit, so that banks are exposed to both liquidity and counterparty risk.

4.3.2 *Transmission through the Corporate Bond Market*

Life insurers are among the largest institutional investors in the corporate bond market. Therefore, any shock to their balance sheets could interact with risk-based capital requirements to cause a significant shift in demand and price impact. Falling bond prices, potentially accompanied by a volatility spike, could cause value-at-risk constraints to bind for other institutional investors, forcing asset sales (Brunnermeier and Pedersen 2009). Thus, shocks to the insurance industry could be transmitted to other parts of the financial sector through fire-sale dynamics in asset markets. This ultimately matters for the real economy through higher borrowing costs for firms.

There is substantial evidence in the literature that shifts in bond demand, when life insurers become financially constrained, have price impact. Ellul, Jotikasthira, and Lundblad (2011) find that financially constrained life insurers sell downgraded corporate bonds to satisfy risk-based capital requirements, temporarily depressing prices. Merrill et al. (2012) find similar evidence for downgraded residential mortgage-backed securities during the financial crisis. Ellul et al. (2015) find that financially constrained life insurers sell corporate bonds with the highest unrealized gains, carried at historical cost according to statutory accounting principles, to improve their capital positions.

These examples show that poorly designed accounting standards and risk-based capital regulation could have unintended consequences. Life insurers may have an incentive to sell bonds in depressed markets, even though they would be the natural long-term investors given their liability structure. Such incentives could exacerbate the transmission of shocks through fire-sale dynamics.

4.3.3 *Transmission to Households*

Any shocks to life insurers could transmit to households through the insurance product market. For example, if households become concerned about the solvency of life insurers because of variable annuity guarantees or shadow insurance, demand could collapse because of a debt overhang problem. Instead of purchasing insurance products, households may self-insure idiosyncratic risk through precautionary saving. This could have a potentially important impact on household welfare and the real economy (Koijen, Van Nieuwerburgh, and Yogo 2016).

Koijen and Yogo (2015) find evidence for the transmission of shocks through annuity and life insurance markets. In ordinary times, life insurers earn an average markup of 6 per cent to 10 per cent on annuities and life insurance. During the financial crisis, life insurers reduced the markup to −19 per cent for annuities and −57 per cent for life insurance, when falling interest rates implied that they should have instead raised prices. In the cross-section of policies, the price reductions were larger for those policies with looser capital requirements. In the cross-section of insurance companies, the price reductions were larger for those companies that suffered larger balance sheet shocks. Insurance companies that reduced prices sold more policies, consistent with a downward shift in the supply curve.

The example in Koijen and Yogo (2015) shows that poorly designed accounting standards and risk-based capital regulation could have unintended consequences. Life insurers may have an incentive to sell policies below actuarial value in order to boost their capital positions in the short run, hurting their solvency in the long run. This issue appears to be relevant to the 'volatility adjustment' under Solvency II, under which regulators would adjust the risk-free term structure of interest rates depending on macroeconomic conditions (European Insurance and Occupational Pensions Authority 2014a). Such adjustments could distort product market outcomes and exacerbate the transmission of shocks to households.

4.4 Implications for Financial Disclosure and Insurance Regulation

The risk profile of life insurers has become increasingly complex and opaque over the last decade because of variable annuities, shadow insurance, securities lending, and derivatives. In this chapter, we have summarized recent trends in exposure to these sources of risk based on public financial statements. To better understand how these sources of risk could lead to overall risk mismatch in the insurance industry, we suggest the following ways to improve financial disclosure.

1. Variable annuities: life insurers could report the type and quantity of guaranteed benefits sold and outstanding for each variable annuity product, which would be useful for understanding potential risk mismatch that arises from equity and interest-rate risk in variables annuity guarantees. Under the current reporting requirements, we only know the aggregate account value associated with guaranteed benefits.
2. Interest-rate risk: life insurers could report the market value and duration of liabilities (e.g. fixed annuities and life insurance), just as they already do for the asset side of the balance sheet. Such data would be useful for assessing the overall risk mismatch, particularly for interest-rate risk. This issue is especially important in the current interest-rate environment, in which there is significant uncertainty over how long interest rates will remain low.
3. Captive reinsurance: state regulators could release the financial statements of captives, following the lead of the Iowa Insurance Division. Furthermore, restated financial statements, in which the entire liability side is reported under statutory accounting principles, would be useful for assessing capital adequacy.
4. Derivatives: life insurers could report their hedging programmes in more detail, which would be useful for assessing their effectiveness. Under the current reporting requirements, we only know how derivatives are used to hedge broad categories of risk (e.g. variable annuities instead of the type of guaranteed benefit).
5. International activity: this chapter and most of the evidence that we cite is for the United States. The main reason is that financial statements at the same level of detail are not publicly available in Europe. Although transparency is expected to improve with Solvency II, we would like to see sufficient detail regarding guaranteed investment products, reinsurance, securities lending, and derivatives to be able to assess overall risk mismatch at the international level.

Recent research summarized in this chapter shows that regulation influences all important functions of the insurance industry including product design, pricing, reinsurance, investment activity, and risk management. Therefore, regulation is not only important for our understanding of insurance markets, but it must be properly designed to ensure both efficient function and future stability of the insurance industry. Yet, little research exists on optimal insurance regulation.

The fact that life insurers have a different liability structure than banks implies that their capital requirements must also be different. Life insurance liabilities are not prone to runs in most countries, so short-term risk constraints designed to prevent bank runs may not be appropriate for life insurers. In fact, short-term risk constraints can actually increase the long-term risk of life insurers if asset prices are mean reverting (Campbell and Shiller 1988). Therefore, life insurers should be assessed by long-term risk measures that are analogous to the short-term measures for banks.

Of course, measurement of long-term risk is challenging and potentially sensitive to reasonable variation in modelling assumptions. A fundamental problem with the insurance industry is that no one knows the market value of liabilities, and the data necessary for doing such calculations are far from complete in the public financial statements. We see the recent trend toward shadow insurance as a step in the wrong direction. Complete and transparent financial statements are necessary to move forward the discussion on optimal insurance regulation.

Acknowledgements

A.M. Best Company owns the copyright to *Best's Statement File* and *Best's Schedule S*, which we use with permission through their license agreement with the Federal Reserve Bank of Minneapolis. Koijen acknowledges financial support from the European Research Council (grant 338082). For comments and discussions, we thank Anders Malmstrom, Anna Paulson, Richard Rosen, and seminar participants at the 2015 Conference on the Economics, Regulation, and Systemic Risk of Insurance Markets at London Business School; the 2015 Banque de France-ACPR Conference on Financial Regulation—Stability versus Uniformity; the 2015 CEPR Financial Regulation Initiative Conference; the European Systemic Risk Board; and SIFR. The views expressed herein are those of the authors and not necessarily those of the Federal Reserve Bank of Minneapolis, the Federal Reserve System, or the National Bureau of Economic Research.

References

Acharya, V.V. and M. Richardson (2014): 'Is the insurance industry systemically risky?' in J. H. Biggs and M. P. Richardson (eds.), *Modernizing Insurance Regulation*, Chapter 9, 151–79. John Wiley & Sons, Hoboken, NJ.

A.M. Best Company (2003–2014a): *Best's Schedule S: Life/Health, United States*. Oldwick, NJ: A.M. Best Company.

A.M. Best Company (2003–2014b): *Best's Statement File: Life/Health, United States*. Oldwick, NJ: A.M. Best Company.
A.M. Best Company (2015): 'Variable annuities: Legacy blocks still represent tail risk', *A.M. Best Special Report*.
Bauer, D., A. Kling, and J. Russ (2008): 'A universal pricing framework for guaranteed minimum benefits in variable annuities', *ASTIN Bulletin*, 38:621–51.
Becker, B., and V. Ivashina (2015): 'Reaching for yield in the bond market', *Journal of Finance*, 70:1863–901.
Becker, B. and M. Opp. (2013): 'Regulatory reform and risk-taking: Replacing ratings', Working Paper No.19257, NBER.
Begenau, J., M. Piazzesi, and M. Schneider (2015): 'Banks' risk exposures', Working Paper No. 21334, NBER.
Berends, K. and T.B. King (2015): 'Derivatives and collateral at U.S. life insurers', *Federal Reserve Bank of Chicago Economic Perspectives*, 39:21–37.
Brunnermeier, M.K. and L.H. Pedersen (2009): 'Market liquidity and funding liquidity', *Review of Financial Studies*, 22:2201–38.
Campbell, J.Y. and R.J. Shiller (1988): 'The dividend-price ratio and expectations of future dividends and discount factors', *Review of Financial Studies*, 1:195–228.
Captives and Special Purpose Vehicle Use Subgroup (2013): 'Captives and special purpose vehicles', Unpublished Manuscript, National Association of Insurance Commissioners.
Credit Suisse (2012): 'US variable annuities', *Credit Suisse Connections Series*.
Cummins, J.D. and M.A. Weiss (2014): 'Systemic risk and the U.S. insurance sector', *Journal of Risk and Insurance*, 81:489–528.
Domanski, D., H. Shin and V. Sushko (2015): 'The hunt for yield: Not waving but drowning?', Unpublished Manuscript, Bank for International Settlements.
Ellul, A., C. Josikasthira, and C.T. Lundblad (2011): 'Regulatory pressure and fire sales in the corporate bond market', *Journal of Financial Economics*, 101:596–620.
Ellul, A., C. Jotikasthira, C.T. Lundblad, and Y. Wang (2015): 'Is historical cost accounting a panacea? Market stress, incentive distortions, and gains trading', *Journal of Finance*, 70:2489–538.
European Insurance and Occupational Pensions Authority (2014a): Consultation paper on a technical document regarding the risk free interest rate term structure. Working Paper 14-042, EIOPA.
European Insurance and Occupational Pensions Authority (2014b): EIOPA insurance stress test 2014. Working Paper 14-203, EIOPA.
European Systemic Risk Board (2015): 'Issues note on risks and vulnerabilities in the EU financial system', Unpublished Manuscript, ESRB.
Foley-Fisher, N., B. Narajabad and S. Verani (2015): 'Self-fulfilling runs: Evidence from the U.S. life insurance industry', Unpublished Manuscript, Board of Governors of the Federal Reserve System.
Froot, K.A. (2007): 'Risk management, capital budgeting, and capital structure policy for insurers and reinsurers', *Journal of Risk and Insurance*, 74:273–99.
Harrington, S.E. (2009): 'The financial crisis, systemic risk, and the future of insurance regulation', *Journal of Risk and Insurance*, 76:785–819.

Iowa Insurance Division (2014): Financial statements—single-state life or property. http://www.iid.state.ia.us/single_state_life_pc.

Kashyap, A.K. (2002): 'Sorting out Japan's financial crisis', *Federal Reserve Bank of Chicago Economic Perspectives*, 26:42–55.

Koijen, R. S. J., S. Van Nieuwerburgh, and M. Yogo (2016): 'Health and mortality delta: Assessing the welfare cost of household insurance choice', *Journal of Finance*, 71: 957–1010.

Koijen, R.S.J. and M. Yogo (2016): 'Shadow insurance', *Econometrica*, 84: 1265–87.

Koijen, R.S.J. and M. Yogo (2015): 'The cost of financial frictions for life insurers', *American Economic Review* 105:445–75.

Lawsky, B.M. (2013): 'Shining a light on shadow insurance: A little-known loophole that puts insurance policyholders and taxpayers at greater risk' Unpublished Manuscript, New York State Department of Financial Services.

Lee, S.-J., D. Mayers and C.W. Smith, Jr (1997): 'Guaranty funds and risk-taking: Evidence from the insurance industry', *Journal of Financial Economics*, 44:3–24.

McDonald, R.L. and A. Paulson (2014): 'AIG in hindsight', *Journal of Economic Perspectives*, 29:81–106.

Merrill, C.B., T.D. Nadauld, R.M. Stulz, and S.M. Sherlund (2012): 'Did capital requirements and fair value accounting spark fire sales in distressed mortgage-backed securities?', Working Paper No.18270, NBER.

National Association of Insurance Commissioners (2011): 'Securities lending in the insurance industry', *NAIC Capital Markets Special Report.*

Novy-Marx, R. and J.D. Rauh (2011): 'Public pension promises: How big are they and what are they worth?', *Journal of Finance*, 66:1211–49.

Peirce, H. (2014): 'Securities lending and the untold story in the collapse of AIG', Unpublished Manuscript, George Mason University.

Roberts, R. (2012): 'Did anyone learn anything from the Equitable Life? Lessons and learning from financial crises', Unpublished Manuscript, King's College London.

Robinson, S. and M. Son (2013): 'The captive triangle: Where life insurers' reserve and capital requirements disappear', Report 156495, Moody's Investors Service.

Schwarcz, D. (2015): The risks of shadow insurance. Unpublished Manuscript, University of Minnesota.

Appendix A

Data Construction

We construct our data from A.M. Best Company (2003–2014b). The relevant schedules and variables are as follows:

1. Summary of Operations:
   (a) Capital and surplus for December 31 of prior year.
   (b) Capital and surplus for December 31 of current year.
2. Analysis of Operations by Lines of Business:
   (a) Individual annuities: Net gain from operations before dividends and taxes.

3. Exhibits of Net Investment Income and Capital Gains (Losses):
   (a) Earned during year: Derivative instruments.
   (b) Realized gain (loss) on sales or maturity: Derivative instruments.
   (c) Realized gain (loss) on sales or maturity: Total capital gains.
   (d) Other realized adjustments: Derivative instruments.
   (e) Other realized adjustments: Total capital gains.
   (f) Change in unrealized capital gain (loss): Derivative instruments.
   (g) Change in unrealized capital gain (loss): Total capital gains.
   (h) Change in unrealized foreign exchange capital gain (loss): Derivative instruments.
   (i) Change in unrealized foreign exchange capital gain (loss): Total capital gains.
   (j) Unrealized increases (decreases) by adjustment: Derivative instruments.
   (k) Unrealized increases (decreases) by adjustment: Total capital gains.
   (l) Net gain (loss) from change in difference between basis: Derivative instruments.
   (m) Net gain (loss) from change in difference between basis: Total capital gains.
4. General Interrogatories:
   (a) Guaranteed benefit: Total related account values.
5. Supplemental Investment Risks Interrogatories:
   (a) Admitted assets subject to agreement at year-end: Securities lending.

In Table 4.1 and Figure 4.1, variable annuity account value associated with guaranteed benefits is 4(a). Net operating gain from individual annuities is 2(a). In Table 4.4 and Figure 4.4, the amount of admitted assets subject to securities lending agreements is 5(a). Total capital gain from investment activity is 3(c)+3(e)+3(g)+3(i)+3(k)+3(m). In Figure 4.5, the change in capital and surplus with derivatives is 1(b)1(a). The sum of net investment income and total capital gain from derivatives is 3(a)+3(b)+3(d)+3(f)+3(h)+3(j)+3(l).

In Table 4.2 and Figures 4.2 and 4.3, our data construction exactly follows Koijen and Yogo (2016), based on A.M. Best Company (2003–2014a).

5

Measuring Systemic Risk for Insurance Companies

Viral V. Acharya, Thomas Philippon, and Matthew Richardson

5.1 Introduction

The question of whether certain insurance companies, or more broadly the insurance sector, may be systemically risky is controversial. This controversy erupted in January 2015 when Metlife Inc. sued the Financial Stability Oversight Council (FSOC) over their decision to designate Metlife a systemically important financial institution (SIFI).[1] Though the lawsuit involves various legal arguments, Metlife's basic case is that the company, and for that matter the industry, is quite different from the banking sector and, in particular, is not systemically risky. The debate is not specific to practitioner and regulatory circles, but also appears in the academic literature.[2] In particular, while the academic literature supports the view that banking (and, for that matter, 'shadow banking') can be systemically risky, there is no such agreement with respect to insurers, asset managers, and other parts of the financial sector. This is partly due to different notions of systemic risk, but also to dissimilar views on the asset and liability side of insurance companies.

One useful way to consider the relative systemic risk of insurance companies is to compare them to banks. Banks have certain characteristics that make

[1] Previously, the FSOC had designated American International Group Inc. and Prudential Financial Inc. as SIFIs, neither of which was contested.

[2] As an example of this literature, see Acharya, Biggs, Richardson, and Ryan (2010), Acharya and Richardson (2014), Cummins and Weiss (2014), Harrington (2014) and Paulson, Plestis, Rosen, McMenamin, and Mohey-Deen (2014).

them relatively systemically risky. One such characteristic is that banks' assets tend to include loans and securities with values that correlate to the performance of the economy as a whole, or to the economic performance of a specific region, industry, or line of business. Put simply, borrowers are more likely to default on a bank loan when times are hard. Another such characteristic is that banks' business model traditionally involves holding short-term liabilities, such as deposits that can be withdrawn on demand or repurchase agreements, which are more liquid than their assets, such as loans to be repaid on a fixed schedule or asset-backed security holdings. Banks are thus vulnerable to 'runs' that occur when depositors or other creditors all withdraw funds at once.

Insurers, traditionally, did not share those characteristics with banks. The underwriting risks of traditional insurers' claim liabilities usually are better diversified than are the credit risks of banks' loan assets. Further, traditional insurers typically experience a loss of liquidity only when they make poor business decisions rather than as an inevitable result of their business model. Traditional insurers tend to write insurance policies that have fairly high policy renewal rates and require policyholders who cash out policies early to be subject to surrender charges or have the investment values of the policies paid out as annuities over prolonged periods. Insurers who issue only policies with those features are less vulnerable to runs and therefore less systemically risky.

There are good reasons to think, however, that parts of the insurance industry are no longer traditional in the above sense and instead have become more similar to banking, and relatively more systemically risky. Insurance companies are now exposed to more aggregate, nondiversifiable risk than would traditionally have been the case. That exposure comes both from their product offerings and from their investment decisions. As for product offerings, in the lead-up to the financial crisis, some large life insurers aggressively wrote investment-oriented life insurance policies with minimum guarantees and other features that exposed them to risk from movements in equity and other investment markets.[3] Such nontraditional policies can lead to large losses when markets decline—and therefore make the companies more systemically risky. The investments of insurance companies also appear to include more exposure to the risk of market movements than would traditionally have been the case. If such risks materialize (and the risks by nature are more likely to do so during conditions of financial and economic stress), then insurance companies collectively will suffer investment losses. Recent studies

[3] For example, some insurers sold financial products protecting against losses due to macroeconomic events and other nondiversifiable risks. In the years leading up to the financial crisis, the monoline insurers and American International Group ('AIG') wrote financial guarantees on structured financial products tied to subprime mortgages. (See Acharya, Biggs, Richardson, and Ryan (2010)).

suggest that life insurers' holdings are sensitive to interest rates and include exposures to mortgage-backed securities.[4] Becker and Opp (2013) document that a reform of capital requirements for U.S. insurers in 2009 and 2010 led those insurers to reduce sharply (from 90 per cent to less than 50 per cent) the share of their mortgage-backed securities that were rated investment-grade, choosing instead to purchase riskier ones. Such risk-seeking again parallels the behaviour of banks in purchasing residential mortgage-backed securities before the financial crisis. Such findings suggest life insurers now invest in ways that leave them exposed to risk based on the poor performance of the economy as a whole.

In addition, insurance companies are now more vulnerable to runs—that is, to the withdrawal of funds by policyholders who lose confidence in a particular insurer or in insurers generally. That vulnerability comes from a rapid rise in the sale of annuities, particularly variable annuities, which are purchased as withdrawable investment accounts. Paulson, Plestis, Rosen, McMenamin, and Mohey-Deen (2014) provide a detailed analysis of this issue, including evidence that approximately 54 per cent of life insurers' liabilities are in moderately to highly liquid categories. The study further estimates that 43 per cent of the life insurance industry's total general-account liabilities would likely be withdrawn in an environment of 'extreme stress', and 31 per cent in an environment of 'moderate stress'. Moreover, over time, some insurance companies have become active in shadow banking which tends to be lightly regulated and subject to significant liquidity and run risks when underlying security or counterparty risks materialise.[5] Examples include insurance companies running large securities lending businesses; using reinsurance to move liabilities from operating companies that sell policies to less regulated (that is, less capitalised) 'shadow insurers' in regulation-friendly U.S. states (such as South Carolina and Vermont), and offshore locales (such as Bermuda and the Cayman Islands);[6] and utilising funding agreements and related products (e.g. funding-agreement-backed notes and funding-agreement-backed commercial paper) which fall into the class of shadow banking activities.

[4] See respectively Brewer, Carson, Elyasiani, Mansur, and Scott (2007) and Baranoff and Sager (2009).

[5] Shadow banking is a system of financial institutions that resemble banks, or transactions that resemble bank services, because they provide the liquidity or maturity transformation services provided by banks. Shadow banking typically involves borrowing short term in rollover debt markets, using significant leverage, and lending to or investing in longer-term and illiquid assets.

[6] See Koijen and Yogo (2013). Because the liabilities transferred through shadow insurance arrangements stay within the insurer's holding company, there is not the usual risk transfer between the insurer and reinsurer. According to Koijen and Yogo, this type of regulatory arbitrage grew from $11 billion to $364 billion between 2002 and 2012. Such arrangements—which are increasingly widespread—functionally resemble the special-purpose vehicles used by large complex banks during the financial crisis.

Motivated by the above description of the possible sources of systemic risk for banks and insurance companies, this chapter describes the systemic risk model of Acharya, Pedersen, Philippon and Richardson (2015, 2016). In particular, we provide a simplified version of the extended model from that article that incorporates externalities arising from both an aggregate capital shortfall in the economy and fire sales as results of runs on financial firms' liabilities. Intuitively, a financial firm contributes to systemic risk through its contribution to the aggregate capital shortfall and the loss of future financial intermediation in the real economy (i.e. as a 'going concern'), and through its liability structure which impacts the likelihood of runs and forced fire sales (i.e. leading to a loss of 'current activities' in the real economy). Our contribution is to provide a framework for considering how systemic risk of an insurance company, relates to runs, the nature of liabilities, fire sales, insolvency, and capital shortfalls.

Our main result demonstrates the sense in which insurance companies, in comparison to banks, may or may not produce systemic risk. For example, we show that traditional insurance companies can be systemic, namely as going concerns because their contribution to an aggregate capital shortfall reduces the amount of financial intermediation undertaken in the economy. In contrast, banks contribute to systemic risk both as going concerns but also with respect to their existing assets and activities, causing fire sales within the financial system to have negative effects on the economy. As discussed above, nontraditional insurance companies may also be systemic to the extent that their liabilities are liquid and therefore runnable. The model provides the relevant parameters to begin thinking practically about the systemic risk of insurance companies. In practice, a comparison across both banks and insurance companies should incorporate the amount of the firm's assets, the systematic risk of those assets, the leverage of the firm, and the firm's liquidity mismatch, that is, the extent to which the firm engages in shadow banking activities and employs short-term financing.

The chapter is organised as follows. In Section 5.2, we provide a detailed discussion of the definition of systemic risk with a specific application to insurance companies. Section 5.3 presents the formal model of systemic risk for financial firms, and compares and contrasts the implications for banks and insurance companies. In Section 5.4, we make some empirical observations. Section 5.5 concludes.

5.2 Defining Systemic Risk

With respect to systemic risk management, the role of a regulatory body is to ensure that stress on the financial system does not prevent any given firm from carrying out its ordinary functions where those functions are critical to the functioning of the real economy. However, in order to regulate and manage systemic risk, one must be able to measure a firm's systemic risk. And in order to measure systemic risk, one needs to be able to take a position and precisely define what it is. In general, a financial firm can be described as systemically risky if it has the potential under stress conditions to cause harm to the broader economy. A conclusion that a firm is systemically risky is different from a conclusion that it is likely to go into financial distress: a firm can be systemically risky but healthy (or can be in poor health but not a significant source of systemic risk). A regulator concerned with systemic risk should ask whether a firm's financial activities could potentially contribute to a system-wide event such as the financial crisis that struck the U.S. economy in late 2008. That can happen when a firm is so positioned in the market that its distress is likely to cause distress in other firms—including its counterparties, creditors, or customers.

In previous work (e.g. Acharya, Pedersen, Philippon, and Richardson 2015), we argue that the above conditions occur when there is an aggregate capital shortfall of the financial sector.[7] Intuitively, systemic risk arises when there is a breakdown in *aggregate* financial intermediation—that is, the ability of financial firms in the economy as a whole to obtain funds from depositors or investors, and to provide financing to other firms. If one financial firm becomes unable to perform intermediation services, but all other financial firms continue to have ready access to capital, the consequences for the economy as a whole are likely to be minimal—the other firms can simply step into the breach. When capital is low in the aggregate, however, that is not possible.[8] Based on this intuition, Acharya, Pedersen, Philippon, and Richardson (2015) build a simple model of systemic risk and show that each financial institution's contribution to systemic risk can be measured as its systemic expected shortfall (SES), i.e. its propensity to be undercapitalised when the system as a whole is undercapitalised.[9] Thus, it is not the individual institution's capital shortfall per se, but its contribution to aggregate capital shortfall that matters when attempting to assess its systemic importance.

[7] An aggregate capital shortfall of the financial sector occurs when the market value of the equity in the sector as a whole falls below a certain fraction of the market value of the assets of the sector as a whole. It can be described as financial firms generally being under stress.

[8] See, for example, Thakor (1996) and Holmstrom and Tirole (1997) on the theoretical side, and Bernanke (1983), Slovin, Sushka, and Polonchek (1993), and Gibson (1995) for empirical observations.

[9] This SES measure of systemic risk has been analysed in a variety of recent papers. (For example, see Acharya, Engle, and Pierret (2013), Acharya, Engle, and Richardson (2012), Adams and Gropp (2010), Allen, Bali, and Tang (2012), Benoit, Colletaz, Hurlin, and Perignon (2012), Bisias, Flood, Lo, and Valavanis (2012), Brownlees, Chabot, Ghysels, and Kurz (2015), Brunnermeier, Dong, and Palia (2011), Engle, Jondeau, and Rockinger (2014), Giesecke and Kim (2011), Hansen (2012), and Huang, Zhou, and Zhu (2012).)

In the academic literature, using alternative measures of systemic risk, the importance of such co-movement is common to most approaches.[10]

The intuition for why the capital shortfall argument carries through to the insurance industry is straightforward.[11] The exposure of insurance companies to various forms of risk, and their potential to contribute to a broader shortfall of capital in the financial sector, gives them the further potential to cause impacts on the real (that is, nonfinancial) economy. Life insurance companies are one of the largest investors in the U.S. capital markets and therefore an important source of funding for the U.S. economy. The American Council of Life Insurers (ACLI) estimates that, at the end of 2013, life insurers held $5.6 trillion in total assets; were 'the largest institutional source of bond financing for American business, holding 20% of all U.S. corporate bonds'; and were a significant player in the commercial mortgage market, 'financing more than $286 billion, or one-eighth, of U.S. commercial mortgages'.[12]

The possibility that a source of financing this large could be withdrawn or significantly impaired is a significant systemic risk; and, of course, the possibility of fire sales of corporate bonds (causing corporate bond prices to fall sharply) would be an even greater risk. Distress in the insurance subsector could make it prohibitively expensive for even AA-rated and AAA-rated firms to issue corporate bonds. There is evidence, for example, that the liquidity of the corporate bond market dropped after the onset of the financial crisis in 2008.[13] Further, there are plausible scenarios in which trouble in the corporate bond market could spread to the banking subsector. Firms unable to obtain financing by issuing bonds would likely draw down on their bank lines of credit as a form of last-resort financing. In doing so, they would trigger massive liabilities for their relationship banks. Healthier banks with adequate capital and deposit bases might be able to meet the sudden drawdowns of credit lines. Moderately risky ones could experience distress. Weakened banks could well

[10] See, for example, Bisias, Flood, Lo, and Valavanis (2012), Brownlees and Engle (2015), Adrian and Brunnermeier (2015), Billio, Getmansky, Lo, and Pelizzon (2011), De Jonghe (2009), Huang, Zhou and Zhu (2009), and Goodhart and Segoviano (2009).

[11] See, for example, Acharya and Richardson (2014).

[12] ACLI, *Assets and Investments in America's Economy*, https://www.acli.com/Tools/ Industry% 20Facts/Assets%20and%20Investments/Pages/ Default.aspx.

[13] See Dick-Nielsen, Feldhutter, and Lando (2012). While it is an open question what role financial disintermediation on the part of distressed insurers played in the credit crunch in the corporate bond market in the fall of 2008, nevertheless, the impact of the insurance sector's inability to participate in the corporate bond market is now well documented, even outside the context of a common shock to the economy. For example, Ellul, Jotikasthira, and Lundblad (2011) show that, when insurance companies are required by regulation to sell downgraded corporate bonds, those bonds show significant price declines. Moreover, Manconi, Massa, and Yasuda (2012) document that in the second half of 2007, bond mutual funds and insurance firms contributed to the illiquidity of the corporate debt market as losses on the holdings of securitised bonds and commercial mortgage-backed securities transmitted in the form of asset sales or reduced purchases in other holdings, notably of lower-rated securitised and corporate bonds.

run aground.[14] It is natural to conclude that such effects would be even stronger if the insurance subsector was distressed; if at the same time there were a wave of downgrades in the economy; and especially if the banking subsector was also experiencing severe distress—a scenario that, taken as a whole, deserves the title of 'systemic risk'.[15]

As described in Section 5.1 Introduction, a growing body of literature recognises that insurance companies, like other financial actors, can be systemically risky when they engage in activities that expose them to risk from distress elsewhere in the economy and when they are positioned to transmit to other actors in the economy any distress they experience. (See, for example, Acharya, Pedersen, Philippon, and Richardson (2015), Billio, Getmansky, Lo, and Pelizzon (2011), Baluch, Mutenga, and Parsons (2011), Acharya and Richardson (2014), and Cummins and Weiss (2014).)[16] Of particular importance, Cummins and Weiss (2014) apply the SES measure specifically to the U.S. insurance industry. While their main conclusion is that core insurance activities tend not to be associated with systemic risk,[17] they find that noncore businesses (such as derivatives trading, offering financial guarantees, asset management, and securities lending) are linked to SES.

Defining a systemic financial crisis so far has focused on a capital shortfall of the aggregate sector. But, more broadly, the failure of a financial firm can be considered *systemic* in nature as long as it has spillover effects on the ability of the financial system as a whole to function. The aforementioned possibility that financial activities could be significantly impaired or asset fire sales could take place does not presuppose an aggregate capital shortfall. Indeed, it is well-known that financial crises can occur when the economy is hit by shocks and financial firms rely sufficiently on short-term financing that there is a risk the financing of these firms does not get rolled over (e.g. Diamond and Dybvig (1983), Allen and Gale (2000) and Diamond and Rajan (2001, 2005)). If a sufficient 'run' on a number of firm's liabilities takes place, these firms will be potentially forced to sell assets to cover the financing at potentially fire sale prices. Moreover, without the availability of long-term capital in the economy, small shocks can lead to runs on the liabilities (Acharya, Gale,

[14] See, for example, Acharya, Almeida, Ippollito, and Perez (2014) and Ivashina and Scharfstein (2010).

[15] Negative effects on the real economy could also follow directly from insurance companies' unwillingness or inability to supply insurance products, which could cause higher prices and an overall loss of economic welfare. There is growing evidence that capital-constrained financial firms, including insurance companies, may reduce the supply of capital in the face of losses, e.g. Froot (2001), Froot, and O'Connell (1999), Garmaise and Moskowitz (2009). It is an open question, however, whether these supply shocks extend beyond catastrophe losses in the insurance area.

[16] That said, there are a number of papers in the literature arguing that insurance companies are *not* systemically risky, see, e.g. Harrington (2009, 2014), Grace (2010) and Park and Xie (2011).

[17] The exception is for some life insurers who specialise in separate accounts and group annuities, and other banking-like products.

and Yorulmazer (2009)). These 'runs' can lead to a reduction in financial activities of the firm and fire sales which amplify throughout the financial sector, not dissimilar from the impact of an aggregate capital shortfall of the financial system.

For example, consider the following impact of fire sales described by Diamond and Rajan (2005, 2011). When fire sales of financial assets occur, the return on capital for these assets is high relative to real assets in the economy. In general equilibrium, fire sales therefore increase the required return on capital for real investments, producing rationing on the real side of the economy. This negative externality that lowers real investment only gets corrected when real and financial returns to capital are equilibrated.

Unlike the argument with respect to capital shortfall, it is difficult to make the case that traditional insurance companies are subject to runs. With little chance of runs by policyholders, it is reasonable to conclude that, *ceteris paribus*, banks (and other runnable institutions) contribute more to the systemic risk of the financial system. For example, Chen, Cummins, Viswanathan, and Weiss (2012) provide evidence that banks tend to create systemic risk for insurers but not vice versa. That said, there are two caveats to this argument. First, as described in the Section 5.1 Introduction, there is strong reason to believe that, for certain life insurers, the growth in variable annuities and shadow banking activities have increased the risk of runs. Second, and to the point of this chapter, even if a financial firm's liabilities are not runnable, the firm can contribute to systemic risk through its contribution to an aggregate capital shortfall.

The discussion above suggests two possible externalities for the systemic risk of financial firms—a firm's contribution to an aggregate capital shortfall and/or a run on its liabilities (resulting in fire sales). As described above in our discussion of the banking versus insurance sectors, it is likely that these two sources of systemic risk differ within and across financial sectors. As a result, the goal of this chapter is to provide a starting framework for analysing the systemic risk of insurance firms by taking into account both externalities.

5.3 A Model for Systemic Risk of Insurance Companies and Banks

In this Section, we describe the model of systemic risk of Acharya, Pedersen, Philippon, and Richardson (2016) that include runnable liabilities. A financial firm contributes to systemic risk through its contribution to two negative externalities—(i) the first corresponds to its contribution to the aggregate capital shortfall ('going concern'), and (ii) the second is based on its liability structure which impacts the likelihood of runs and forced fire sales ('current activities'). Our contribution is to explain how systemic risk of a financial firm, whether it be a bank or insurance company, relates to runs, the nature of liabilities, fire sales, insolvency, and capital shortfalls.

5.3.1 *Assets and Solvency*

We consider N financial firms, indexed by $i = 1, \ldots N$ and three dates $t = 0, 1, 2$, and we normalise the risk free rate to zero. At time 0, firm i has inside equity $w_{i,0}$, issues face value of debt d_i worth b_i, and buys assets worth a_i, subject to the budget constraint, $w_{i,0} + b_i = a_i$. At time 2, the assets pay off $q_i a_i$ but the random gross return q_i is learned at time 1, and the net worth of the firm is $q_i a_i - d_i$.

Once the returns are realised, we group firms into solvent and insolvent ones. We define the insolvency indicator as: $\delta_i \equiv 1 \leftrightarrow q_i a_i < d_i$. The owner of the firm is protected by limited liability and can consume $max\ (q_i a_i - d_i, 0)$. We also assume that assets have a capital requirement of z. The free or excess capital of firm i at time 1 is therefore $w_i = max\ (q_i a_i - d_i - z a_i, 0)$.

A firm can therefore be in one of three states:

- solvent with free capital if $q_i > {}^{d_i}/_{a_i} + z$,
- solvent without free capital if ${}^{d_i}/_{a_i} < q_i < {}^{d_i}/_{a_i} + z$,
- insolvent if $q_i < {}^{d_i}/_{a_i}$.

We define aggregate assets as $A \equiv \sum_i a_i$ and aggregate free capital as $W \equiv \sum_i w_i$.

5.3.2 *Runs*

We assume that a fraction γ of the liabilities can be withdrawn at time 1, and that creditors choose to withdraw when firms are insolvent. To meet the redemptions, the firm must sell a fraction α of its assets at unit price p: $\alpha_i = \min\left(1; \frac{\gamma d_i}{p a_i}\right)$.

Creditors anticipate potential losses and price the debt fairly. We assume that γ is an exogenous industry-specific parameter. To be concrete, we will assume that γ is large for banks and small for traditional insurance companies. Note that we select the best equilibrium. Short-term creditors run only on insolvent firms. Equilibria with self-fulfilling runs are also possible and would only reinforce our results.

5.3.3 *Market for Existing Assets*

The assets of insolvent firms can either be sold to solvent firms, or they can be liquidated. For simplicity, we assume that recovery values do not depend on the idiosyncratic component of asset returns (the general case is treated in

Acharya, Pedersen, Philippon, and Richardson (2016)). Asset buyers receive a return s and liquidation delivers l with $l < s$. To summarise, asset payoffs are given by:

- q_i if the assets stay inside the firm,
- s if the assets are *bought by another firm,*
- l if the assets are *liquidated.*

Let p be the price at which assets are sold. Because liquidation is always feasible and because buyers must at least break even, we must have $l \leq p \leq s$.[18] We assume a form of cash-in-the-market pricing. The equilibrium price p depends on whether there is enough free capital to buy the assets of insolvent firms (firms that are solvent but without excess capital do not participate in the market). The market clearing condition is $W \geq zp(\int \delta_i \alpha_i a_i - \mathrm{L})$, where L is the quantity of assets that are liquidated (instead of being bought by another firm). We assume the same type of requirement for the firms' own assets and for the purchase of assets from other firms.

5.3.4 *Discussion of the Model and Systemic Externalities*

The key contribution of our chapter is to distinguish two types of negative externalities in the financial system.

EXTERNALITY BASED ON EXISTING ACTIVITIES

This corresponds to the disruption of existing activities. It occurs when existing assets are liquidated. We draw a sharp distinction between sales and liquidations. If a financial firm is liquidated, the failure of its critical infrastructure leads to a negative externality and we assume that the externality is proportional to the quantity of liquidated assets. In other words, the externality is fundamentally linked to the short-term nature of liabilities. In our model, this happens only where there is a run.

As described in Section 5.2, fire sales that result in the liquidation of assets can imply that current activities of the firm are interrupted. Examples of such activities include: (i) existing loans are not properly monitored anymore; (ii) revolving credit is interrupted; and (iii) existing policies are disrupted. Note that though we define A to be the firm's assets, the real meaning of A is as the sum of the current activities of the firms.

[18] We consider equilibria where solvent firms do not want to sell their assets. This holds as long as leverage is higher than the benchmark return, a condition that is easily satisfied in equilibrium. Formally, we want $\delta_i = 0 \rightarrow q_i > s$, and $\frac{d_i}{a_i} > s$ is a sufficient condition for this to be true.

GOING CONCERN EXTERNALITY

The going concern externality arises when financial firms cannot provide some critical new services. The main difference with the previous externality (in Section 5.3.4 above) is that the externality can occur even if there are no runs. We assume that the going concern externality arises from an aggregate capital shortfall. For instance, as mentioned earlier, life insurance companies are important buyers of corporate bonds and commercial mortgages. Distress in the entire life insurance industry can then trigger a credit crunch even if insolvent insurers are not forced to liquidate their assets. Acharya, Pedersen, Philippon, and Richardson (2016) show how this externality arises naturally in a model with ongoing investment demand. In this case, an aggregate shortfall pushes up the required return on new project, leading to a fall in investment.

THE EXTERNALITY CONDITION

We incorporate both types of disruptions by assuming that aggregate externalities are given by:

$$Externality = fL + g\psi[1_{W<\bar{W}}(\bar{W} - W)]$$

The fire sale externality is simply proportional to the amount of liquidated assets L, which is endogenously determined. The going concern externality depends on the aggregate shortfall of free capital relative to some benchmark $\bar{W}$ (which depends on the size of the economy, etc). The parameter ψ reflects the fact that not all assets of a firm are devoted to systemically risky activities and thus is defined as the fraction of a firm's assets devoted to financial intermediation. For example, $\psi = 1$ is likely for banks while $\psi < 1$ is probably more reasonable for other firms with large financial operations, such as General Electric or General Motors or insurance companies for that matter. For the case of insurance companies, some portion of their assets is devoted to traditional insurance operations which may be uninterrupted even if the insurance company fails and there is an aggregate capital shortfall. That said, for the purposes of the model below, for ease of exposition, we assume all firms are governed by $\psi = 1$. The parameters f and g capture the severity of the two externalities. A final point is important. In this simple setup the two externalities are independent, although of course correlated because triggered by some of the same shocks. We will later discuss endogenous interactions between the two externalities based on marking to market and fire sales discounts.

EQUILIBRIUM AT TIME 1

For simplicity we will consider an *ex-ante* symmetric equilibrium where all firms within the same industry choose the same leverage. This implies that, conditional on distress, the liquidation rate is the same. We then define the aggregate rate of distress as $\bar{\delta} \equiv \sum_i \frac{\delta_i a_i}{A}$ and we can then write $W \geq zp(\bar{\delta}\alpha A - L)$.

Our main task is to determine the equilibrium prices at which assets are sold or liquidated. There are two types of equilibria depending on the nature of liabilities. If $s < \gamma \frac{D}{A}$, there is no partial sale because the price is never high enough to pay the short-term creditors. Since $s < \frac{D}{A}$, partial sale requires that γ be low enough. The banking model in Acharya, Pedersen, Philippon, and Richardson (2015), with $\gamma = 1$, is always in this category. If $s > \gamma \frac{D}{A}$, however, a partial sale is possible when the price is high enough. This new possibility captures some features of the traditional insurance market where liabilities are relatively stable.

In all cases, we will describe the equilibrium with the random variable λ defined as $\lambda \equiv \frac{W}{z\bar{\delta}A}$. This is the ratio of the free capital (potentially levered) to the potential quantity of assets that need to be reallocated. When it falls below 1, there is a shortfall of buyers.

Full liquidation equilibria

When $s < \gamma \frac{D}{A}$, then there is no partial liquidation equilibrium and we have $\alpha = 1$ for all insolvent firms. There are three regions:

- if $\lambda > s$, then $p = s$ and $L = 0$: no crisis;
- if $l < \lambda < s$, then $p = \lambda$ and $L = 0$: fire sales, but no liquidation;
- if $\lambda < l$, then $p = l$ and $L > 0$: liquidation creates systemic costs.

The quantity of liquidated assets is given by $L = 1_{\lambda < l}\left(\bar{\delta}A - \frac{W}{zl}\right)$.

Partial liquidation equilibria

If $\gamma \frac{D}{A} < s$, then partial liquidation is possible. The structure of the equilibrium depends on the value of the liquidation price l. If $l < \gamma \frac{D}{A} < s$, then the equilibrium is as follows:

- if $\lambda > \gamma \frac{D}{A}$, then $p = s$ and $L = 0$;
- if $l < \lambda < \gamma \frac{D}{A}$, then $p = \lambda$ and $L = 0$;
- if $\lambda < l$, then $p = l$ and $L > 0$.

If $\gamma \frac{D}{A} < l$, then the equilibrium is as follows:

- if $\lambda > \gamma \frac{D}{A}$, then $p = s$ and $L = 0$;
- if $\lambda < \gamma \frac{D}{A}$, then $p = l$ and $L > 0$.

By combining the various cases, we obtain the following generic proposition:

Proposition: Equilibrium at time 1

if $\lambda > min\left(\gamma \frac{D}{A}; s\right)$, then $p = s$ and $L = 0$;

if $min(\gamma\frac{D}{A};l) < \lambda < min(\gamma\frac{D}{A};s)$, then L=0 and $p=\lambda$;
if $\lambda < min(\gamma\frac{D}{A};l)$, then $p=l$ and $L<0$.

The quantity of liquidated assets is given by $L = 1_{\lambda<\min(\gamma\frac{D}{A};l)}\left(\bar{\delta}\min\left(\frac{\gamma D}{l};A\right) - \frac{W}{zl}\right)$.

EQUILIBRIUM AT TIME 0 AND THE OPTIMAL TAXATION OF SYSTEMIC RISK

As explained, systemic externalities come from liquidation and from going concern externalities. The planner cares about the externality while private agents do not. Below, we characterise the equilibrium at time 0.

The *ex-post* value for the owner is the sum of the returns on her own assets $\max(q_i a_i - d_i, 0)$ and the return on her acquisition $w_i({}^s/_p - 1)/z$. The programme of a bank owner is therefore

$$\max_{d_i, \tilde{q}_i} -w_{0,i} - \tau_i + \mathbb{E}\left[(1-\delta_i)\left(q_i a_i - d_i + w_i({}^s/_p - 1)/z\right)\right],$$

subject to the time 0 budget constraint. Note that we allow the manager to choose a portfolio of assets, i.e. to have an endogenous return chosen in some specified set.

From the planner's perspective, because bondholders are assumed to break even, welfare is measured by equity value net of externalities. The planner's problem is therefore to maximise $P^1 + P^2 + P^3$, with $P^1 = \sum_i \mathbb{E}\left[(1-\delta_i)\left(q_i a_i - d_i + w_i({}^s/_p - 1)/z\right)\right] - w_{0,i} - \tau_i$, and the externalities $P^2 = -f\mathbb{E}\left[1_{\lambda<min(\gamma\frac{D}{A};l)}\left(\bar{\delta}min\left(\frac{\gamma D}{l};A\right) - \frac{W}{zl}\right)\right]$ and $P^3 = -g\psi\mathbb{E}[1_{W<\bar{W}}(\bar{W} - W)]$.

With respect to the fire sale externality, P^2, to shorten the notation, let us denote by χ the occurrence of a fire sales crisis: $\chi \equiv \{\lambda < \min\left(\gamma\frac{D}{A};l\right)\}$. Then we can rewrite $P^2 = -f\mathbb{E}\left[\bar{\delta}min\left(\frac{\gamma D}{l};A\right) - \frac{W}{zl}|\chi\right]\Pr(\chi)$. Recall that $A \equiv \sum_i a_i$, and $W \equiv \sum_i w_i$, and $\bar{\delta} \equiv \sum_i \frac{\delta_i a_i}{A}$. Therefore, $\bar{\delta}\min\left(\frac{\gamma D}{l};A\right) - \frac{W}{zl} = \min\left(1;\frac{\gamma D}{lA}\right)\sum_i \delta_i a_i - \frac{1}{zl}\sum_i w_i$. The planner's solution can therefore be decentralised with the following tax system:

$$\tau_i^f = f\Pr(\chi)\left(\min\left(1;\frac{\gamma D}{lA}\right)a_i \Pr(\delta_i|\chi) - \frac{1}{zl}\mathbb{E}[w_i|\chi]\right)$$

where $w_i = \max(q_i a_i - d_i - z a_i, 0)$ is the free capital of firm *i*.

The tax has two parts because, during a crisis, a firm may either contribute to systemic risk through being 'forced' to liquidate assets at a cost to the overall system or mitigate systemic risk by being healthy enough to purchase some of the assets, thus avoiding liquidation. In the context of the model, the first expression is captured by $a_i \Pr(\delta_i|\chi)$ and represents the amount of assets dumped in a saturated market. It is equal to current assets times the probability of insolvency, conditional on a systemic crisis. It is not linear in negative equity as, for example, marginal expected shortfall would be. This is because, in the model, we assume that default creates a discrete jump in liquidation.

The second expression $\mathbb{E}[w_i|\chi]$ is the expected excess capital of the firm in a systemic crisis. It contributes negatively to the tax since it gives credit to the firm for its contribution to clearing the takeover market if the firm is solvent despite the systemic crisis.

With respect to the going concern externality, it is possible to show that the tax is equivalent to the systemic risk tax solved for and presented in our previous work (Acharya, Pedersen, Philippon, and Richardson (2015)). Specifically, the systemic risk tax associated with the aggregate capital shortfall externality is

$$\tau_i^g = g\psi \Pr(W < \bar{W})\mathbb{E}\left[\frac{\bar{W}}{N} - w_i | W < \bar{W}\right] .$$

In the cross-section, the optimal tax is directly proportional to systemic expected shortfall, i.e. the firm's expected capital shortfall in a crisis, namely when there is an aggregate capital shortfall.

The above breakdown of systemic risk is useful for analysing and comparing the banking sector to the insurance sector. A defining feature of the banking sector is that most liabilities are runnable (γ is large) and assets are illiquid (l is low), implying $\min\left(1; \frac{\gamma D}{lA}\right) = 1$, whereas, for traditional insurance companies, liabilities are more stable and assets more liquid, implying $\min\left(1; \frac{\gamma D}{lA}\right) = \frac{\gamma D}{lA} < 1$. *Ceteris paribus*, this means that banks may impose higher systemic risk than insurance companies even if the banks have less assets and less chance of insolvency, i.e. $a_{banks}\Pr(\delta_{banks}|\chi) < a_{insur}\Pr(\delta_{insur}|\chi)$.

Therefore, in comparing insurance companies to banks, we have provided a formal framework that explains how traditional insurance companies can be systemic, namely as going concerns because their contribution to an aggregate capital shortfall reduces the amount of financial intermediation undertaken in the economy. Of course, as described above, a particular insurance company's contribution depends on whether their assets are involved in the financial intermediation process. Consider the case of a poorly capitalized insurance company which collects premiums and simply pays them out to policyholders as these holders' claims become due. With little involvement in financial intermediation, such as an investor in corporate bonds and mortgage-backed securities or offering financial guarantees, it is not clear that this firm's distress in a time of crisis has systemic consequences. This insurance company is arguably no different from any other corporation engaged in real economy activities. Rather, it is the role of insurance companies in the financial intermediation process that highlights their importance as a going concern.

In contrast, banks contribute to systemic risk both as going concerns but also with respect to legacy assets, causing fire sales within the financial system with knock-on effects to the economy. Nontraditional insurance companies may be systemic to the extent that their liabilities are liquid. In practice, a comparison across both banks and insurance companies should incorporate their contribution to an aggregate capital shortfall, and the extent to which they engage in shadow banking activities and employ short-term financing.

Note that an interesting point of comparison between banks and traditional insurers can be seen in comparing the two extremes of whether the liabilities can be run on, i.e. $\gamma = 1$ versus $\gamma = 0$. In the latter case, insurers never engage in fire sales and can potentially help mitigate the crisis by purchasing assets. For example, the firm, Berkshire Hathaway, which has considerable insurance operations, might be considered an example of this type of firm. However, the insurance firm can still become insolvent and contribute to an aggregate capital shortfall.

This chapter has presented the simplified version of the model of Acharya, Pedersen, Philippon, and Richardson (2016) in order to analyse systemic risk with the possibility of both capital shortfalls and of runs and fire sales. In the setting above, the two externalities are assumed to be independent. However, there are two important reasons why these externalities may not be independent in practice, namely marking to market with endogenous runs, and strategic capital allocations with fire sales. With respect to the former reason, we have assumed that runs only take place if the firm is insolvent, based on long-run true value. If instead we assume insolvency on a mark-to-market basis, then the fire sale price would in fact matter for solvency. This would increase the runs and make them endogenous to the fire sales. It would also deplete capital and increase the going concern externality. With respect to the latter reason, the two externalities could interact to the extent that the same capital could be used to make new loans or to buy distressed assets. Fire sales then create an opportunity cost for making new loans. We could extend the model in our framework by modelling explicitly the new loans, with return R. The arbitrage condition would be $R=s/p$. Any fire sale, even before it hits the price l, would then raise the cost of fund for new loans (see, for example, Diamond and Rajan (2011)).

5.4 Empirical Implications

In this section, we briefly describe empirical implications of the model. Taking the model literally, the systemic risk of a financial firm is comprised of two components:

- Going Concern Externality × (fraction of assets involved in financial intermediation) × (probability of an aggregate capital shortfall) × (firm's expected capital shortfall conditional on a crisis, i.e., when there is an aggregate capital shortfall).

- Runs Externality × (probability of a fire sale crisis) × (a firm's quantity of assets) × (probability of insolvency conditional on a fire sales crisis) scaled by the fraction of assets that must be sold minus (the expected capital of the firm relative to required capital conditional on a fire sales crisis).

This result highlights the particular functional role of runnable liabilities, liquidity of assets, the quantity of assets, leverage, capital requirement, probability of insolvency in a crisis, probability of a crisis, and expected capital shortfall of a firm in a crisis. The result incorporates in a specific way, therefore, how the systemic risk of a firm is related to standard intuitive measures such as high leverage, systematically risky assets and/or activities, and liquidity mismatch.

Putting aside the issue of how to measure the relative cost of the going concern externality versus the runs externality, all the other parameters of the model are in theory measurable, albeit some with substantial noise such as the probability of a crisis. Importantly, because parameters like the probability of a crisis do not vary across firms, relative measures of systemic risk across firms can be developed.

Indeed, NYU Stern's Systemic Risk Rankings published by NYU's Volatility Institute provide estimates of the expected capital shortfall of global financial firms given a systemic crisis. (See http://vlab.stern.nyu.edu/welcome/risk/.) NYU Stern Systemic Risk Rankings approximate this amount of capital (i.e. SRISK) by estimating how much (if any) does a firm's market value of equity fall below a fraction of the firm's total assets when a crisis hits. Figure 5.1 provides time-series estimates of SRISK for the current three most systemic insurance companies, Metlife, Prudential, and Lincoln National, taken from NYU's site. Note these measures of systemic risk focus just on the going concern externality and assume the same ψ in Section 5.3.4 in the discussion on the externality condition (in other words, the same fraction of assets tied to financial intermediation).

There are two interesting points from Figure 5.1. First, there is considerable difference in magnitude of the going concern risk for Metlife and Prudential versus Lincoln National. This difference has grown since the financial crisis. Interestingly, FSOC has designated Metlife and Prudential as SIFIs but not Lincoln National. Second, unlike the banking sector, the SRISK does not decrease after the financial crisis, but instead has been at a similar or higher level since 2011. In a similar vein, Acharya and Richardson (2014) show that, before the crisis, the insurance subsector's percentage of the U.S. financial sector's total quasi market value of assets and total SRISK are similar (approximately 20 per cent). After the crisis, however, the insurance has become—on a relative basis, in terms of its total assets—a more systemically risky financial subsector. That is, whether due to regulation or to voluntary risk reduction in

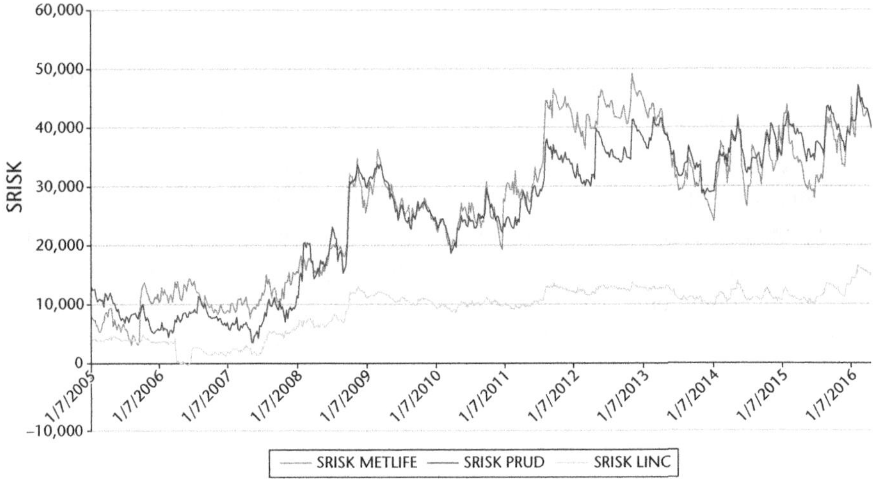

Figure 5.1. The relative going concern externality of insurance companies

Figure 5.1 graphs the SRISK over the last decade for the three insurance companies with the highest SRISK as of May 2015. We approximate this amount of capital by estimating how much, if any, does a firm's market value of equity fall below a fraction of the firm's total assets. We can estimate this measure econometrically using market data on equities and balance sheet data on liabilities. It is possible to show that[1]

$$SRISK_{it} = E(Capital\ Shortfall_i|Crisis) \approx [k(1 - L_{it}) - (1 - k)(1 - LRMES_{it})L_{it}]A_{it}$$

where k is the prudential level of equity relative to assets (8% in this example), L is the ratio of market value of equity to quasi-market value of assets of the firm (i.e. market value of equity plus book value of assets minus book value of equity) defined as A, and $LRMES$ is the long-run marginal expected shortfall (i.e. the decline in expected equity value if there is another financial crisis).

[1] See http://vlab.stern.nyu.edu/welcome/risk/.

the after-effect of the crisis, the banking subsector has become (and, since that time, has generally remained) *better* capitalised and *less* risky relative to the insurance subsector.

Tables 5.1A and 5.1B demonstrate this result in a slightly different way. Taking the current twelve most systemic financial firms in terms of a going concern, Tables 5.1A and 5.1B document how these firms' SRISK has changed compared to before and after the financial crisis. Some observations are in order. First, of the twelve firms with highest SRISK, six of them are now insurance companies, the most over the last decade. It is certainly true that the fraction of insurance company assets involved in financial intermediation may be less than banking and therefore the going concern externality due to insurance may be somewhat lower. Nevertheless, the delta of systemic risk of the insurance sector has been increasing. Second, this finding is confirmed in

Table 5.1. Changes in SRISK from A: 1/31/2007 and B: 8/31/2009 to 8/21/2015

Table 5.1A: 1/31/2007

Institution	SRISK (t)	SRISK (t − 1)	Δ SRISK	Δ(DEBT)	Δ(EQUITY)	Δ(RISK)
Bank of America Corp.	69,365.4	−41,273.2	110,638.5	45,832.8	37,108.3	27,697.5
Citigroup Inc.	41,170.7	−23,491.2	64,661.9	−12,368.4	63,051.5	13,978.8
Prudential Financial Inc.	40,021.9	6,176.3	33,845.7	24,495.7	3,507.0	5,843.0
MetLife Inc.	39,247.3	20,087.6	19,159.7	26,872.2	−3,641.2	−4,071.3
JPMorgan Chase & Co.	36,517.1	−24,215.2	60,732.2	77,813.1	−38,709.9	21,629.0
Morgan Stanley.	27,068.5	56,162.3	−29,093.8	−26,803.6	8,477.3	−10,767.5
Lincoln National Corp.	12,714.3	2,877.3	9,837.0	5,437.7	3,052.1	1,347.2
Goldman Sachs Group Inc./The	12,301.2	32,859.6	−20,558.4	−2,503.8	2,508.9	−20,563.6
Principal Financial Group Inc.	7,095.2	458.7	6,636.5	6,142.4	452.6	41.5
Genworth Financial Inc.	6,580.4	−2,550.0	9,130.4	−328.3	7,072.1	2,386.5
State Street Corp.	5,973.1	−2,991.0	8,964.1	13,822.2	−3,238.4	−1,619.7
Hartford Financial. Services Group Inc./The	4,494.5	7,026.3	−2,531.8	−7,034.5	6,732.4	−2,229.7

Table 5.1B: 8/31/2009

Institution	SRISK (t)	SRISK (t − 1)	Δ SRISK	Δ(DEBT)	Δ (EQUITY)	Δ(RISK)
Bank of America Corp.	69,365.4	102,499.0	−33,133.7	−8,149.4	−6,889.8	−18,094.5
Citigroup Inc.	41,170.7	114,845.2	−73,674.5	−6,754.8	−47,508.9	−19,410.8
Prudential Financial Inc.	40,021.9	24,637.2	15,384.8	24,922.3	−6,132.1	3,105.5
MetLife Inc.	39,247.3	27,905.0	11,342.3	27,726.0	−10,170.6	−6,213.1
JPMorgan Chase & Co.	36,517.1	72,134.0	−35,616.9	26,921.4	−34,222.4	−28,316.0
Morgan Stanley	27,068.5	32,592.6	−5,524.1	10,017.8	−12,865.5	−2,676.4
Lincoln National Corp	12,714.3	10,448.3	2,266.0	6,103.6	−1,938.0	−1,899.6
Goldman Sachs Group Inc./The	12,301.2	22,174.4	−9,873.2	−4,754.7	1,112.6	−6,561.1
Principal Financial Group Inc.	7,095.2	7,055.4	39.8	7,011.8	−3,241.0	−3,731.0
Genworth Financial Inc.	6,580.4	6,656.2	−75.7	−113.5	682.4	−644.6
State Street Corp.	5,973.1	582.6	5,390.5	10,524.9	−1,972.4	−3,161.9
Hartford Financial Services Group Inc./The	4,494.5	19,217.8	−14,723.3	−4,520.1	−6,063.9	−4,139.3

Tables 5.1A and 5.1B document the SRISK changes of the ten highest SRISK financial firms (as of 8/21/2015) from two dates: A: 1/31/2007 (before the financial crisis) and B: 8/31/2009 (after the financial crisis). We estimate SRIS econometrically using market data on equities and balance sheet data on liabilities. It is possible to show that[19]

$$SRISK_{it} = E(Capital\ Shortfall_i|Crisis) \approx [k(1 - L_{it}) - (1 - k)(1 - LRMES_{it})L_{it}]A_{it}$$

where k is the prudential level of equity relative to assets (8% in this example), L is the ratio of market value of equity to quasi-market value of assets of the firm (i.e., market value of equity plus book value of assets minus book value of equity) defined as A, and LRMES is the long-run marginal expected shortfall (i.e. the decline in expected equity value if there is another financial crisis).

[19] See http://vlab.stern.nyu.edu/welcome/risk/.

Tables 5.1A and 5.1B. The SRISK of five of six insurance companies has increased since before the crisis and four of six since after the crisis. This contrasts with the five large banking institutions. While three of the banks' SRISK has increased since before the crisis, all of the banks' SRISK has declined subsequent to the crisis. The fact that there has been a 'changing of the guard' so to speak should not be surprising. If the amount of financial assets are somewhat fixed, and the banking sector has reduced its role, then other parts of the financial system must pick up the slack. Insurance companies are clearly part of the story. Finally, Table 5.1B shows that the increase in SRISK of the insurance sector is not because market equity values have declined or asset risk has increased, but rather higher SRISK is due to an increase in leverage. In other words, systemic risk (in the form of going concern risk) has been transmitted to the insurance sector through leverage which may be a red flag for regulators.

Along with the going concern externality, it is possible to make progress on whether there is a run externality for insurance companies. Two key parameters are (i) whether an insurance company's liabilities are runnable, and (ii) the probability of an insolvency in a crisis. With respect to (i), most notably, Paulson, Plestis, Rosen, McMenamin, and Mohey-Deen (2014) provide an algorithm for analysing runs by developing a framework for breaking life insurers' liabilities into categories of illiquid, moderately liquid and highly liquid. They document that over 50 per cent of liabilities are in the moderate to high categories, and estimate that over 40 per cent of the life insurance industry's liabilities would likely be withdrawn in an environment of 'extreme stress'. Rather than performing a full-blown analysis of runnable liabilities, however, we instead simply comment on one firm, namely Metlife. According to FSOC's filings on Metlife, as of December 2013, Metlife had written approximately $100 billion of variable annuities; had $49 billion of $308 billion general account liabilities withdrawable without penalty; had $52 billion of funding agreements and $35 billion of funding agreement backed notes and commercial paper; and securities lending of around $30 billion. These magnitudes are consistent with the aforementioned general findings on liabilities of the life insurance sector by Paulson, Plestis, Rosen, McMenamin, and Mohey-Deen (2014).

It is sometimes argued that runnable liabilities are not important for insurance companies because many of the relevant state regulators have authority to step in and prevent redemptions. This argument actually reinforces the case for some insurance companies contributing to systemic run risk in much the same way that deposit insurance for banks is a regulatory response to possible bank runs. Whether these regulations are optimal is an open question, but they exist because of the run threat. Setting up gates to prevent redemptions, however, has clear costs. It reduces liquidity by tying up the funds of the policyholders, and, because of this cost, may make runs more likely. That is,

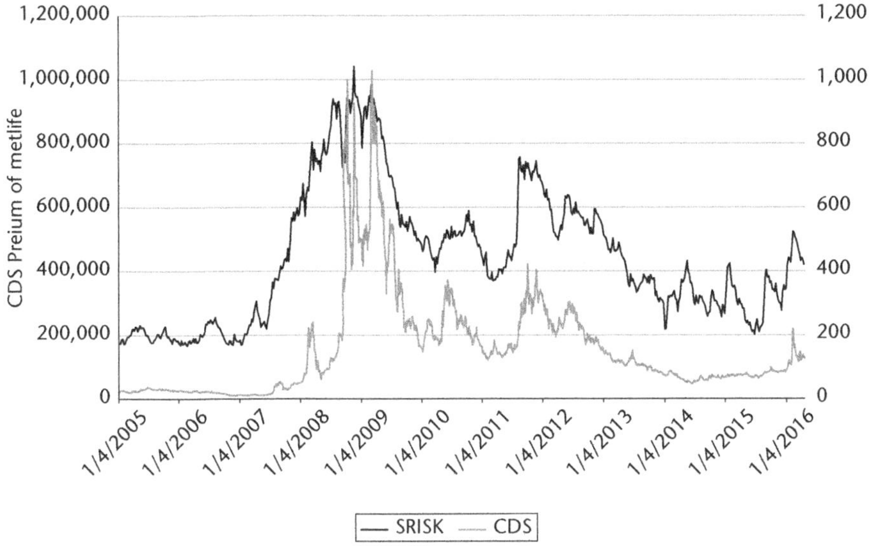

Figure 5.2. CDS Premium of Metlife

Figure 5.2 graphs the CDS premium of Metlife alongside the aggregate SRISK of the U.S. financial sector over the last decade. The CDS premium of Metlife represents that of a five-year CDS contract and is represented on the right-hand side in basis points, while the aggregate SRISK is simply the sum of the SRISKs of each financial firm in the U.S. and is represented on the left-hand side in $1,000s.

the regulation encourages policyholders to be the first to redeem before the gates are set up, leading many policyholders to run prematurely.

As a final comment on the run externality, note that the second key parameter is the probability of insolvency conditional on a crisis. This is also measurable. Putting aside the price of risk, the simplest way would be to back out the probability of default from traded securities such as credit default swaps. To coincide with the above focus on Metlife, Figure 5.2 documents Metlife's CDS premium over the past decade alongside the total SRISK of the U.S. financial system (which represents the estimate of the financial sector's undercapitalisation in a stress situation). Two points are of interest. First, from 30 September 2008, through 1 June 2009, the premium never fell below 400 basis points. For comparison purposes, over the last twenty years, the median spread of high-yield (so-called junk) bonds has been 560 basis points. Second, there is a remarkable relation between MetLife's CDS and the financial sector's SRISK throughout the ten-year period. That suggests MetLife's financial distress is at its highest when the estimate of aggregate capital shortfall is high. As seen by the systemic risk model's formula at the beginning of this section, higher insolvency probability *ceteris paribus* increases the run externality. Acharya and Richardson (2014) document a similar finding by comparing the average CDS premium of insurance firms against aggregate stock market values.

5.5 Conclusion

On the one hand, a growing body of literature recognises that insurance companies, like other financial actors, can be systemically risky when they engage in activities that expose them to risk from distress somewhere in the economy and when they are positioned to transmit this distress to other actors in the economy. On the other hand, insurance companies, especially those engaged in purely traditional activities, would seem to be quite different from banks in this regard. This chapter provides a theoretical framework to analyse and compare different types of financial firms along a number of dimensions.

Working off the systemic risk model of Acharya, Pedersen, Philippon, and Richardson (2010, 2016), we propose and implement a more precise definition of systemic risk. Our model incorporates two negative externalities arising respectively from an aggregate capital shortfall in the economy and fire sales as results of runs on financial firms' liabilities. A financial firm contributes to systemic risk through its contribution to the aggregate capital shortfall and the loss of future financial intermediation in the real economy (i.e. as a 'going concern'), and through its liability structure which impacts the likelihood of runs and forced fire sales (i.e. leading to a loss of 'current activities' in the real economy).

The resulting model highlights the conditions under which one firm may be more systemically risky than another firm. Specifically, a comparison across both banks and insurance companies should incorporate the firm's size, the risk of the firm's assets in a crisis, the leverage of the firm, and the firm's liquidity mismatch, that is, the extent to which the firm engages in shadow banking activities and employs short-term financing. Since many of these characteristics are publicly available for financial firms, the model in this chapter has practical consequences. We provide several empirical observations to illustrate this point.

References

Acharya, Viral, Heitor Almeida, Filippo Ippollito, and Ander Perez (2014): 'Credit Lines as Monitored Liquidity Insurance: Theory and Evidence', *Journal of Financial Economics*, 112: 287–319.

Acharya, Viral, Robert Engle, and Diane Pierret (2013): 'Testing Macroprudential Stress Tests: The Risk of Regulatory Weights', *Journal of Monetary Economics*, 65: 36–53.

Acharya, Viral, Robert Engle, and Matthew Richardson (2012): Capital Shortfall: A New Approach to Ranking and Regulating Systemic Risks, *American Economic Review, Proceedings & Papers*, 102: 59–64.

Acharya, Viral, Douglas Gale, and Tanju Yorulmazer (2009): 'Rollover Risk and Market Freezes', *Journal of Finance*, 2011, 66: 1175–207.

Acharya, Viral and Matthew Richardson, (2014): 'Is the Insurance Industry Systemically Risky?', Chapter 9 in John Biggs, Matthew Richardson, and Ingo Walter (eds.), *Modernizing Insurance Regulation*. John Wiley & Sons, Hoboken, NJ.

Acharya, Viral, John Biggs, Matthew Richardson, and Stephen Ryan (2010): 'Systemic Risk and the Regulation of Insurance Companies,' in Viral V. Acharya, Thomas Cooley, Matthew Richardson, and Ingo Walter (eds.), *Regulating Wall Street: The Dodd-Frank Act and the New Architecture of Global Finance*, p. 242.

Acharya, Viral, Lasse H. Pedersen, Thomas Philippon, and Matthew Richardson (2015): 'Measuring Systemic Risk', *The Review of Financial Studies*, forthcoming.

Acharya, Viral, Lasse H. Pederson, Thomas Philippon, and Matthew Richardson (2016): *Measuring Systemic Risk* II (January 2016), mimeo.

Adams, Z., R. Füss, and R. Gropp (2010): 'Modeling Spillover Effects Among Financial Institutions: A State-Dependent Sensitivity Value-at-Risk (SDSVaR) Approach', Working Paper, European Business School.

Adrian, Tobias and Markus Brunnermeier (2015): *CoVaR. American Economic Review*, forthcoming.

Allen, Franklin and Douglas Gale (2000): Financial Contagion, *Journal of Political Economy*, 108: 1–33.

Allen, Linda, Turan G. Bali, and Yi Tang (2012): 'Does Systemic Risk in the Financial Sector Predict Future Economic Downturns?' *Review of Financial Studies*, 25(10): 3000–36.

American Council of Life Insurers, *Assets and Investments in America's Economy*, https://www.acli.com/Tools/Industry%20Facts/Assets%20and%20Investments/Pages/Default.aspx

Baluch, Faisal, Stanley Mutenga, and Chris Parsons (2011): 'Insurance, Systemic Risk and the Financial Crisis', *The Geneva Papers on Risk and Insurance Issues and Practice*, 36(1): 126–163.

Baranoff, Etti G. and Thomas W. Sager (2009): *The Impact of Mortgage-Backed Securities on Capital Requirements of Life Insurers in the Financial Crisis of 2007–2008*, 34 Geneva Papers on Risk & Ins. pp. 100–18.

Benoit, S., G. Colletaz, C. Hurlin, and C. Perignon (2012): A Theoretical and Empirical Comparison of Systemic Risk Measures, working paper.

Bernanke, Ben (1983): Nonmonetary Effects of the Financial Crisis in the Propagation of the Great Depression. *The American Economic Review*, 73(3): 257–76.

Billio, Monica, Mila Getmansky, Andrew Lo, and Loriana Pelizzon (2011): Econometric Measures of Connectedness and Systemic Risk in the Finance and Insurance Sectors. Ca' Foscari University of Venice, Department of Economics Working Paper No. 21/WP/2011.

Bisias, Dimitrios, Mark Flood, Andrew Lo, and Stavros Valavanis (2012): A Survey of Systemic Risk Analytics. Office of Financial Research Working Paper No. 0001.

Becker, Bo and Marcus Opp (2013): 'Regulatory Reform and Risk-Taking: Replacing Ratings', Working Paper No, 19257, NBER (July 2013).

Brownlees, Christian and Robert Engle (2015): 'SRISK: A Conditional Capital Shortfall Index for Systematic Risk Assessment', *The Review of Financial Studies*, forthcoming.

Brownlees, Christian, Ben Chabot, Eric Ghysels, and Christopher Kurz (2015): 'Back to the Future: Backtesting Systemic Risk Measures during the Great Depression and Historical Bank Runs', Working paper, Federal Reserve.

Brunnermeier, M. K., G. N. Dong, and D. Palia (2011): 'Banks Non-Interest Income and Systemic Risk', Working Paper, Princeton University.

Chen, Hua, J. David Cummins, Krupa S. Viswanathan, and Mary A. Weiss (2014): 'Systemic Risk and the Inter-Connectedness between Banks and Insurers: An Econometric Analysis,' *Journal of Risk and Insurance*, 81(3): 623–52.

Cummins, J. David and Mary Weiss (2014): 'Systemic risk and Regulation of the U.S. Insurance Industry', Chapter 7 in John Biggs, Matthew Richardson and Ingo Walter (eds.), *Modernizing Insurance Regulation*. John Wiley & Sons, Hoboken, NJ.

De Jonghe, Olivier (2009): 'Back to the Basics in Banking? A Micro-analysis of Banking System Stability', National Bank of Belgium Working Paper No. 167.

Diamond, Douglas W. and Phillip H. Dybvig (1983): 'Bank Runs, Deposit Insurance, and Liquidity', *Journal of Political Economy* 91, 401–19.

Diamond, Douglas W. and Raghuram G. Rajan (2001): 'Liquidity Risk, Liquidity Creation, and Financial Fragility: A Theory of Banking', *Journal of Political Economy* 109(2): 287–327.

Diamond, Douglas W. and Raghuram G. Rajan (2005): 'Liquidity Shortages and Banking Crises', *The Journal of Finance*, 60(2): 615–47, April 2005.

Diamond, Douglas W. and Raghuram G. Rajan (2011): 'Fear of Fire Sales, Illiquidity Seeking, and Credit Freezes', *The Quarterly Journal of Economics*, 126(2): 557–91.

Dick-Nielsen, Jens, Peter Feldhutter, and David Lando (2012): 'Corporate Bond Liquidity Before and After the Onset of the Subprime Crisis', *J. Fin. Econ.*, 103: 471–92.

Elijah Brewer III, James M. Carson, Elyas Elyasiani, Iqbal Mansur, and William L. Scott (2007): 'Interest Rate Risk and Equity Values of Life Insurance Companies: A GARCH-M Model', *J. Risk & Ins.* 74: 401–23.

Ellul, Andrew, Chotibhak Jotikasthira, and Christian T. Lundblad (2011): 'Regulatory Pressure and Fire Sales in the Corporate Bond Market', *J. Fin. Econ.* 101: 596–620.

Engle, Robert, Eric Jondeau, and Michael Rockinger (2014): 'Systemic Risk in Europe', *Review of Finance*, 19: 145–90.

Froot, Kenneth A. (2001): 'The Market for Catastrophe Risk: A Clinical Examination', *J. Fin. Econ.* 60: 529–71.

Froot, Kenneth A. and Paul G. J. O'Connell (1999): 'The Pricing of U.S. Catastrophe Reinsurance,' Chapter 5 in Kenneth A. Froot (ed.), *The Financing of Catastrophe Risk*. University of Chicago Press.

Garmaise, Mark J. and Tobias J. Moskowitz (2009): 'Catastrophe Risk and Credit Markets', *J. Fin.* 64: 657–707.

Gibson, Michael (1995): 'Can Bank Health Affect Investment? Evidence from Japan', *The Journal of Business*, 68(3): 281–308.

Giesecke, Kay and Baeho Kim (2011): 'Systemic Risk: What Defaults Are Telling Us', *Management Science*, 57: 1387–405.

Goodhart, Charles and Miguel Segoviano (2009): 'Banking Stability Measures. IMF', Working Paper No. WP/09/4.

Grace, Martin F. (2010): 'The Insurance Industry and Systemic Risk: Evidence and Discussion', Working Paper, Georgia State University.

Hansen, Lars P. (2012): 'Challenges in Identifying and Measuring Systemic Risk', Working Paper, NBER.

Harrington, Scott (2009): 'The Financial Crisis, Systematic Risk, and the Future of Insurance Regulation', *Journal of Risk and Insurance* 76, 785–819.

Harrington, Scott E. (2014): 'Designation and Supervision of Insurance SIFIs', Chapter 8 in John H. Biggs and Matthew P. Richardson (eds.), *Modernizing Insurance Regulation.* John Wiley & Sons, Hoboken, NJ.

Holmstrom, Bengt and Jean Tirole (1997): 'Financial Intermediation, Loanable Funds, and the Real Sector', *The Quarterly Journal of Economics*, 112(3): 663–91.

Huang, Xin, Hao Zhou, and Haibin Zhu (2009): 'A Framework for Assessing the Systemic Risk of Major Financial Institutions', Finance and Economics Discussion Series, Divisions of Research and Statistics and Monetary Affairs, Federal Reserve Board of Washington DC, No. 2009–37.

Huang, Xin, Hao Zhou, and Haibin Zhu (2012): 'Systemic Risk Contributions', *Journal of Financial Services Research*, 42(1): 55–83.

Ivashina, Victoria and David S. Scharfstein (2010): 'Bank Lending During the Financial Crisis of 2008'. *Journal of Financial Economics* 97(3) (September): 319–38.

Koijen, Ralph S. J. and Motohiro Yogo (2013): 'Shadow Insurance', Working Paper No. 19568, NBER (Oct. 2013).

Manconi, A. M. Massa and A. Yasuda (2012): 'The Role of Institutional Investors in Propagating the Crisis of 2007–08,' *Journal of Financial Economics*, 104(3): 491–518.

Paulson, Anna, Thanases Plestis, Richard Rosen, Robert McMenamin, and Zain Mohey-Deen (2014): 'Assessing the Vulnerability of the U.S. Life Insurance Industry', Chapter 6 in John H. Biggs and Matthew P. Richardson (eds.), *Modernizing Insurance* Regulation. John Wiley & Sons, Hoboken, NJ.

Park, Sojung Carol and Xiaoying Xie (2011): 'Reinsurance and Systematic Risk: The Impact of Reinsurer Downgrading on Property-Casualty Insurers', Working Paper, California State University, Fullerton.

Slovin, Myron, Marie Sushka, and John Polonchek (1993): 'The Value of Bank Durability: Borrowers as Bank Stakeholders', *The Journal of Finance* 48(1): 247–66.

Thakor, Anjan (1996): 'Capital Requirements, Monetary Policy, and Aggregate Bank Lending: Theory and Empirical Evidence', *The Journal of Finance*, 51(1): 279–324.

The Volatility Inst., NYU Stern, http://vlab.stern.nyu.edu/welcome/risk/.

6

Measuring Interest Rate Risk in the Life Insurance Sector

The U.S. and the U.K.

Daniel Hartley, Anna Paulson, and Richard J. Rosen

6.1 Introduction

Interest rates have decreased to levels at or near historical lows in many countries around the world including the U.S., the U.K. and continental Europe in recent years (see Figure 6.1). The interest rate environment is important for life insurance firms because they typically use fixed-income markets to hedge the implicit or explicit return that they promise on core products—life insurance policies and annuities. However, hedging interest rate risk for insurance policies and annuities is not always straightforward. Many life insurers use hedging strategies such as duration matching. These techniques generally do a good job of hedging interest rate risk when rates are relatively stable and near historical averages, as they were in the early part of the century in the United States and Europe. But, these strategies may not do as well when there is a large change in interest rates such as the sustained decrease in rates that occurred after the 2008 financial crisis. In this chapter, we measure the interest rate risk exposure of insurers in the U.S., the U.K., and continental Europe during the rate decrease and the subsequent period when interest rates have continued to be very low by historical standards. We compare these measures to measures of their interest rate risk exposure during the more normal interest rate period prior to the financial crisis.

Figure 6.1. Ten-year constant maturity government bond yields

Life insurance firms sell products that promise payments in the future. Most products sold by life insurers offer some combination of protection—either from loss of life (a life insurance policy) or from outliving financial resources (an annuity)—and savings (often in a tax-advantaged way). All of these products involve policyholders paying in funds before, often well before, insurers make any payments. This pattern exposes insurers to interest rate risk. Exposure to interest rate risk varies with the features of particular products. We exploit differences in the features of life insurance products across countries to examine the importance of product features in determining life insurance exposure to interest rate risk.

One important dimension across which life insurance products differ is the degree to which policyholders are guaranteed minimum returns on the savings elements of their policies. In many countries such as the United States, annuities and other savings products offered by life insurers are generally sold with minimum rate guarantees. So, for example, a policyholder might be offered an annuity that guarantees a minimum return of 4 per cent per year on all invested funds. In other countries such as the United Kingdom, it is more common for the return on savings elements in life insurance products to be a function of the return insurers earn on investments.[1] All else equal,

[1] Moody's (2015) estimates that guaranteed products account for between 60% and 80% of U.S. life insurance industry reserves and for 40% of U.K. life insurance reserves. However, many of the guarantees in the U.K. are made at interest rates well below market rates at the time they are

products with guarantees are more exposed to interest rate risk than products with no guarantees.

Of course, all else is not equal. Life insurers can choose assets and use derivatives to hedge the interest rate risk introduced by their liabilities.[2] The task of asset liability management is an important function at these firms. Insurers seek to invest in a way that ensures that funds are available when they are due to policyholders. This generally leads life insurers to invest heavily in fixed-income assets such as bonds. For example, according to data from SNL Financial, over 87 per cent of Prudential Financial's investment assets were fixed-income securities in 2014. Life insurers may choose assets to back their liabilities with interest rate risk in mind but may choose not to—or may not be able to—completely balance the interest rate sensitivity of their assets and liabilities. This conflict arises in part because assets with maturities as long as those of some insurance liabilities are not always available. This often leads life insurers to manage interest rate risk through approximate hedges such as duration matching. Duration matching is effective for hedging small changes in interest rates, but can leave insurers unhedged if interest rates move substantially (the so-called convexity problem).

Another important factor in evaluating interest rate risk is that life insurers can be exposed to interest rate risk through the behaviour of policyholders, especially through products with guaranteed returns. Some insurance products offer policyholders the option to contribute additional funds at their discretion (possibly only in specific circumstances) or to close out a contract in return for a predetermined payment (in the latter case, the policyholder is said to surrender the contract). When interest rates change, it is more likely that policyholders will act on these options. For example, they may contribute more to an annuity with a high guaranteed return when interest rates are low or surrender an annuity with a low return guarantee when interest rates rise significantly. The key is that the combined effect of guarantees and policyholder behaviour can make hedging interest rate risk much more complex. This can lead life insurers to leave themselves more exposed to changes in interest rates that are large enough to substantially affect policyholder behaviour. We examine whether differences in guarantees and policyholder behaviour across countries are related to the interest rate sensitivity of life insurers in those countries.

We propose a measure of the residual interest rate risk that life insurers retain after taking into account their efforts to reduce interest rate risk through asset-liability management and other hedging activities. We then examine

granted and essentially provide protection against a loss on the policyholders' investments (guarantees are made at 0–1% even when market interest rates are much higher).

[2] See Berends and King (2015) for a discussion of derivatives usage by U.S. life insurers.

how this measure has changed in recent years as interest rates decreased and then remained low. The evolution of interest rates has been similar in many countries, including in the U.S. and the U.K., which are the focus of this study (see Figure 6.1). Despite being exposed to similar changes in interest rates, the residual exposure of life insurers to interest rate risk may differ by country due to differences in the characteristics of products sold across countries. The primary focus of this chapter is a comparison of interest rate risk for insurance firms in the U.S. and the U.K. We compare the residual exposure to interest rate risk for firms in the U.S. to that of firms in the U.K. In the U.S., guarantees and policyholder options are common and in the U.K. they are not, so our study design helps to shed light on the role of guarantees in generating interest rate risk.[3]

There are two potential approaches to measuring the interest rate exposure of life insurance firms: bottom-up and top-down. A bottom-up measure would make use of detailed data on insurance assets and liabilities and would involve estimating the interest rate risk of each on an individual- or product-basis. This approach is impractical for us as it would require detailed information that is not publicly available. However, stock analysts and ratings agencies pay close attention to the product mix of insurers and interest rate guarantees of the products that insurers sell. Thus, the interest rate sensitivity of an insurer's liabilities is likely to be factored into the price of their stock. For these reasons, we use a top-down approach that relies on the sensitivity of life insurer stock returns to interest rates.

The top-down measure of interest rate exposure that we use is based on a two-factor market model of insurer stock returns. We include a broad stock market return factor to control for changes in the overall economy as well as an interest rate factor. The coefficient on the interest rate factor, which is allowed to vary through time, is our measure of the exposure to interest rate risk.

In order to see how interest rate sensitivity is related to the product-specific features of life insurance and annuities, we compare the U.S., where many insurance products have guarantees and some policyholder flexibility, to the U.K., where the combination of both guarantees and policyholder options is much less common. We examine residual interest rate risk exposure for insurers in the two countries along multiple dimensions. However, we are particularly interested in the period beginning in July 2010. This period was after the financial crisis and was when long-term interest rates decreased significantly before levelling off at a historically low level. We refer to this as

[3] Many annuities in the U.K. were compulsory for our sample period. Policyholders in the U.K. had little optionality in their investments (Oliver Wyman 2014) and surrenders are not possible for U.K. annuities (Geneva Association 2012).

the low-rate period. During this period, we find that the stock prices of U.K. life insurers were not significantly impacted by small changes in interest rates, suggesting they were not particularly exposed to interest rate risk. Over the same time period, U.S. life insurers' stock prices increased significantly when interest rates increased, implying that U.S. life insurers faced considerable interest rate risk and that, in particular, the duration of their liabilities exceeded that of their assets. We interpret this finding to mean that the guarantees and policyholder options that are common to U.S. life insurance products exposed them to considerable interest rate risk in the period following the financial crisis when interest rates fell significantly and stayed low.

We test our interpretation and ensure these results are not due to omitted factors, through a two-stage difference-in-differences test for both U.S. and U.K. firms. First, we compare the low-rate period to a period when interest rates were 'normal', that is to say within historical norms. We define the normal-rate period as beginning in 2002 and continuing through June 2007 (ending before the financial crisis). During this period, we find that small changes in interest rates had no effect on life insurer stock prices in *either* the U.K. or the U.S. Next, we compare changes in interest rate sensitivity between the normal period and the low-rate period for the two countries. We find that interest rate risk increased for U.S. life insurers between the normal period and the low-rate period. But, there was no change in interest rate risk for U.K. life insurers between the same two time periods.

The second stage of the difference-in-differences analysis focuses on ensuring that the differences that we observe between the U.S. and the U.K. are due to differences in the life insurance industry in the two countries. In this stage, we compare the changes in interest rate risk exposure for life insurers in the two countries to changes in interest rate risk exposure for a control group of firms. Specifically, we examine the interest rate risk for non-life insurers (primarily property and casualty insurance firms) during the 'normal-rate' period and the 'low-rate' period for the U.S. and the U.K. Non-life insurers typically have liabilities of a much shorter duration (auto or business continuity insurance, for example) and their products do not have a savings element or a guaranteed return. Consistent with intuition, we find that non-life insurers' stock prices had little reaction to small interest rate changes in either the low-rate period or the normal-rate period for either U.K. or U.S. insurers. Thus, the second stage of the analysis shows that life insurers in the U.S. had an increase in interest rate risk in the low-rate period relative to the normal-rate period when compared to non-life insurers in the U.S., while there was no such pattern in the U.K.

As a robustness check, we conduct a similar analysis using a sample of large insurers based in continental Europe. This analysis is complicated by two factors: first, there is no clear way to assess the prevalence of a combination of guarantees and policyholder options in life insurance products for most European countries. Second, large continental European insurance firms often have significant cross-border activities. To address the second factor, we evaluate insurers by the source country for premiums, not where the firm is headquartered. Then, we split our sample based on the share of life insurance premiums that each insurer earns from Germany. While there is not a perfect consensus regarding the degree to which the life insurance products of each European country combine guarantees and options in a manner similar to U.S. products, there is broad agreement that the products offered in Germany are more similar to those in the U.S. than to those in the U.K. Consistent with the results in our main analysis, we find that life insurers with larger shares of German premiums experienced increases in interest rate risk during the low-rate period relative to life insurers with smaller shares of premiums from Germany, although the difference is statistically significant for only a portion of the low-rate period.

As a further check that our top-down procedure captures residual interest rate risk, we compare the residual interest rate risk from our model to country-level bottom-up measures derived from the European Insurance and Occupational Pensions Authority (EIOPA) 'low for long' stress scenario for European countries. Despite large differences between our approach and the EIOPA procedure, we find that our measure of risk is correlated with interest rate risk estimated from the EIOPA results.

Our overall findings are consistent with life insurance firms in the U.S. retaining a portion of the interest rate risk associated with interest rate guarantees and policyholder options. One interpretation is that during the normal interest rate period insurers successfully hedged themselves against small movements in interest rates using duration matching or something similar. They did not, however, hedge themselves against the effects of rate guarantees and the exercise of policyholder options under the low-probability scenario that interest rates decreased significantly. When this event came to pass, policyholders with guarantees elected to keep their policies longer and, when possible, increased their savings rate. Keeping policies longer effectively delays the expected pattern of payments from the insurer to policyholders and forces the insurer to pay an above-market interest rate during this extra time. The effect of this was to increase the duration of insurers' liabilities by more than the amount of a fixed-rate coupon bond with the same duration prior to the rate drop. If insurers had assets (which, recall, are primarily fixed-rate coupon bonds) of the same duration as the liabilities before interest rates decreased, this would leave them unhedged.

In contrast to the U.S., in the U.K., where insurers have more flexibility to pass lower returns on to policyholders and where policyholders have much less flexibility to change investments or surrender, insurers were less exposed to the effect of lower interest rates. Our results suggest that these product features allowed U.K. life insurers to remain largely hedged to interest changes across both the normal and the low-rate period.

We consider two potential alternative explanations for why the sensitivity of life insurers' stock prices to interest rates might increase when interest rates decrease significantly. The first is that duration matching is only an approximate hedge against interest rate risk (the convexity problem). Given life insurance balance sheets, if insurers do not adjust their asset portfolios as rates fall, the duration of liabilities will increase faster than the duration of assets.[4] This is true even when there are no guarantees and policyholder behaviour does not change. Convexity is an issue in both the U.S. and the U.K., yet we find that the sensitivity of life insurers' stock prices to interest rates only increased in the U.S. and not in the U.K. This suggests that convexity from duration matching is not the major driver of our results, perhaps because insurers dynamically adjusted their portfolios as interest rates decreased.

A second potential explanation for why a top-down measure of interest rate sensitivity based on stock prices could be larger in the low-rate period is that some insurance products can be difficult to sell at a profit when interest rates are very low. Since insurers' profit is equal to the return they earn on assets plus payments from policyholders less payments to policyholders, a decrease in interest rates lowers asset returns and induces insurers to either increase prices or reduce benefits, making insurance products generally less attractive to customers. Lower demand will show up in insurer stock prices and hence impact our top-down measure of interest rate risk. This effect is likely to impact both U.S. and U.K. life insurers, so it may not seem like an obvious explanation for our findings. However, the combination of guarantees and policyholder options means that insurers have to price in the ability of policyholders to switch out of a product if interest rates rise significantly. This may make it relatively more difficult for life insurers to sell certain product classes in the U.S. relative to those in the U.K. To the extent that this is true, it reinforces our interpretation that the combination of guarantees and policyholder options left U.S. insurers relatively more exposed to residual interest rate risk.

The rest of the chapter is organized as follows. Section 6.2 describes our top-down measure of interest rate risk. Section 6.3 describes the data we use in the analysis. Our main hypotheses and findings for the U.S. and the U.K. are described in Section 6.4. In Section 6.5, we present a robustness check of our results using a sample of European insurers. Section 6.6 concludes.

[4] This is true because of the structure of assets and liabilities in life insurers' portfolios. See Section 6.4 for more details.

6.2 Measuring Exposure to Interest Rate Changes

To assess how the interest rate environment affects the exposure of insurance firms to interest rate changes, we use a top-down model that relates stock returns to changes in bond prices. Specifically, we estimate a two-factor model of insurer stock returns where the factors are a broad market factor and a government bond factor. Previous studies of the sensitivity of life insurance firms to interest rate risk have used a similar approach to measure the correlation between insurers' stock returns and interest rate changes (Brewer, Mondschean, and Strahan 1993; Brewer et al. 2007; Carson, Elyasiani, and Mansur 2008; Berends et al. 2013). In contrast to Fama and French (1992; 1993) we retain the panel structure of the data rather than forming portfolios of stock returns. The results are robust to using portfolios. The benefit of retaining the full information contained in the panel of returns is shown in Ang, Liu, and Schwarz (2010) in the context of testing factor models. The panel data approach allows us to implement difference-in-differences estimates that exploit the full variation in the share of insurance premiums that are due to life insurance products.

We are interested in the coefficient on the government bond return but we include the stock market index to control for common factors such as macroeconomic shocks that influence all equity prices. Thus, our two-factor model gauges the extent to which changes in the ten-year rate that are uncorrelated with moves in the overall market are associated with changes in insurance firm stock prices. For a panel of insurer stocks indexed by i, we estimate:

$$R_{i,t} = \alpha + \beta R_{m,t} + \gamma R_{10,t} + \epsilon_{i,t}, \tag{1}$$

where

$R_{i,t}$ = the return (including dividends) on stock i in week t,

$R_{m,t}$ = the return on a value-weighted stock market portfolio in week t,

$R_{10,t}$ = the return on a government (either U.S. or U.K.) bond with a ten-year constant maturity in week t, and

$\epsilon_{i,t}$ is a mean zero error term.

We estimate the model using weekly (Friday through Friday) data and value weight the regressions using the stock market capitalization of insurers as of the year-end prior to each observation as the weight.[5]

Since we are interested in how the interest rate sensitivity of insurance firms has changed over time, we estimate the coefficients using a window consisting of two years of weekly return data. We re-estimate the coefficients on a rolling

[5] We have also estimated the model in terms of excess returns by subtracting the three-month government bond return from each of the total returns as in Fama and French (1992, 1993). The results are almost exactly the same in the pre- and post-crisis periods.

basis, sliding the window forward by one week each time. In choosing a window of two years, we are trading off having a long enough window to deliver enough data for estimation with having a short enough window so that the business environment and interest rates can be considered reasonably stable during each window.

Assuming that market expectations for future interest rate movements can be described as a random walk at short horizons (such as a week), we can interpret, γ, the coefficient on the return on the ten-year interest rate, as a measure of how news about changes in interest rates are capitalized into the stock prices of insurance firms. If γ is different from zero, the market perceives there to be some interest rate sensitivity in the insurance firms' profits. For example, if γ is negative, the market believes that the insurance firms' future profits will increase when returns on the ten-year government bond decrease, that is, when interest rates increase.

6.3 Data

We examine data on insurance firm stock returns from January 2002 through July 2015.[6] Our objective is to determine whether interest sensitivity is different in the recent period of decreasing and low interest rates than it would be in a period of 'normal' interest rates. It would be natural to compare the low-rate period to the years immediately preceding it, but that period included the financial crisis when interest rates and stock returns were likely moving for reasons that are outside the focus of this chapter. For that reason, we define the time period immediately before the financial crisis (which we assume starts in July 2007), from January 2002 to June 2007 as the normal period.

The sample of insurance firms includes all publicly-traded insurers based in the U.S. or the U.K. that are included in the SNL Financial dataset and that have stock price data extending back in time to at least two years before the financial crisis.[7] Many of the larger insurance firms in both the U.S. and the U.K. have a mix of life insurance and other types of insurance. We use insurance premiums to divide firms into those that are predominately life insurers and those that are not. Firms are categorized as life insurers if they derive at least fifty per cent of their premiums from life insurance.[8] Firms are

[6] We do not look back further than 2002 because before that there are not enough insurance firms with traded stock to conduct our analysis. Mutual insurance firms are excluded because they do not have publicly traded stock.

[7] We include Manulife, a firm based in Canada, in the U.S. sample since most of its premiums are from John Hancock, its U.S. subsidiary. We exclude American International Group (AIG) since the market's perception of its interest rate risk may be distorted due to government intervention.

[8] We measure premiums using GAAP or IFRS accounting figures, as appropriate (one Swiss company uses Swiss GAAP). Because GAAP revenue does not include fixed and variable annuity

Table 6.1. Insurer sample statistics

Insurer Type	Life Insurers			Non-life Insurers		
	U.S.	U.K.	Europe	U.S.	U.K.	Europe
Size—total assets (millions of $)	189	209	141	152	8	24
Financial leverage—assets (net of separate accounts) to equity ratio	9.6	13.6	13.6	3.7	4.5	6.7
Profitability—net income before taxes to equity ratio	6%	21%	12%	14%	28%	14%
Number of companies	21	6	12	57	4	13

Note: This table shows sample report the sample mean of size, financial leverage, and profitability as of the end of 2014 for the six samples analysed in this chapter. The number of insurers in each sample is reported in the last row.

divided based on 2014 premium data to keep the portfolios consistent over time. Very few firms would switch groups if we were to reclassify them every year. Note that most of non-life premiums are for property and casualty (P&C) insurers, so the non-life group is largely P&C insurers.

In our main analysis, we focus on four samples: U.S. life insurers; U.S. non-life insurers; U.K. life insurers; and U.K. non-life insurers. In a robustness exercise discussed in Section 6.5, we examine the interest sensitivity of continental European insurers. Descriptive statistics on the sample of life and non-life insurers for the U.S., the U.K., and continental Europe are shown in Table 6.1. As measured by total assets, the average size of life insurers in all three samples as well non-life insurers in the U.S. were of a similar magnitude during our sample period. The U.K. and continental European non-life insurers were much smaller. A rough measure of leverage, the ratio of assets (excluding separate account assets) to equity, was larger for U.K. and continental European life insurers than for U.S. life insurers. As is to be expected due to the shorter duration of non-life liabilities, on average, non-life insurers had lower asset-to-equity ratios than life insurers. U.K. life and non-life insurers showed the highest profitability among the six samples, while U.S. life insurers showed the lowest profitability, as of the end of 2014.

Tables 6.2 and 6.3 list the companies in the U.S. and U.K. samples, respectively. They also report the share of premium income that each insurer earned from life and health insurance products in 2014, the number of weekly stock return observations available for each insurer, and the market capitalization of each insurer as of the end of 2014. We use market capitalization as reported by SNL Financial to form weights, which vary at an annual frequency. All reported regressions are weighted by market capitalization.

premiums, we may understate the extent to which U.S. insurers are involved in interest rate sensitive life insurance activities. This should tend to make the non-life insurance sample more sensitive to interest rate risk. We exclude premiums from reinsurance of life insurers' products because life reinsurance predominantly covers mortality risk.

Table 6.2. U.S. insurer sample

Company Name	Premium income from life and health insurance	Observations	Market capitalization, year-end 2014 (millions of $)
Aetna Inc.	4%	661	31,070
Affirmative Insurance Holdings, Inc.	0%	540	20
Aflac Incorporated	98%	661	27,029
Alleghany Corporation	0%	661	7,441
Allstate Corporation	7%	661	29,365
American Equity Investment Life Holding Company	99%	567	2,220
American Financial Group, Inc.	2%	661	5,326
American Independence Corp.	43%	661	83
American National Insurance Company	23%	661	3,070
Assurance America Corporation	0%	661	14
Atlantic American Corporation	63%	661	83
Baldwin & Lyons, Inc.	0%	661	386
CNA Financial Corporation	5%	661	10,451
CNO Financial Group, Inc.	93%	579	3,501
Centene Corporation	0%	661	6,150
Chubb Corporation	0%	661	24,050
Cincinnati Financial Corporation	4%	661	8,485
Citizens, Inc.	96%	661	381
Donegal Group Inc.	0%	661	432
EMC Insurance Group Inc.	0%	661	481
Erie Indemnity Company	2%	661	4,746
FBL Financial Group, Inc.	56%	661	1,434
Federated National Holding Company	0%	661	329
First Acceptance Corporation	0%	661	105
GAINSCO, INC.	0%	661	50
Genworth Financial, Inc.	56%	544	4,222
HCC Insurance Holdings, Inc.	35%	661	5,166
Hallmark Financial Services, Inc.	0%	661	232
Hanover Insurance Group, Inc.	0%	661	3,131
Hartford Financial Services Group, Inc.	22%	661	17,694
Health Net, Inc.	0%	661	4,179
Horace Mann Educators Corporation	15%	661	1,358
Independence Holding Company	78%	661	242
Infinity Property and Casualty Corporation	0%	605	887
Investors Heritage Capital Corporation	78%	661	24
Investors Title Company	0%	661	148
Kansas City Life Insurance Company	75%	661	520

Kemper Corporation	28%	661	1,893
Kingstone Companies, Inc.	0%	661	60
Lincoln National Corporation	33%	661	14,795
Loews Corporation	5%	661	15,671
MBIA Inc.	0%	661	1,831
MGIC Investment Corporation	0%	661	3,155
Manulife Financial Corporation	100%	671	35,739
Markel Corporation	0%	661	9,534
Mercury General Corporation	0%	661	3,124
MetLife, Inc.	86%	661	61,226
Molina Healthcare, Inc.	0%	588	2,662
National Interstate Corporation	0%	513	590
National Security Group, Inc.	10%	661	34
National Western Life Insurance Company	10%	661	979
Navigators Group, Inc.	0%	661	1,047
Old Republic International Corporation	1%	661	3,818
Phoenix Companies, Inc.	69%	661	393
Principal Financial Group, Inc.	90%	661	15,265
ProAssurance Corporation	0%	661	2,553
Progressive Corporation	0%	661	15,865
Prudential Financial, Inc.	95%	661	41,144
RLI Corp.	0%	661	2,129
Radian Group Inc.	0%	661	3,194
Reinsurance Group of America, Incorporated	95%	661	6,026
Safety Insurance Group, Inc.	0%	617	961
Security National Financial Corporation	98%	661	71
Selective Insurance Group, Inc.	0%	661	1,538
StanCorp Financial Group, Inc.	94%	661	2,940
State Auto Financial Corporation	0%	661	909
Stewart Information Services Corporation	0%	661	889
Torchmark Corporation	100%	661	6,930
Travelers Companies, Inc.	0%	661	34,105
Triad Guaranty Inc.	0%	661	2
UTG, Inc.	73%	661	53
Unico American Corporation	0%	661	61
United Fire Group, Inc.	7%	661	744
Universal American Corp.	3%	661	777
Universal Insurance Holdings, Inc.	0%	661	697
Unum Group	96%	661	8,801
W. R. Berkley Corporation	0%	661	6,497
WellCare Health Plans, Inc.	0%	541	3,604

Table 6.3. U.K. insurer sample

Company Name	Premium income from life and health insurance products	Observations	Market capitalization, year-end 2014 (millions of $)
Admiral Group Plc	0%	538	5,744
Amlin Pc	0%	672	3,738
Aviva Plc	58%	672	22,268
Chesnara Plc	100%	556	669
Legal & General Group Plc	96%	672	22,917
Old Mutual Plc	76%	672	14,573
Personal Group Holdings Plc	0%	672	220
Prudential Plc	99%	672	59,491
RSA Insurance Group Plc	0%	672	6,879
St James's Place Plc	100%	672	6,549

6.4 Hypotheses and U.S.–U.K. Comparison

6.4.1 *Hypotheses*

We focus on a comparison of the U.S. and the U.K. because it provides a useful contrast in the types of products sold by life insurance firms. In the U.S., many life insurers offer guaranteed minimum rates of return on the savings elements of whole life policies, fixed-rate annuities, and variable annuities. In addition, policyholders often have the right to withdraw the savings embedded in these policies (sometimes after a penalty) or to borrow against the savings. Policyholders may also have the right to adjust the flow of new savings. Obviously, the value of these options depends on how the current interest rate (and expectations of future rates) compares to the guaranteed rate. As interest rates decrease, there is more incentive for policyholders to increase their savings or to delay plans to surrender policies. This has the effect of increasing the duration of liabilities. By contrast, in the U.K. most products with a savings element offered by insurance firms have either no or de minimus guarantees. This means that for U.K. policyholders, the return on their savings is proportional to the return that insurers earn on assets financed by policyholders' premiums. This gives policyholders less incentive to time savings to changes in interest rates. As a result, when interest rates decrease, liabilities in the U.K. should lengthen less than those in the U.S. This motivates our main difference-in-differences hypothesis:

> Life insurance firms in the U.S. should become more sensitive to interest rates relative to life insurance firms in the U.K. as interest rates decrease. This should

be reflected in a larger decrease in γ, the coefficient on the bond return in the two-factor model, for U.S. life insurers than for U.K. life insurers between the normal and the low interest rate periods.

Since most life insurance products are fairly long term, we expect that this increased interest rate sensitivity could persist for a while if rates remain low after a large decrease.

One complication to a simple test of the difference in interest rate sensitivity between U.S. and U.K. life insurance firms is that conditions for insurance firms in the U.S. and the U.K. might otherwise differ. Some of these differences should be captured by the stock market index variable. However, some insurance-specific factors may not be captured by the broad stock market indices we use. To account for this, we compare life insurance firms to other insurance firms. If there are factors in the U.S. or the U.K. that impact returns to the insurance industry in each country generally, this comparison will ensure that we are focused on differences due to interest rate sensitivity and not to other factors influencing the evolution of returns in each country. As noted earlier, this comparison group of firms is primarily P&C insurers. P&C insurance products typically have a much shorter duration than life insurance products and, partially as a result, P&C insurers typically have fewer fixed-income assets and the fixed-income assets they do have are shorter maturity than those held by life insurers. In addition, return guarantees and policyholder options are not relevant for P&C insurers. Thus, we expect that the non-life insurance firms will be less sensitive to interest rate changes and will be more similar between the U.S. and the U.K. compared to life insurance firms. Still, the non-life firms will be responsive to changes in the local environment for insurers, and that may differ across the two countries. We can refine our difference-in-differences hypothesis as follows:

> The difference between the change in γ for U.S. life insurers and the change in γ for U.S. non-life insurers from the normal-rate period to the low-rate period should be more negative than the difference between the change in γ for U.K. life insurers and the change in γ for U.K. non-life insurers.

We also expect that:

> The difference between the change in γ for U.S. life insurers and the change in γ for U.S. non-life insurers from the normal-rate period to the low-rate period should be negative.

A substantial decrease in interest rates can affect the interest rate sensitivity of life insurers even if they hedge risk using an approximate method such as duration matching. Life insurance liabilities often have a very long duration. People purchase life insurance policies well before they are likely to die.

Similarly, they invest in annuities that are often established prior to retirement and that are expected to make payouts for many years. While insurers would presumably like to hedge these risks by investing in assets of a similar duration to the liabilities, there is often a shortage of high-quality, long duration, fixed-income assets. This is one of the reasons that insurers frequently choose to hedge by matching the overall duration of their asset portfolio to the overall duration of their liabilities. This is in essence hedging a mixture of new (long-term) and old (shorter-term) liabilities with assets whose duration is somewhere in the middle. If insurers do not adjust these hedges when interest rates decrease, the duration of liabilities will increase more than the duration of assets does. This is the so-called convexity problem. Insurers can mitigate this problem by dynamically re-hedging their portfolios as rates change. We expect the convexity problem to be largely similar in the U.S. and the U.K. except for the impact of guarantees and policyholder behaviour given guarantees. As a result, any changes in γ in the U.S. relative to the U.K. should not be driven by convexity, apart from the effects of guarantees and policyholder optionality.

Low interest rates can also affect the ability of life insurance firms to profitably sell certain products. For products with a savings element, it is difficult for an insurer to profitably offer a significant return (whether guaranteed or not) when interest rates are very low. There is little incentive for potential policyholders to lock their money into an annuity or to tie it up through the savings elements of a life insurance contract when the rate of return is mere basis points. This means that the profitability of life insurers may decrease when interest rates decrease because of a reduced ability to sell products. To the extent that this is broadly true for both the U.S. and the U.K., it should affect the interest rate sensitivity of life insurers in both countries. However, there is an additional factor that affects profitability: for products where policyholders have options, insurers have to price in the effect of those options. If interest rates increase, policyholders are more likely to exercise options to leave or reduce payments. This means a policy with those features will have to be priced higher (or offer a lower guaranteed rate), all else equal, than one without those features. Guarantees and policyholder options are present more often in the U.S. than the U.K., so some of what we measure might come from the inability to sell products. Still, this is consistent with our broader story that the complications from guarantees and policyholder options meant that U.S. insurers did not hedge the residual interest rate risk of a large decrease in interest rates, where the risk of not being able to sell products is one component of interest rate risk. Our top-down approach does not allow us to determine the exact sources of the interest rate risk.

6.4.2 *U.S.–U.K. Comparison*

Figure 6.2 plots the estimates of γ from the rolling regressions for the sample of U.S. insurance firms. We use the S&P 500 as our market index. Each point in the black line reflects a point estimate using the past two years of weekly returns data. The light grey bands reflect 95 per cent confidence intervals constructed from heteroskedasticity-robust standard errors. The dark grey line shows the mean of the ten-year U.S. government bond yield over the past two years.

Panel A of Figure 6.2 shows the estimates for life insurers. As the figure illustrates, in the normal-rate period estimates of γ are very close to zero with very tight confidence intervals. As data from the financial crisis (beginning roughly in July 2007 and continuing through June 2010) become fully incorporated into the two-year window, the point estimates rise and the confidence intervals expand dramatically. Finally, as the crisis abates, the confidence intervals become smaller and the point estimates drop. By 2012, yields on a ten-year U.S. government bond were historically low, and the estimates of γ from the past two years of data were negative and statistically different from zero. By the end of the sample period the point estimate of γ was about -1, indicating that a one percentage point increase in ten-year U. S. government bond returns was associated with a one percentage point decrease in the stock market value of life insurance firms. Using the July 2015 yield on a ten-year U.S. government bond of 2.32 per cent, our results imply that a one percentage point decrease in the yield of the ten-year bond is associated with an 8.8 per cent drop in the stock market value of life insurers.

Panel B of Figure 6.2 shows that U.S. non-life insurance firms displayed a somewhat similar degree of interest rate sensitivity to the life insurance firms in the period prior to the financial crisis, but were much less interest rate sensitive in the period following the financial crisis. The point estimates of γ in the post-crisis period are small in magnitude and statistically indistinguishable from zero for most of the period after the crisis.

To complete our difference-in-differences estimates, we compare the changes at life insurers to the changes at non-life insurers by pooling the life and non-life samples used to estimate Panels A and B and adding interaction terms to the specification shown in Equation (1):

$$\begin{aligned} R_{i,t} = {} & \alpha + \beta_1 R_{m,t} + \beta_2 R_{m,t} \times \mathit{Life\ share}_{i,t} \\ & + \gamma_1 R_{10,t} + \gamma_2 R_{10,t} \times \mathit{Life\ share}_{i,t} + \epsilon_{i,t}, \end{aligned} \tag{2}$$

where $\mathit{Life\ share}_{i,t}$ is the share of the premiums at firm i that are from life insurance products. Panel C of Figure 6.2 is from an estimation of (2). The Figure plots γ_2, the coefficient on the interaction between the government bond return factor and the share of premiums from life insurance. In essence,

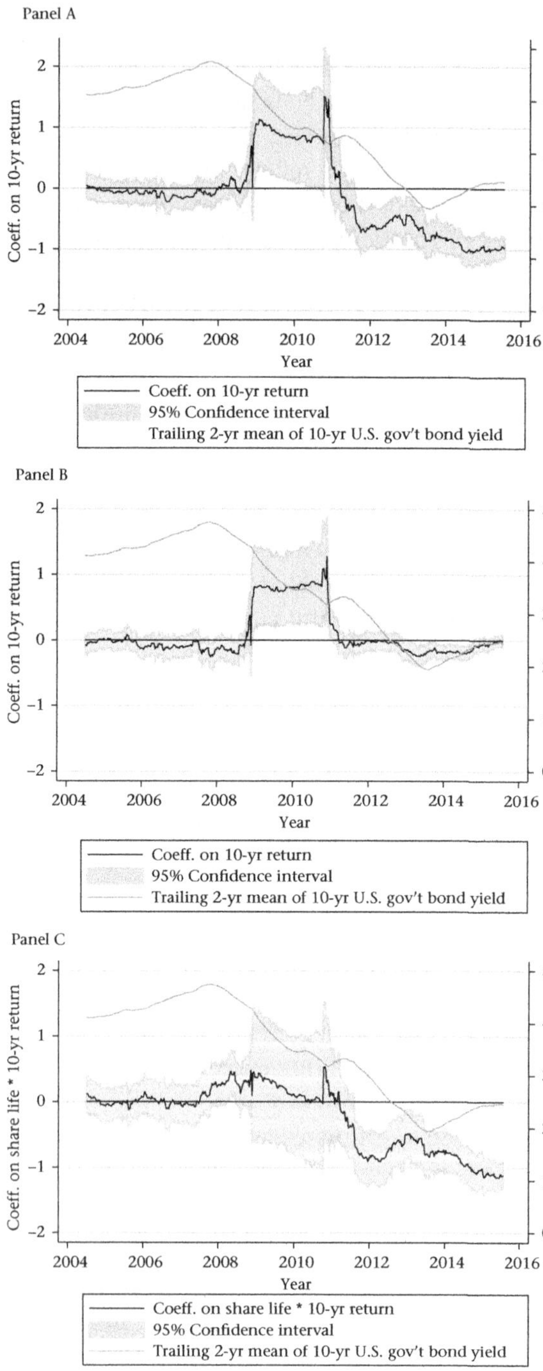

Figure 6.2. Estimates of interest rate sensitivity for U.S. insurers

Panel A. Life insurers
Panel B. Non-life insurers
Panel C. All insurers (difference)

Panel C shows the difference between panels A and B in that it shows how interest rate sensitivity for a pure life insurance firm changed relative to a pure non-life insurance firm. The Figure clearly shows that during the low-rate period in the U.S., life insurers became more interest rate sensitive than non-life insurers.

Figure 6.3 shows a similar set of plots to those shown in Figure 6.2, but for U.K. insurance firms. Again the samples are split into life insurers (Panel A) and non-life insurers (Panel B). We estimate the regressions in the same manner that we do for the U.S. sample, except that we use the weekly returns on the FTSE100 and the ten-year U.K. government bond as explanatory variables rather than the S&P 500 and ten-year U.S. government bond returns. While the number of firms in both the life and non-life insurance samples is much smaller for the U.K. than for the U.S., which contributes to the larger confidence intervals, the estimates of γ in both the pre- and post-crisis periods are almost always statistically indistinguishable from zero for the life insurance sample (Panel A). The same is largely true for the non-life insurance sample (Panel B), except for a short period during 2013. Furthermore, the difference-in-differences estimate shown in Panel C is statistically indistinguishable from zero, indicating that any changes in interest rate sensitivity over time were due to factors that affected both life and non-life insurers similarly.

Comparing the results for the U.S. and the U.K., we find support for our main hypothesis. Running through the pieces of our triple difference hypothesis: in the U.S., the change in γ for life insurers from the normal-rate period to the low-rate period is significantly more negative than the change for non-life insurers. However, in the U.K., there is no significant change in γ for life insurers from the normal-rate period to the low-rate period and the change relative to non-life insurers is, if anything, positive. We argue that this evidence is consistent with guarantees and policyholder options making U.S. life insurers more sensitive to interest rates in the current low-rate period as compared with the normal-rate period. We are agnostic as to the extent to which this is due to imperfect hedging of pre-existing liabilities versus incomplete hedging of differences in the ability of life insurers to profitably sell new policies when interest rates are low.

We do not explicitly consider differences in the incentives for life insurance firms to hedge across countries. Of course, life insurers in the U.S. understand their potential exposure from a large interest rate decrease. We would expect this to give them a greater incentive than U.K. life insurers to hedge against interest rate decreases. Nonetheless, we find that the residual exposure to interest rates in the low-rate period is larger in absolute value for U.S. firms than for U.K. firms even after any aggressive hedging by U.S. life insurers.

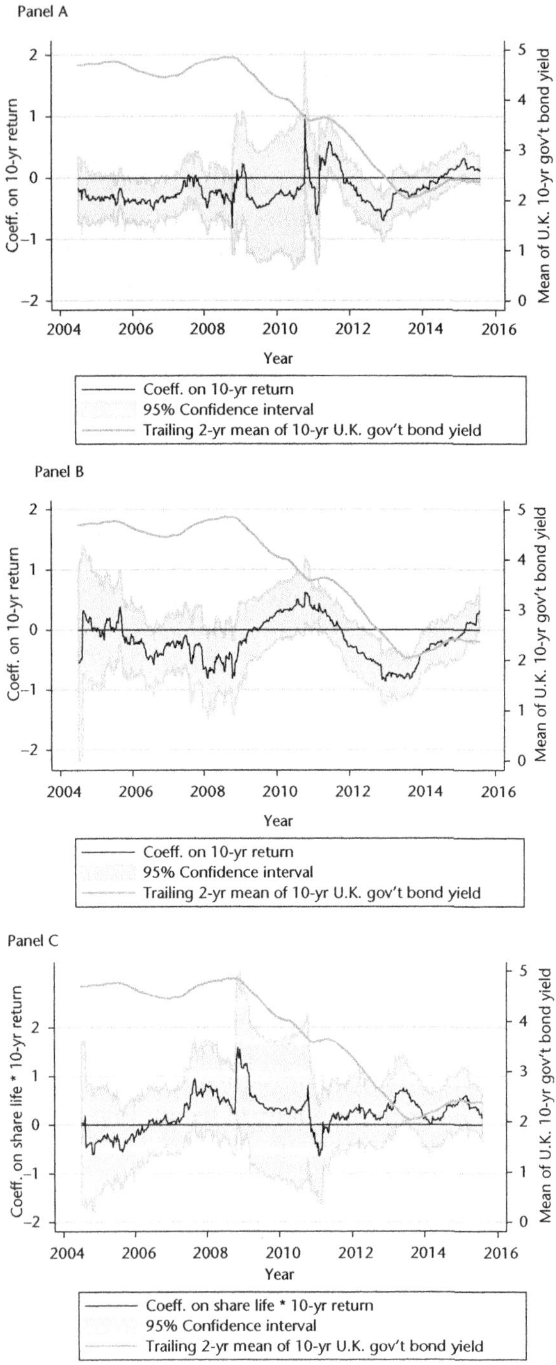

Figure 6.3. Estimates of interest rate sensitivity for U.K. insurers

Panel A. Life insurers

Panel B. Non-life insurers

Panel C. All insurers (difference)

6.5 Interest Rate Risk in Continental Europe

In this Section we turn to continental Europe. We show results that are consistent with our findings for the U.S. and the U.K. using a sample of European insurers and describe how our top-down measure of interest rate sensitivity compares to a bottom-up measure which is uniquely available for Europe.

6.5.1 *Baseline Analysis of Europe*

Extending our analysis to continental Europe is complicated by several factors, the first of which is that, as in the U.K., there are relatively few large insurers. The second factor that complicates our analysis is that the insurance market in Europe is more integrated than in the U.S. or the U.K. A firm based in one country may sell the majority of its products in other countries and thus be exposed to the guarantees and options that are prevalent in the countries where they sell policies rather than the country in which they are headquartered. Finally, for a number of countries there is no clear consensus regarding the prevalence of products that contain both guarantees and options. Given these constraints, we create a panel including all publicly-traded insurers based in Austria, France, Germany, Italy, Spain, and Switzerland.[9] We then group these firms based on their exposure to German and U.S. life insurance customers, since there is a consensus that German insurance products contain long-lived guarantees to policyholders that make their exposure to interest rate risk from life insurance liabilities similar to that of U.S. insurers.

The continental European sample is constructed in a similar manner to our U.S. and U.K. samples. We select insurance firms that are included in the SNL Financial dataset and that have stock price data extending back in time to at least two years before the financial crisis. Again, for each firm, we calculate the share of life and health insurance premiums, net of reinsurance. Since life insurance markets in continental Europe are more integrated than those in the U.S. and the U.K., we construct country-specific measures of interest rate risk exposure by calculating the share of life insurance premiums that each company receives from each of the countries in our continental European sample (Table 6.4).[10] Our premium-based measure is likely to reflect the exposure that a given firm has to the types of life insurance products that are sold in a given country. Our maintained hypothesis is that the extent of guarantees

[9] We focus on this set of countries because the sample is deepest in these countries and there is a good mix of life and non-life insurance companies in these countries.

[10] We calculated the share of life insurance premiums that each company earned from each country in our sample using each company's 2014 annual report (see Table 6.4).

Table 6.4. European insurer sample

Country	Company name	Premium income from life and health insurance products	Share of life and health insurance premium income from Germany and U.S.	Observations	Market capitalization, year-end 2014 (millions of $)
Austria	UNIQA Insurance Group AG	52%	0%	635	2,915
Austria	Vienna Insurance Group AG	50%	2%	635	5,773
France	AXA	59%	33%	667	56,764
France	April SA	63%	0%	667	611
France	CNP Assurances SA	90%	0%	667	12,231
France	Euler Hermes Group	0%	0%	667	4,560
France	SCOR SE	0%	0%	667	5,676
Germany	Allianz Group	34%	64%	659	75,883
Germany	Hannover Rück SE	0%	0%	659	10,996
Germany	Münchener Rückversicherungs-Gesellschaft	26%	60%	659	33,972
Germany	Nürnberger Beteiligungs-AG	80%	98%	659	999
Germany	Wüstenrot & Württembergische AG	61%	98%	659	2,030
Italy	Assicurazioni Generali SpA	69%	28%	651	32,181
Italy	Mediolanum SpA	99%	4%	651	4,742
Italy	Società Cattolica di Assicurazione -Società Cooperativa	64%	0%	655	1,207
Italy	Unipol Gruppo Finanziario SpA	49%	0%	651	3,563
Italy	UnipolSai Assicurazioni SpA	47%	0%	651	7,066
Spain	Grupo Catalana Occidente SA	26%	0%	653	3,427
Spain	MAPFRE SA	24%	0%	653	10,486
Switzerland	ACE Limited	20%	0%	661	37,756
Switzerland	Bâloise Holding AG	53%	14%	654	6,070
Switzerland	Helvetia Holding AG	61%	7%	654	4,729
Switzerland	Swiss Life Holding Limited	97%	9%	654	7,625
Switzerland	Vaudoise Assurances Holding SA	34%	0%	654	1,331
Switzerland	Zurich Insurance Group Ltd	23%	29%	654	46,772

and of policyholder optionality is related more to the common products typically sold in the country where the policyholder lives than to those sold in the country where a firm has its headquarters.

We then split our sample by exposure to Germany and the U.S. and by whether a firm is predominantly a life insurer. Using data from annual reports, we calculate the share of life insurance premiums from either Germany or the U.S.[11] Firms that earned more than 25 per cent of their life insurance premiums from Germany and the U.S. are categorized as high German exposure firms, and those that earned less are categorized as low German exposure firms.[12] Splitting the sample this way classifies seven firms as having high German exposure and eighteen firms as having low German exposure.

Panels A and B of Figure 6.4 show the results of estimating the same specifications as were presented for the U.S. and U.K. samples in Figure 6.2 Panel C and Figure 6.3 Panel C, respectively, except that in Figure 6.4 the samples used are the high German exposure companies (Panel A) and the low German exposure companies (Panel B). When estimating Equation (2) for the continental European sample, we use German government bond returns to avoid picking up the effects of sovereign credit risk that might influence interest rates in some of the European countries. We use the return on the ten-year German government bond as the bond return factor ($R_{10,t}$) and the return on the German stock market as measured by the DAX as the market return factor ($R_{m,t}$) for all of the countries in our continental European sample.

Panel C of Figure 6.4 adds another dimension of differencing. We compare the changes at life insurers to the changes at non-life insurers in the high and low German exposure companies by pooling the high and low German exposure sample used to estimate Panels A and B and adding additional interaction terms to the specification shown in Equation (2):

$$\begin{aligned} R_{i,t} = \alpha &+ \beta_1\, R_{m,t} + \beta_2\, R_{m,t} \times \mathit{Life\ share}_{i,t} + \beta_3\, R_{m,t} \times \mathit{German}_{i,t} \\ &+ \beta_4\, R_{m,t} \times \mathit{Life\ share}_{i,t} \times \mathit{German}_{i,t} + \gamma_1\, R_{10,t} + \gamma_2\, R_{10,t} \times \mathit{Life\ share}_{i,t} \\ &+ \gamma_3\, R_{10,t} \times \mathit{German}_{i,t} + \gamma_4\, R_{10,t} \times \mathit{Life\ share}_{i,t} \times \mathit{German}_{i,t} + \epsilon_{i,t}, \end{aligned} \quad (3)$$

where $\mathit{Life\ share}_{i,t}$ is (as previously defined) the share of the premiums at firm i that are from life insurance products, and $\mathit{German}_{i,t}$ is an indicator variable

[11] We lump the U.S. and Germany together since they have similar products. However, only AXA and Zurich, Insurance Group, Ltd. (at 21% and 6%, respectively) earn more than 5% of life premiums from the U.S. For this reason, we refer to this measure as 'German exposure'.

[12] We were unable to find information with the split of life insurance premiums by country of origin in annual reports for Nürnberger Beteiligungs-AG. We assume that it earns the same share of life premiums from Germany and the U.S. (98%) as Wüstenrot & Württembergische AG which is the German firm that most resembles Nürnberger Beteiligungs-AG in terms of the share of premiums earned from life insurance and market capitalization. Our results are robust to assuming that Nürnberger Beteiligungs-AG earns 0%, 50%, or 100% of its life premiums from Germany and the U.S.

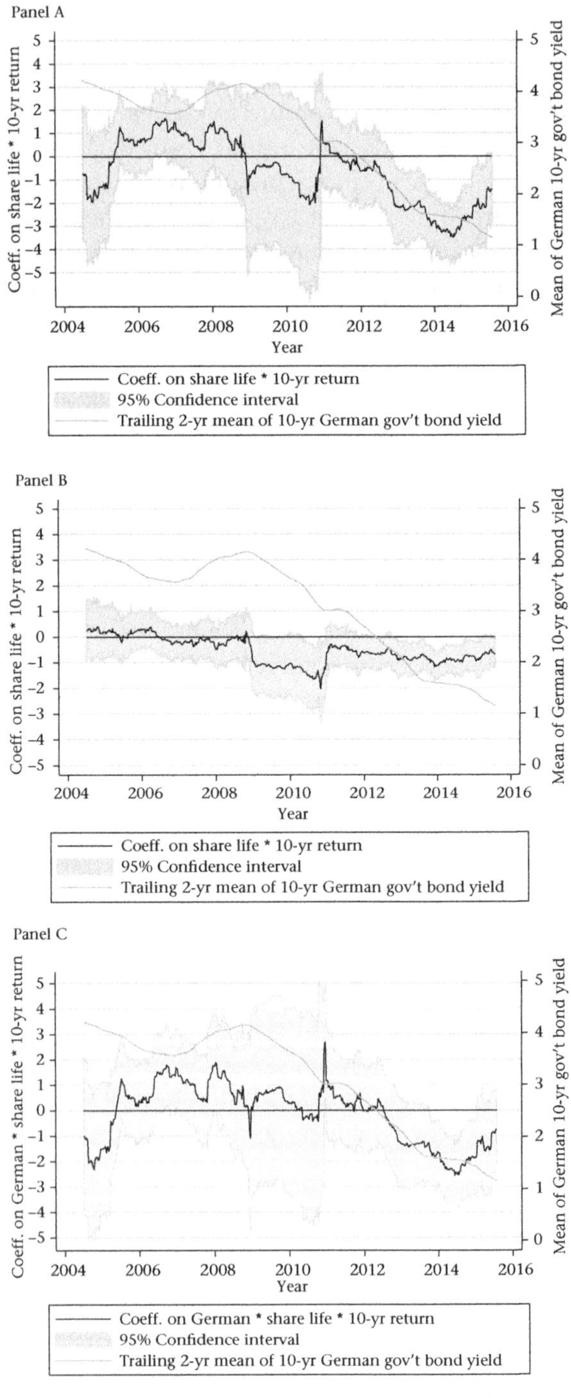

Figure 6.4. Estimates of interest rate sensitivity for continental European insurers

Panel A. High German exposure (difference)
Panel B. Low German exposure (difference)
Panel C. All insurers (difference in differences)

which is equal to 1 if the share of life insurance product premiums from Germany and the U.S. is greater than 25 per cent at firm *i*, and 0 otherwise. Panel C of Figure 6.4 plots γ_4 estimates from (3), where γ_4 is the coefficient on the interaction between the government bond return factor and the share of premiums from life insurance and the high German exposure indicator. This coefficient measures the effect of life insurance exposure to bond returns over and above the effect of non-life insurance exposure for firms more exposed to Germany relative to those less exposed to Germany. We interpret this coefficient as measuring how interest rate sensitivity for a pure life insurance firm highly exposed to German products changed relative to a pure life insurance firm with low exposure to German products. In other words, it captures the difference between Panels A and B in Figure 6.4. While the results are somewhat noisy, the figure clearly shows that during the low-rate period, continental European life insurers with higher German exposure became more interest rate sensitive than continental European life insures with lower German exposure. Due to the complications of small sample sizes and a noisy measure of the extent of guarantees and of policyholder optionality, we are not surprised by the noisiness shown in Figure 6.4 Panel C. However, we are reassured by the fact that the point estimates change from positive to negative from the normal-rate to the low-rate period. We view this as a robustness check to our main results which compare the U.S. and U.K.

6.5.2 *Comparison to a Bottom-Up Measure of Interest Rate Risk*

Finally, we consider how our top-down measures of the change in interest rate sensitivities align with a bottom-up measure that simulates the durations of the specific assets and liabilities that insurance companies hold. Bottom-up measures exist for a set of European insurance companies which participated in EIOPA stress tests (see EIOPA 2014) and the results are publicly available at the country level.

In order to measure the change in interest rate risk from the normal-rate to the low-rate period at a country level, we run country-specific, value-weighted panel regressions using samples of life and non-life insurer stock returns. Again, we split the sample based on whether 50 per cent or more of premiums come from life and health insurance. We form the country-specific weights by multiplying the market capitalization of each company by the share of life insurance premiums that the company earns from the specific country that we are considering.[13] We estimate life insurance and non-life insurance regressions for each country. In order to summarize the difference-in-differences

[13] Based on 2014 premiums converted to a common currency using the exchange rate at the end of the year.

measure of the change in interest rate risk in each country with a single coefficient, we estimate a model using returns data from the normal-rate and the low-rate periods (excluding the financial crisis period), and include an interaction term between an indicator for the low-rate period and the return on the ten-year government bond. Specifically, we estimate:

$$R_{i,t} = \alpha + \beta_0 R_{m,t} + \beta_1 L_t{}^* R_{m,t} + \gamma_0\ R_{10,t} + \gamma_1 L_t{}^* R_{10,t} + \epsilon_{it}, \tag{4}$$

where $R_{i,t}$, $R_{m,t}$, $R_{10,t}$, $\epsilon_{i,t}$ are defined as before and L_t is an indicator variable which is equal to 1 in the low-rate period and 0 in the normal-rate period.

The coefficient γ_1 in equation (4) is a country-specific measure of the change in interest rate sensitivity between the normal and the low interest rate period for life and non-life insurers. We compare this top-down measure to the bottom-up measures reported by country from the EIOPA 2014 stress test scenario that investigated the impact of a 'low for long' interest rate scenario (see Table 6.5). Importantly, for the sake of comparability, EIOPA conducted their stress tests at the undertaking-level, meaning that the country-specific duration mismatches that they report in the low for long scenario reflect

Table 6.5. Comparison of interest-rate factor to EIOPA results for the continental European sample

Country	Coefficient on bond factor (γ)		EIOPA duration mismatch, years
	Life insurers	Non-life insurers	
Austria	−1.00***	0.35	11.33
France	−0.60***	−0.35	5.58
Germany	−0.68***	−0.28	11.32
Italy	−0.84***	−0.25	1.16
Spain	−0.59**	−0.47**	0.89
Switzerland	−0.39	−0.20	—
Correlation with EIOPA duration mismatch	−0.40		

Note: This table shows point estimates from twelve separate panel regressions. Two regressions are estimated for each country. One regression is for the life insurance sample and one is for the non-life insurance sample. In each regression the dependent variable is the weekly stock return of the insurance companies in our continental European sample. Each regression is weighted. The weights are formed by multiplying the market capitalization of each company (expressed in a common currency) by the share of life insurance premiums that the firm earned from the country which the regression is for. The explanatory variables consist of the same two factors contained in our main specifications, the return on the stock market, and the return on the ten-year government bond (as noted in the text we use the German stock and government bond return for the continental European sample). We have also added an indicator variable for the low-rate period and an interaction term between the return on the ten-year government bond and an indicator variable for the low-rate period. We can interpret the coefficient on this variable as the change in interest rate sensitivity of insurance company stock returns from the normal-rate to the low-rate period. The sample includes only observations from the normal-rate and low-rate periods. For comparison, duration mismatch measured in years from the low yield module A of the EIOPA 2014 stress tests are also shown. The mismatch figure captures the number of years by which the simulated duration of liabilities exceeds the simulated duration of assets. No EIOPA data are available for Switzerland. The correlation between the mismatch numbers and the life insurer interest rate sensitivity change coefficients is shown below the coefficients. A negative correlation indicates that countries with larger increases in interest rate sensitivity (more negative coefficients) were deemed to have liabilities of a longer duration than their assets.

the participating business-units operating in a particular country and thus insurance products that are sold in that country (rather than firms that are headquartered in the country).

For the five countries in both our continental European sample and the EIOPA sample, we find a correlation of −0.40 between our top-down interest rate risk measure and EIOPA's duration mismatch measure.[14] A negative correlation indicates that countries with larger increases in interest rate sensitivity (more negative coefficients) according to the top-down analysis were deemed to have liabilities of a longer duration than their assets in the bottom-up EIOPA stress tests. This suggests that the top-down approach and EIOPA's bottom-up approach of measuring interest rate risk are aligned. We do not report the correlation between the EIOPA duration mismatch numbers and our interest rate risk measures for the non-life sample due to the fact that the coefficients on our interest rate risk measure are small in magnitude and mostly statistically indistinguishable from zero as we would expect for the non-life insurers.

6.6 Conclusion

We use a two-factor model of life insurer stock returns to measure interest rate risk at U.S. and U.K. insurers. We find that interest rate risk among U.S. life insurers has increased in the recent period of decreasing and low interest rates. In the U.K., in contrast, life insurer interest rate risk has been low in this period and roughly similar to the period prior to the financial crisis when long-term interest rates were in their usual historical ranges. We attribute the difference in interest rate risk between the U.S. and the U.K. to the heavier use of guarantees and policyholder options among U.S. life insurers relative to their U.K. counterparts.

Acknowledgements

We are grateful for helpful comments from Thomas King, Ralph Koijen, Zain Mohey-Deen, Moto Yogo, and the participants at The Economics, Regulation and Systemic Risk of Insurance Markets conference at the London Business School, and for excellent research assistance from Tyna Eloundou and Teddy Kalambokidis. The views expressed in this chapter are our own and do not necessarily reflect those of the Federal Reserve Bank of Chicago or the Board of Governors of the Federal Reserve System.

[14] Switzerland did not participate in the EIOPA stress test.

References

Ang, Andrew, Jun Liu, and Krista Schwarz (2010): 'Using Stock or Portfolios in Tests of Factor Models', Unpublished manuscript.

Berends, Kyal and Thomas King (2015): 'Derivatives and Collateral at U.S. Life Insurers', *Economic Perspectives,* 39/1.

Berends, Kyal, Robert McMenamin, Thanases Plestis, and Richard J. Rosen (2013): 'Sensitivity of Life Insurance Firms to Interest Rate Changes', *Economic Perspectives,* 37/2.

Brewer, Elijah III, James M. Carson, Elyas Elyasiani, Iqbal Mansur, and William L. Scott (2007): 'Interest Rate Risk and Equity Values of Life Insurance Companies: A GARCH–M model', *Journal of Risk and Insurance,* 74/2: 401–23.

Brewer, Elijah III, Thomas H. Mondschean, and Philip E. Strahan (1993): 'Why the Life Insurance Industry did not Face an "S&L-type" Crisis', *Economic Perspectives,* 17/5: 12–24.

Carson, James M., Elyas Elyasiani, and Iqbal Mansur (2008): 'Market Risk, Interest Rate Risk, and Interdependencies in Insurer Stock Returns: A System-GARCH Model', *Journal of Risk and Insurance,* 75/4: 873–91.

EIOPA (2014): 'EIOPA Insurance stress test 2014', Technical report.

Fama, Eugene F. and Kenneth R. French (1992): 'The Cross-Section of Expected Stock Returns', *The Journal of Finance,* 47/2: 427–65.

Fama, Eugene F. and Kenneth R. French (1993): 'Common Risk Factors in the Returns on Stocks and Bonds', *Journal of Financial Economics,* 33/1: 3–56.

Geneva Association (2012): 'Surrenders in the Life Industry and Their Impact on Liquidity', Technical report.

Moody's (2015): 'Low Interest Rates are Credit Negative for Insurers Globally, but Risks Vary by Country', Moody's Investors Service, Global Insurance Themes, 26 March, Technical report.

Oliver Wyman (2014): 'The Future of the U.K. Life Industry. Time to Invest in Mass Market Retirement', Technical report.

Part 3
Regulation

7

How the Insurance Industry's Asset Portfolio Responds to Regulation

Bo Becker

7.1 U.S. Insurers' Fixed Income Holdings

The U.S. insurance industry holds large quantities of fixed income assets. In 2012, the industry reported fixed income holdings of $3.63 trillion (at book values; $3.97 trillion at market values). The largest categories, in order, were corporate bonds, structured securities, treasuries, and municipal bonds. Life insurance generates around three-quarters of the assets. Because of the size of these holdings, the insurance industry is of critical importance to fixed income markets in the United States.[1] Most of the assets are investment grade, meaning that risk is generally limited.

In this chapter, we discuss how insurance regulation depends on the composition of the large fixed income portfolios owned by insurers, and some of the (unintended) consequences of these regulations. We begin by a brief overview of insurance regulation, and in particular how capital requirements depend on the composition of insurers' asset portfolios.

7.1.1 *Why Insurers Invest in Risky Assets*

Before considering what limits insurance risk taking, it is worth stopping to consider why insurers may like to take risk. A standard concern is risk shifting, i.e. firms acting on an incentive to take on such large risks that the firm will

[1] One sign of the industry's importance is the impact on pricing of insurance industry trades; see Ellul, Jotikasthira, Lundblad (2011, and this volume).

default in adverse scenarios, leaving someone other than the firm's owners to absorb losses (see, e.g. Allen and Gale 2000). Equity-holders get the upside, but do not worry about the downside. Risk shifting is only in the interest of owners if there is default risk, and the value created is related to the magnitude of the default risk. In other words, risk shifting can only motivate risk taking in distressed insurers. Additionally, insurers are likely interested in taking risk outside of distress, as a part of their regular investment operations, in order to receive higher expected returns. This means taking on priced risk (other priced features, such as illiquidity, may also be attractive to insurers). The risk premium motivation may be more general than risk shifting, since it does not depend on insurer distress. Taxpayers should be concerned about risk taking motivated by risk premiums as well as that motivated by risk shifting, since either can affect insurers' insolvency risk.

7.1.2 *Regulation of Insurance Companies' Assets*

Insurance companies in the U.S. face regulation requiring minimum capital levels. Insurance companies are a concern for taxpayers because of the risk that a failure will result in the use of public resources. Just as for banks, whose deposits are insured, and who as a result face regulation limiting the risks they can take, insurers' risk exposures are regulated.[2] Insurance industry regulation is aimed at reducing the likelihood that a state fund or taxpayers will have to bail out insurance policies, and also the expected shortfall in case of a state take-over.

One key feature of these regulations is that regulators (state insurance commissioners) are meant to intervene before an insurer is insolvent. Regulators get some oversight rights already if reported capital is below two times the regulatory minimum capital. As solvency declines (measured by book value of capital relative to the requirement), the regulatory oversight is gradually tightened. When capital is below the required minimum, the insurer can be taken over.

Another key feature of capital regulation of U.S. insurers is that the amount of capital depends on both assets and liabilities. For property and casualty insurers, who may face large undiversified risks in the policies they write (e.g. if natural disasters cause large-scale property damage), and who hold relatively small asset portfolios relative to the size of annual premium revenue, capital requirements are largely determined by the liability side. On the other hand, life insurers face much lower risk of large unforeseen payout on policies, but they do hold very

[2] The taxpayers' exposure to insurers is more indirect than that to banks, because a first line of defence if an insurance company is unable to meet its liabilities is a state insurance fund, financed by fees levied on the insurers of that state. Only as a backstop to that fund are the state taxpayers exposed to industry losses.

large asset portfolios (relative to annual premium revenue). Therefore, their capital requirements depend heavily on risk in asset portfolios. Some fixed income assets, notably treasuries, have no capital requirement. Equities are risky, but make up a smaller share of portfolios (as of 2015 Q2, U.S. Flow of Fund data showed that property and casualty and life insurance companies had around four and a half trillion dollars of fixed income securities, mortgages, and loans, and around two trillion dollars of corporate equities). Thus, life insurers' capital requirements are heavily influenced by the risk profile of their holdings of corporate bonds, municipal bonds, and structured assets.[3]

7.1.3 *Capital Requirements by Category*

Capital requirements for all fixed income assets except treasuries have historically depended on credit ratings. Under this system, bonds are grouped into broad buckets based on ratings, and a capital requirement is calculated for each bond based on the category it belongs to. The details of capital requirements are set by the National Association of Insurance Commissioners (NAIC). As an example, in 2008, structured securities rated between A- and AAA faced requirements of 0.40 per cent of face value (an insurance company needed 40 cents of equity for every $100 of book value of bonds in this range of ratings) if held by a life insurer, and 0.30 per cent, if held by a non-life insurer. For bonds rated BBB, the capital requirement was 1.3 per cent (1 per cent for non-life) of book value; for BB, 4.6 per cent (2 per cent); for B 10 per cent (4.5 per cent); for CCC 23 per cent (10 per cent); for a rating below CCC, the capital requirement was 30 per cent. This system still applies to municipal bonds, corporate bonds, and non-MBS (mortgage-backed securities) structured assets. The new system for MBS is discussed below in Section 7.2.3.[4]

7.2 The Impact of Capital Regulation on Insurers' Asset Portfolios

How does the capital requirement of an asset affect investment choices? In particular, does the system effectively limit risk taking? Several features of the current system are important for understanding insurer incentives.

[3] Obviously, the shares of various asset classes in the aggregate industry asset portfolio will in part be determined by capital requirements. The low equity share, for example, may reflect both high capital requirements for shares, and the good match between fixed income assets and the large fixed long-term liabilities of the industry.

[4] The capital requirement for an insurance company is not a linear combination of the requirements for individual assets. See Becker and Opp (2014) for a more detailed discussion. Note also that while the ratings cutoffs have remained unchanged, the exact requirements are adjusted over time.

First, capital requirements are based on the risk of individual assets, not the entire portfolio. Since covariance is a fundamental feature of asset risks; this means that the system appears flawed by design. However, rating agencies may compensate for this by considering systematic risk when assigning rating (see Hilscher and Wilson 2013). Also, there are rules (aside from the rating-dependence of capital requirements) which penalize portfolio concentration (for example, the ten largest holdings face a multiplier on their capital requirements). Finally, idiosyncratic risks are presumably rewarded less than exposures to broad risk factors in fixed income markets.[5] This means that there is a stronger incentive to take on systematic (priced) risks in solvent insurance companies, and we expect diversification based on insurers' own interests. For insolvent companies, which would like to risk shift, risk premiums may matter less. However, the ability to risk shift may be limited by the regulatory powers granted over non-insolvent but stressed insurers.

Second, capital requirements are imposed infrequently, only at year-end. There is therefore ample room to vary risk taking over the year in order to 'window dress' measured risks at year-end.

Third, current capital regulation is also short term in that any shortfall must be addressed immediately. The system does not have any 'shock absorbers' when asset markets move, apart from those provided by traditional accounting rules (see Ellul et. al. 2014). When a shortfall has to be addressed quickly, it is not possible to use operating profits to replenish equity, or even to issue new equity over a drawn-out period. It is not clear that it is optimal to force such a short cycle in solvency regulation.

Fourth, because the system uses broad categories for defining asset risk (e.g. bonds rated A- through AAA are treated the same way), there is leeway to vary risk: within each bucket of assets facing the same capital requirement, there is a range of assets of varying risk and expected returns.

Several recent studies examine some of the implications of these features of insurance regulation on asset portfolios. We discuss some of these in the following sections.

7.2.1 *Corporate Bonds Through the Recent Cycle*

Given capital requirement rules that treat broad groups of bonds equally, insurers could reach for yield by selectively buying the riskiest bonds within a given category, thus increasing the risk of the portfolio without raising capital requirements. Becker and Ivashina (2015a) study such reaching for yield in the corporate bond market in a sample period covering the pre-crisis

[5] However, see Campbell and Taksler (2003).

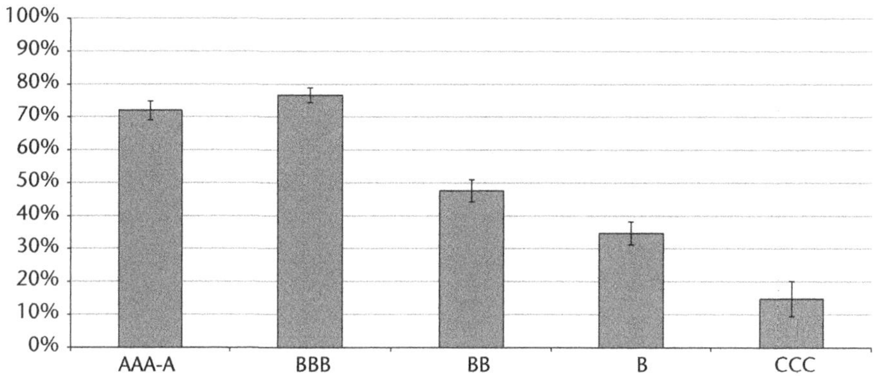

Figure 7.1. Insurance companies' holdings of newly issued corporate bonds, 2004: Q2–2007: Q2, by rating category

This figure is based on Becker and Ivashina (2015a).

The figure plots the (equal-weighted) fraction of institutional purchases of newly issued bonds that are acquired by insurance companies between 2004:Q2–2007:Q2, sorted by NAIC risk category. The fraction of holdings is computed with respect to the total acquisitions of insurance companies, pension and mutual funds. We report equally-weighted averages across bonds. Bars correspond to 95% confidence intervals (based on the standard deviation across individual bonds).

period of low rates and compressed spreads, the financial crisis itself, and the beginning of the recovery.

Insurers mostly buy investment grade bonds. Becker and Ivashina examine acquisitions of investment grade bonds at issue within this universe. Mutual funds and pension funds which are not subject to capital requirements, serve as benchmark. In the thirteen quarters preceding the financial crisis (2004: Q2 to 2007: Q2), insurers exhibit a preference for investment grade bonds, dominating pension funds and mutual funds in this category. This is plotted in Figure 7.1. That is, across risk categories, insurers exhibit the risk aversion that capital requirements are meant to induce. Yet, *within* capital requirement buckets, risk preferences are reversed, as shown by Figure 7.2. The share of newly-issued corporate bonds acquired by insurers in the same time frame *increases* in risk (as measured by yield to maturity at issue, or the CDS spread) within the AAA to A category.[6] Thus, insurers appear to reach for yield in a way that is invisible to the standard metric on which they are evaluated. The pattern is robust to inclusion of duration and liquidity controls. Importantly, the risk taking does not generate 'alpha', i.e. excess returns relative to other assets with similar risk. The reaching for yield pattern is stronger in firms where the regulatory capital requirement is more binding, supporting the

[6] The same is true for BBB, but for high yield bonds, there is insufficient data to estimate a preference with any precision. See Becker and Ivashina (2015a) for details.

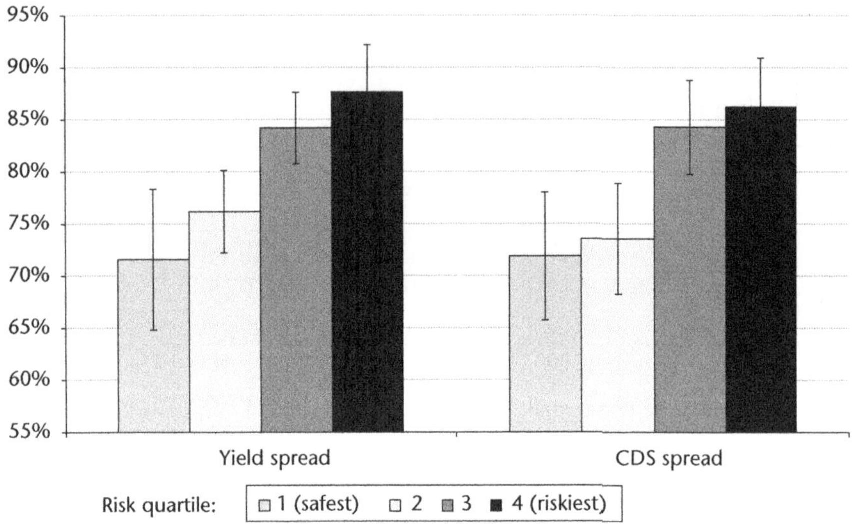

Figure 7.2. Insurance companies' holdings of newly issued highly rated corporate bonds, 2004: Q2–2007: Q2

This Figure is based on Becker and Ivashina (2015a), Figure 1B. The figure plots the (equal-weighted) fraction of newly issued bonds acquired by insurance companies out of total institutional purchases (insurance, mutual funds, pension funds), for the period 2004:Q2–2007:Q2. Bonds are sorted by promised yields and by issuer CDS spreads. Bars correspond to 95% confidence intervals (based on the standard deviation across individual bonds. Investment grade bonds (NAIC 1 and 2) are sorted into quartiles of offering yield or CDS Spread.

conclusion that tension between regulatory capital requirements and risk appetite can explain this type of reaching for yield.

Becker and Ivashina (2015a) also document that reaching for yield disappears in the crisis period. To examine the time patterns of reaching for yield in more detail, they calculate that changes in holdings of each outstanding bond are related to the bond's yield, with a coefficient allowed to vary by quarter. The pattern, shown in Figure 7.3, demonstrates not only that the crisis appears to have reduced the risk appetite of insurers, but that this was temporary: reaching for yield recommenced after the crisis. One interpretation of these patterns is as follows: insurers primarily search for risk in order to gain risk premiums, not for risk shifting purposes (since the pattern only exists during favourable periods). When they are under stress, insurers invest more carefully, to the point where capital requirements are not constraining their risk exposures.

7.2.2 *The 'High Yield Premium'*

Becker (2015) follows up the Becker Ivashina (2015a) results by looking for signs of price impact on high yield corporate bonds. If insurers' reaching for

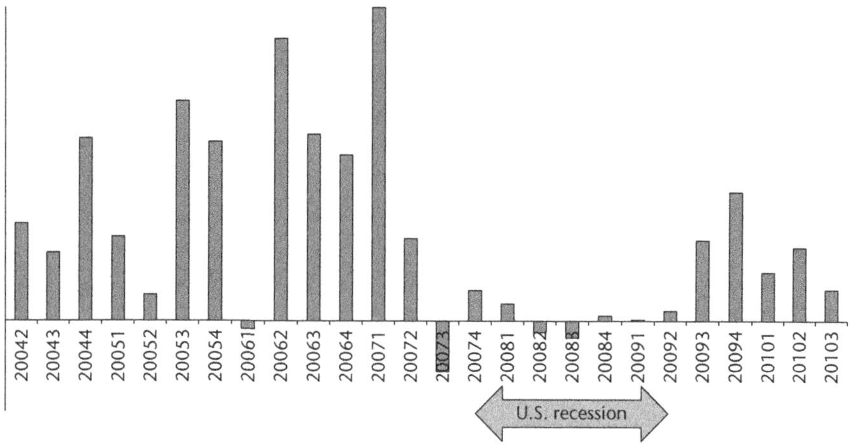

Figure 7.3. Reaching for yield by U.S. insurance companies through time

This figure is based on Becker and Ivashina (2015a), Figure 7. The figure shows the strength of insurance companies' preference for higher yielding investment grade bonds by quarter. This preference is estimated from a panel regression where the quarterly change in log holdings of all non-maturing corporate bonds is regressed on yield. If the coefficient is positive, insurers accumulate higher yield bonds relative to others.

yield is large enough to have price impact, we would expect the safest investment grade bonds to see artificially reduced expected returns, while the safest high yield bonds should see correspondingly inflated expected returns (see Frazzini and Pedersen 2014 for more details).

Whether BB+ bonds receive low returns relative to BBB– bonds, given the difference in risk is hard to decide because both risk and expected returns are hard to estimate. Two indirect implications may be easier to test, based on the nature of capital requirements. Insurers should care more about capital requirements in periods of financial stress, and only at year-ends, when requirements are imposed. There is evidence of both in the pricing of new corporate bond issues.

First, as Figure 7.4 shows, the risk-adjusted difference in yields between BBB– and BB+ is high at times when financial industry stock prices are low, and vice versa. This is consistent with avoidance of the high yield label specifically when the industry is troubled, such as in the wake of recessions.

Second, there should be seasonality in the high yield premium if it is driven by insurers. Capital requirements are imposed at calendar year-ends. Since portfolios can be adjusted over time, high yield bonds might be bought in the spring and sold in the summer. Becker (2015) uses yields to maturity of newly issued bonds to look for such seasonality. As Figure 7.5 shows, the difference in yields between BBB– and BB+ is high around year-ends, but low in the summer. It is highest in December but insignificantly different from zero in May. These seasonal patterns suggest that credit pricing is indeed affected by insurers who avoid assets with the high yield label around the year-end.

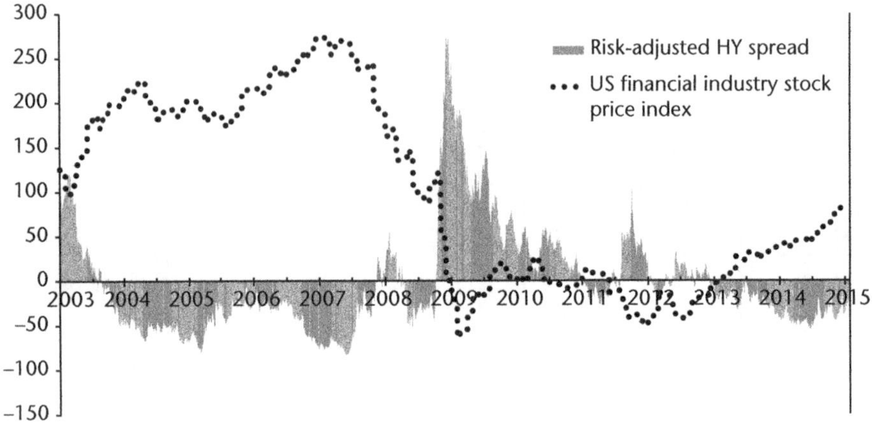

Figure 7.4. The risk-adjusted high yield premium, 2003–2015

This figure is based on Becker (2015), Figure 1. The figure plots the average excess yield spread of the highest rated high yield corporate bonds (BB) relative to a polynomial fit of bond yield spreads to rating categories AA+ through B−. This excess yield on high yield assets relative two fitted values is the high yield premium. The dotted line shows the index of S&P 1500 financial companies' stock prices (renormalized). The correlation is −0.52.

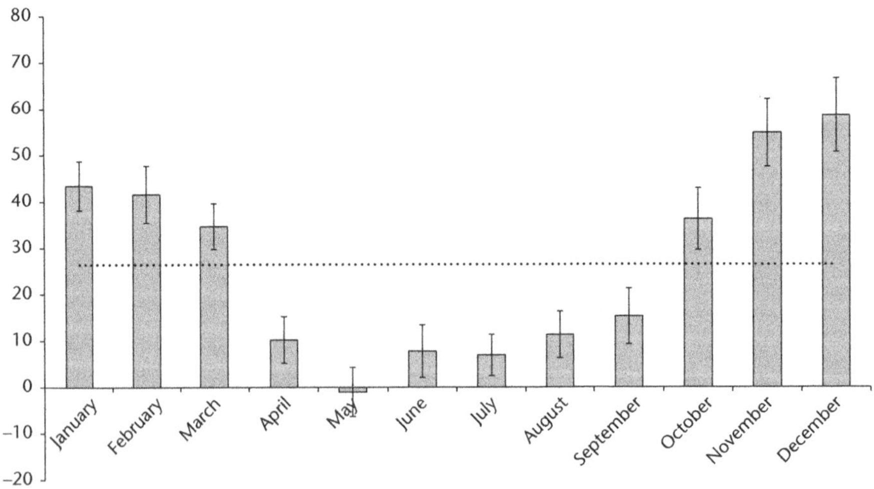

Figure 7.5. Seasonality of the risk-adjusted high yield premium

This figure is based on Becker (2015), Figure 2. The figure plots the monthly averages of the average high yield spread (the excess yield on BB-rated bonds relative to a polynomial fit of bond yield spreads to rating categories AA+ through B−). The dotted line indicates the average for all months (26.4 bps). The underlying data covers January 2003 to January 2015; 95% confidence intervals are indicated with bars for each month.

These results confirm that the desire of insurers to take risks without increasing regulatory capital requirements is large enough to impact pricing in the corporate bond market.

7.2.3 *The 2009–2010 regulatory experiment in capital requirements for mortgage-backed securities*

The credit ratings-based system used for fixed income assets was replaced in 2009 and 2010 for mortgage-backed securities (first residential MBS, then commercial MBS). Becker and Opp (2014) analyse this shift. The new system relies on measures of credit risk called expected loss, ELOSS; these are produced by Blackrock (previously also by PIMCO). ELOSS represents the present value of expected future losses of principal, based on macroeconomic scenarios defined by the regulator. The ELOSS of individual securities is correlated with credit ratings but not perfectly so. On balance, ELOSS appears slightly more optimistic in the sample period studied by Becker and Opp. Most importantly, the new system adjusts for book values, so that if an asset is held at a book value which is equal to par value less expected losses, no capital is needed. Becker and Opp show that this new rule has had a dramatic effect on capital requirements. For both MBS classes, ELOSS was stable during the period, whereas credit ratings deteriorated substantially. All told, by 2012, aggregate capital requirements for mortgage-backed securities had been reduced from $19.4 billion to $3.7 billion.

Did the lower capital requirements affect portfolio decisions of insurers? Exploiting that the change did not affect other asset classes, Becker and Opp compare the patterns in new asset acquisitions by insurers around the time of the changes. Indeed, there was a large change. In the two years leading up to the new rules, purchases of newly issued CMBS by insurance companies were 7.5 per cent speculative grade (value weighted), but in the two years following the shift, investment was only 53.0 per cent in investment speculative grade assets.[7] For comparison, corporate bond purchases, which were unaffected by the regulatory change, were 8.7 per cent investment grade before the change, and 10.9 per cent after. Municipal bonds showed patterns similar to corporates.

The fact that only the asset class with a change in capital requirements shows evidence of increased risk appetite in 2009–2010 suggests that the new, low capital requirements were indeed the driver. Becker and Opp conclude that insurers' risk taking was distorted and increased by the new regulation. Given the size of insurers' portfolios and their slow turnover, the full

[7] Interestingly, this confirms trade rumours at the time (Morgan Stanley 2014).

impact of this changed behaviour will take a long time to be manifested in asset portfolios.

7.3 Conclusion

The capital regulation system used for insurance U.S. companies has had several important effects on long-term asset allocations.

First, insurance companies accumulate more risk than intended. In good times, they reach for yield in choosing their fixed income investments, both across asset classes and within. Because they are evaluated with imperfect risk metrics they face an incentive to buy assets that comply with a set benchmark but have 'hidden risk.' This leads to higher risks than may have been expected. And when risk is easier to take on (requires less capital) in a certain market, insurers load up on risk in that market. The extra risk may destabilize credit markets and the broader financial system, and may, in an adverse scenario, impose large costs on taxpayers.

Second, regulation-driven investment practices may distort investment. Assets or issuers who happen to fit into low capital requirement categories will be able to raise funds at lower cost. This may distort the capital allocation in the economy. Indeed, Becker and Ivashina detect issuance patterns in corporate bonds which may be driven by reaching for yield. Similarly, the large increase in risk taking by insurers buying commercial mortgage-backed securities documented by Becker and Opp may also drive issuance volumes.

It is worth pointing out that it is the imperfect measurement of risk which makes it inevitable that there will be some scope for risk taking in financial intermediaries. This is a principal-agent problem. The party desiring to control risks (the 'principal') does not observe perfectly what risks are taken by the manager (the 'agent'). Thus, the prevalence of ratings as a sorting device in credit markets means that they may impact asset pricing even in the absence of regulation.[8]

While the regulation of risks is inherently imperfect, recent experience points to several lessons for the design regulation. Rules that treat asset classes differently can have a large impact on investment flows. The recent MBS experience in the U.S., like the favourable treatment of sovereign debt under Basel rules for banks, points to large potential consequences when the financial sector faces strong regulatory incentives. Additionally, changes in

[8] For example, Chernenko and Sunderam (2012) document that issuance volumes respond to the availability of funds to different institutional investors. Becker and Ivashina (2015b) show that contracting (covenants) also depend on such flows.

regulation are subject to various political pressures including lobbying by industry and special interests, and the political economy when time pressure is added. Hurried implementation of new rules may lead to oversights and shortcuts. A case can be made for moving slowly.

Speculating about the reasons behind the problematic change in capital requirements for MBS, Becker and Opp suggest that that the introduction of the new rules was (partially) motivated by a desire to reduce the need for insurers to issue equity and perhaps sell distressed MBS into a poor market. The financial crisis has depleted financial resilience of the insurance industry, and mortgage-backed securities represented a large chunk of unrealized losses. As ratings were downgraded, there was pressure to reduce capital requirements in order to avoid a large squeeze on insurers, potentially even a wave of forced state takeovers. If this is accurate, the new system was a success in avoiding some of the short term pressures. However, the new system also dramatically reduced the capital requirements for new acquisitions of MBS, and the industry took advantage in the reviving MBS market. The long-term scenario if insurers can take credit risk with impunity in this particular area is ominous. Not only is the allocation of capital in U.S. financial markets disturbed, but the overall risk in insurers may rise considerably over time.

References

Allen, Franklin, and Douglas Gale (2000): 'Bubbles and crises', *The Economic Journal*, 110 (460): 236–55.

Becker, Bo (2015): 'Reaching for yield, avoiding high yield: the price impact' in Martin Fridson (ed.), *High Yield, Future Tense—Cracking the Code of Specualtive Debt*. New York Society of Security Analysts Publishing, New York, NY.

Becker, Bo and Victoria Ivashina (2015a): 'Reaching for yield in the bond market', *Journal of Finance*, 70(5): 1863–1902.

Becker, Bo and Victoria Ivashina (2015b): 'Covenant-light contracts and creditor coordination'. Working Paper.

Becker, Bo and Marcus Opp (2014): 'Regulatory reform and risk-taking: replacing ratings', Working Paper.

Campbell, John Y., and Glen B. Taksler (2003): 'Equity volatility and corporate bond yields', *Journal of Finance*, 58(6)a: 2321–50.

Chernenko, Sergei, and Adi Sunderam (2012): 'The real consequences of market segmentation', *Review of Financial Studies*, 25(7): 2041–69.

Ellul, Andrew, C. Jotikasthira, and C. T. Lundblad (2011): 'Regulatory pressure and fire sales in the corporate bond market', *Journal of Financial Economics*, 101(3), 596–620.

Ellul, Andrew, C. Jotikasthira, and C. T. Lundblad (2014): 'Is historical cost accounting a panacea? Market stress, incentive distortions, and gains trading', Working Paper.

Frazzini, Andrea, and Lasse Heje Pedersen (2014): 'Betting against beta', *Journal of Financial Economics*, 111(1): 1–25.

Hilscher, Jens and Mungo Wilson (2013): 'Credit ratings and credit risk: Is one measure enough?', Working Paper.

Morgan Stanley Research (2014): 'Are insurance companies buying CMBS 2.0 B-pieces?', January.

8

Spillover Effects of Risk Regulation on the Asset Side to Asset Markets

Andrew Ellul, Chotibhak Jotikasthira, and Christian T. Lundblad

8.1 Introduction

A fundamental objective of risk regulation is to force financial institutions (banks and insurance companies) to internalize potential social costs associated with their failure. This goal is largely achieved, in principal at least, through the capital adequacy requirements imposed on these financial institutions. However, externalities associated with the transmission of distress from one financial institution to others and, potentially, to the broader economy, are not confined to the extreme outcome of failures. In this chapter, we focus on the asset fire sale externality, which has been identified by regulators (Brunnermeier et al. 2009) as a very important rationale for risk regulation but ironically can be triggered or exacerbated by the regulation itself. Such an externality arises in situations when an institution is forced to sell assets, especially at times when counterparties' liquidity is low, and without taking into account the price spiral dynamic that its actions can generate and from which other institutions' balance sheets can suffer.

Stiglitz (1982) and Geanakoplos and Polemarchakis (1986) were among the first to investigate this issue, and their analysis shaped the subsequent theoretical literature. However, the potential triggers of asset fire sales have been largely under-researched, and until recently, have been perceived as largely exogenous to the regulatory environment and mostly the product of investors' redemptions unrelated to the fundamental value of assets.[1,2] Here, we present evidence to demonstrate that, contrary to this traditional view, fire sales in financial institutions can occur precisely due to regulatory constraints.

The underlying assumption of the risk regulatory framework that has emerged over the last two decades is that keeping the financial soundness of *each individual financial institution* will lead to a *healthy and stable financial system*. While this assumption seems reasonable enough, it has been found to be wanting, not just in the 2007–2009 financial crisis but also in other major crises. The main reason is that this assumption is vulnerable to the fallacy of composition (Brunnermeier et al. 2009) caused precisely by the regulatory framework itself. That is, the actions taken by one institution to satisfy its regulatory requirements during a period of market stress may end up causing system-wide damage and thus leading to lower, not higher, stability. A financial institution that is hit by a price shock to the assets on its balance sheet will likely react by selling these assets if such declining valuations impact its relevant regulatory metrics (or its perceived solvency). If these sales occur when potential buyers are unable to provide liquidity, perhaps because they also hold these, or similar, assets on their balance sheets, a fire sale feedback effect may result. This forced selling will end up damaging the financial soundness of other institutions, making the regulatory constraints even more binding.

The distress faced by European life insurance companies in 2002 is a clear example of these fire sale externalities caused by regulatory constraints. The large stock market declines in the summer of 2002 had a devastating impact on European life insurers' balance sheets and their regulatory capital metrics.[3] Each insurer's response to the binding capital regulations was to sell stocks to re-establish its financial health. This made sense from the point of view of an individual insurer, but the collective selling—and the lack of potential buyers—generated large-scale sales that put further downward pressure on prices and regulatory metrics. The response of regulators was to suspend the solvency tests until the crisis resolved itself.[4]

[1] Shleifer and Vishny (1992) show that forced selling of industry-specific assets may yield transaction prices that are significantly below fundamental values.

[2] There are several examples of asset fire sales in the finance literature. Coval and Stafford (2007) investigate equity transactions induced by open-end mutual fund redemptions. Mitchell, Pedersen, and Pulvino (2007) explore the price reaction of convertible bonds around hedge fund redemptions. Pulvino (1998) studies commercial aircraft transactions initiated by (capital) constrained versus unconstrained airlines. Campbell, Giglio, and Pathak (2011) consider forced selling in the real estate market due to events such as foreclosures.

[3] For example, in the U.K. the 'resilience test' applied to life insurers (for insurers to show solvency in the case of an additional 25% stock market decline) was beginning to bind. The German and Swiss insurers were even more constrained than their U.K. counterparts.

[4] The U.K. Financial Services Authority diluted the requirements of the resilience test to pre-empt the potential destabilizing effects resulting from fire sales of stocks.

We use the U.S. insurance industry, for which we have detailed balance sheet data, as a laboratory to study the fire sale externality caused by regulatory requirements. While insurers are neither highly leveraged institutions nor interconnected through the funding side as banks are, they face very similar regulatory requirements to those faced by banks. High leverage in financial institutions and their balance sheet interconnectedness are seen by many as causing, or at the very least exacerbating, asset fire sales since a healthy asset base is necessary to obtain funding, especially at times of market stress. In the case of banks, it is hard to disentangle whether high leverage or regulatory constraints trigger fire sales and exacerbate the consequent externality. Since the insurance industry has lower leverage than the banking industry, it allows us to better isolate the effects of risk regulations on financial institutions' trading behaviour.

We consider two separate, but related, aspects of the regulatory framework designed to maintain financial stability—capital adequacy requirements, and the accounting rules used in determining whether such requirements are fulfilled. In the insurance industry, the risk-based capital (RBC) ratio is a critical metric used by a whole gamut of agents, from regulators to credit rating agencies, in determining capital adequacy and financial health of individual insurers.[5] It is calculated as the ratio of *statutory* (equity) capital to required *regulatory* capital or RBC, and in this sense is very similar to the capital ratios employed by bank regulators.[6] Our aim is to show how the use of this reasonably sound regulatory metric may create unintended consequences in the form of fire sales.

First, we examine how the *interactions between regulatory capital requirements and the statutory accounting rules* for booking financial assets (mark-to-market (MTM) or historical cost (HCA) accounting) may affect insurers' trading incentives and portfolio choice. Our analysis exploits the significant downgrades of asset-backed securities (ABS) during the 2007–2009 financial crisis and the sharp heterogeneity in U.S. insurance regulation with regard to accounting rules used for the downgraded ABS: life insurers have greater flexibility to hold speculative-grade assets at historical cost than property and casualty (P&C) insurers. Drawing on the evidence of Ellul et al. (2015), and using detailed data on insurers' transactions and portfolio positions, including the accounting treatment *for each security* held, we show that life and P&C insurers respond differently to the significant downgrades of their ABS holdings. To improve their capital positions, P&C insurers rush to sell their ABS holdings. In contrast,

[5] When an insurer's RBC ratio falls below a certain threshold, the insurer is put on a regulatory watch and immediate actions will be taken by regulators.

[6] In banking, the capital ratio is the ratio of statutory capital over risk-weighted assets. In the insurance business, the statutory capital is set in relation to risk-based capital with a required ratio of at least 2.

life insurers largely continue to hold their downgraded securities (at historical cost) and instead *selectively sell* their corporate and government bond holdings with the highest unrealized gains. This so-called 'gains trading' is particularly widespread among life insurers that face regulatory capital constraints and that are heavily exposed to ABS. These trading incentives, induced by the interplay between HCA and capital regulations, alter financial institutions' portfolio allocations, potentially engender distortions in key regulatory metrics, and transmit shocks across otherwise unrelated markets.

Having established that the interactions between the regulatory framework and accounting rules can engender forced selling *during the crisis*, we proceed to ask whether financial institutions internalize these interactions in the *pre-crisis period*. While MTM may generate higher probabilities of fire sales during a crisis, forward-looking institutions may rationally internalize such probability and thus have the right incentives to adopt a more prudent investment strategy during normal times. This means that institutions facing MTM may have safer portfolios entering the crisis. Drawing on Ellul et al. (2014), we show that insurers that faced HCA engaged in greater degrees of regulatory arbitrage (such as 'reaching-for-yields') before the crisis and limited loss recognition during the crisis, and the *ex ante* incentives for insurers facing MTM to be more prudent are at least large enough to offset the fire sale problem. Thus, contrary to popular beliefs, HCA does not necessarily avoid fire sales and result in a more stable financial system.

We then proceed to explore the second channel through which risk regulation may induce fire sales: *regulations governing the investing behaviour of insurance companies may effectively force the sale of assets reclassified into a higher risk category* and simultaneously prevent other insurers from stepping in as buyers. The capital requirements set by regulators for investment- and speculative-grade bonds differ dramatically. When a bond is downgraded, insurers holding the bond will be required to hold a significantly larger amount of capital.[7] In such a scenario, an affected insurer has two options: either raising more equity to offset the higher required capital or selling the downgraded bond to remove it from the required capital calculation. When raising new equity is difficult, the affected insurer will be forced to sell the downgraded bond. Thus, forced selling is most likely to occur when the downgraded bonds are held by regulatory-constrained insurers such as those with low RBC ratios. Further, when coupled with a relative lack of liquidity, forced selling is likely to generate significant price pressure. Using the evidence in Ellul et al. (2011),

[7] Insurance companies are regulated at the state level but states often adopt the guideline prescribed by the National Association of Insurance Commissioners (NAIC) or variants of it. Under the NAIC guideline, the capital requirements are 4.6% and 10% for BB-rated and B-rated bonds, respectively, significantly higher than the 1.3% requirement for BBB-rated bonds and the 0.4% requirement for bonds rated A or above.

we focus on the downgrades of corporate bonds from investment to speculative grades. As insurance companies are the largest single group of investors holding investment-grade corporate bonds (about one-third of bonds outstanding), the bonds' downgrades are often followed by a *collective* need to divest and limited counterparties. We show that more constrained insurers are more likely to immediately sell their holdings of downgraded corporate bonds, and most importantly, the immediacy required by these sellers induces significant, but temporary, price declines. For many downgraded corporate bonds, even a limited amount of forced selling produces very significant price declines and subsequent reversals, suggesting that liquidity provision is limited. This is likely due to the fact that the very same regulation may also prevent other insurers (and other financial institutions in general) from buying the downgraded bond.

Overall, our findings call for a deeper analysis of the trading behaviour of insurers during a crisis. It is likely through this trading activity (associated with regulatory capital constraints) that systemic risk may arise or be amplified, with a consequent negative spiral of prices and liquidity.

Our findings also speak to the limitations of the domino model of financial contagion, which seem to have been discredited by the events of the 2007–2009 financial crisis. Under the domino model, one needs an implausibly large exogenous shock to the financial industry (relative to its collective capital) for such a contagion effect to arise. This conclusion was predicated on the view that financial institutions are passive agents that do not act in response to other institutions' actions or expected actions. The financial crisis has revealed that this is not the case: financial institutions do react because of their worsening regulatory constraints, even to anticipated actions of other agents, and by doing so place greater pressure on the system. Importantly, default itself (actual or expected) may not necessarily be the only trigger for such behaviour: price changes, coupled with ratings changes, will directly affect the regulatory capital positions of institutions, inducing them to trade in ways that further transmit the shocks across different asset markets and different financial institutions.

8.2 Interaction between Regulatory Capital Requirements and Accounting Rules

Most of the theoretical literature that links the propagation of systemic risk to accounting rules (Allen and Carletti 2008; Plantin, Sapra, and Shin 2008; and Sapra 2008) argues that the specific nature of MTM leads to the fire sale externality problem whereby *heightened* selling pressure by financial institutions arises during market stress because of feedback effects between asset prices and financial institutions' capitalization. These authors argue that HCA, in contrast, may limit such downward spirals by avoiding these feedback effects. We challenge this view on HCA and argue that a crucial issue in the debate, largely ignored thus far, relates to the *interaction between the accounting rules and the capital regulatory framework*.

The accounting rules followed by financial institutions may have real impact on economic fundamentals. When markets are under stress, with low liquidity and elevated trading frictions, financial assets may temporarily trade at prices well below their fundamental values (Duffie 2010). In this environment, write-downs will cause a significant erosion of financial institutions' capital base, which may force them to liquidate some of the impaired assets. The traditional view argues that precisely because of this mechanism, MTM will lead to fire sales as price declines lead to asset liquidation, which then leads to further price declines and more liquidation, etc., ultimately leading to a downward price and liquidity spiral. In other words, MTM engenders excessive volatility in prices, degrades their information content, and potentially causes sub-optimal decisions by financial institutions. Under this view, HCA is a remedy as it will avoid fire sales; institutions book their assets at historical costs and are unaffected by asset price declines. While we agree that MTM may induce fire sales and a host of inefficiencies, especially during periods of market stress, we show that HCA also engenders inefficiencies. Specifically, insurers using HCA will have an incentive to engage in selective asset sales aimed at the early realization of earnings (see Laux and Leuz 2009 for a discussion of this so-called gains trading). These inefficiencies are not due to the accounting rules per se, but rather due to the way they interact with the capital regulations. Below, we will first show how such interactions will impact the trading behaviour of insurers during the *financial crisis* and then shift our focus to the *pre-crisis period*.

8.2.1 *Mechanism Inducing Fire Sales*

Let us begin by explaining how the use of MTM and HCA can influence financial institutions' capital positions. Consider securitized assets (referred to as ABS) that experienced substantial downgrades during the 2007–2009 crisis. Under the risk-based capital requirements, the severe downgrades of ABS, often from investment to speculative grades, significantly increased the required capital of various financial institutions holding these securities. The capital ratios of these institutions thus deteriorated. Furthermore, the downgraded ABS also suffered significant price declines. Each affected institution faces a stark decision: either keep the downgraded ABS and raise additional equity capital, potentially difficult during a crisis, or sell the downgraded ABS to reduce the required capital by swapping for low-risk assets like

U.S. Treasuries. This is where the accounting rules used for the ABS should have a first-order effect on trading incentives.

Consider the case where an institution holds the downgraded ABS at market values. In this case, the price decline is automatically reflected in the balance sheet, and the loss directly reduces the institution's equity capital. While the institution, from a purely accounting point of view, will be indifferent between keeping the assets on its balance sheet and selling them, selling the downgraded assets for cash or lower-risk assets will reduce the required capital and hence improve financial health as measured by the RBC ratio (or other similar regulatory metrics). In this case, one institution's desire to satisfy its regulatory constraints by selling the distressed assets may create negative externalities for other institutions holding the same assets, and thus MTM may lead to a downward spiral of prices.

Consider another case where the institution holds the downgraded ABS at historical cost: the price decline does not affect its equity capital unless it sells the downgraded ABS. Due to the increase in required capital, however, the institution still experiences a deterioration of its capital ratios and may need to act to recover its previous measurement of financial health. Selling the downgraded ABS is not attractive as it will force the institution to realize losses and take a further hit on its capital ratios. A common alternative that the institution using HCA often resorts to is to engage in gains trading, where it *selectively sells other risky assets on its balance sheet to recognize gains* and increase its statutory capital.

8.2.2 *Accounting Rules in the Insurance Industry*

Here, we turn to the accounting rules that insurers use for speculative-grade assets. To focus ideas, let us consider the crisis period from 2007 to 2009 where thousands of ABS were sharply downgraded, capital constraints became practically binding, and so the effects of accounting rules were likely to be most pronounced. In the case of an ABS downgraded from investment to speculative grades, P&C insurers have to immediately recognize the value of the ABS as the lower of the book value (based on HCA) or the market price (or model price, in case no market price is available). On the other hand, life insurers can continue to hold the downgraded ABS under HCA except in the extreme case when it is classified as 'in or near default' (Class 6).[8] Given the observed large downgrades among insurers' holdings in ABS during the financial crisis, these

[8] To put the definitions of the risk classes in perspective, a 'Class 5' security is one that corresponds to a CCC/Caa credit rating; even in such cases life insurers can continue to hold the asset under HCA while P&C insurers have to book the same asset at the market price if it is below the amortized historical value.

accounting variations, as they interact with regulatory capital requirements, are likely to induce significantly different trading behaviours and portfolio choices among life and P&C insurers, particularly those that are the most capital-constrained and the most exposed to the ABS market.

8.2.3 *Evidence of Fire Sales during Market Stress*

Using *portfolio-security level* data provided by the National Association of Insurance Commissioners (NAIC), we investigate how the significant downgrades of ABS held by the two groups of insurers affected their behaviour during the 2007–2009 crisis. Our empirical investigation employs a panel of 1,882 life and P&C insurers.[9] As of 2007, life and P&C insurers held roughly the same amount of non-agency ABS as a percentage of their total bond portfolios (around 5–7 per cent). During the financial crisis, the downgrades of some of these ABS were severe, with many falling to speculative grades.[10] We start by investigating the differences between life and P&C insurers in their subsequent accounting treatment of the downgraded ABS. This analysis is shown in Figure 8.1, for the downgrades from investment to speculative grades.

There are striking differences between life and P&C insurers. Focusing on the downgrades in the fourth quarter in which the changes in accounting treatment are immediate, life insurers had a total of 5,161 affected positions that were previously held under HCA. Once the downgrade occurred, life insurers kept 74 per cent of these securities at amortized historical costs and revalued 14 per cent to market values. In contrast, P&C firms had 327 affected positions, of which they kept only 20 per cent under HCA, revalued 60 per cent to market values (four times as much as life firms did), and sold 20 per cent. Note that the statutory capital of life insurers, due to the use of HCA, is much less affected by the downgrades than the capital of P&C insurers. For both groups, however, the *required regulatory capital* increased. The question is then how the different accounting treatments influence the incentives of life and P&C insurers to respond to this increase.

We start by assessing whether the P&C firms' revaluation of downgraded ABS to market values makes them more likely to directly sell the downgraded

[9] Using S&P's Ratings IQuery, we construct a dataset of 34,957 downgrades of non-agency ABS to speculative grade by S&P over the period 2005–2010. We combine information on these securities with *firm-level* observations, provided by the NAIC, on insurance companies' holdings of and transactions in individual ABS and corporate bonds. Further, for each ABS and corporate bond position, insurance companies provide, under statutory accounting principles prescribed by insurance regulatory authorities, both fair and book values to the NAIC. We obtain data on the financial position and strength of each insurance company from Weiss Ratings, LLC. We thank Professor Yihui Wang for giving us access to the S&P's Ratings IQuery.

[10] From the 1,238 ABS held by insurance companies that were downgraded to BB status, 946 were previously rated in the top three credit rating classes, with 451 coming straight from the highest AAA rating class.

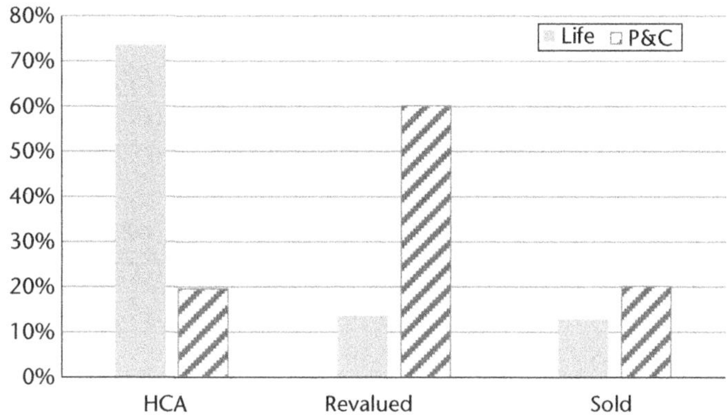

Figure 8.1. Accounting treatment of downgraded ABS

This graph plots the frequencies (in % of total) that downgraded ABS, previously held at modified historical costs, are (i) kept at historical cost (HCA), (ii) kept but revalued to the year-end fair value, and (iii) sold after the downgrade. The sample includes only the ABS that are downgraded by S&P from investment to speculative grades in the fourth quarter of each year during the sample period 2005–2010.

Source: Authors' calculation based on NAIC Schedule D's position data

ABS (relative to their life counterparts). We calculate the probability of selling the downgraded ABS within three months after the downgrade and examine whether such probability differs between the two types of insurers.[11] Table 8.1 reports the results.

In columns (1) and (2), we consider all downgrades from investment to speculative grades, and find that P&C insurers have a higher propensity to sell the downgraded ABS (rather than keeping these ABS on their books) relative to life insurers. This is confirmed for the more severe, and in some sense surprising, downgrades from AAA to speculative grade (columns (3) and (4)). For these AAA-to-speculative-grade downgrades, and controlling for the revaluation effects, we find that the selling probability of P&C firms exceeds that of life firms by 5.8 per cent (Panel B). This difference is highly economically significant, given that the average selling probability is 7.3 per cent for these downgraded ABS.

The results from Table 8.1 exhibit a sharp contrast between P&C and life firms: P&C firms disproportionately sell their downgraded ABS holdings. Since P&C insurers already recognize the losses associated with these holdings, selling them has no further effects on the insurers' balance sheets but has an important advantage from the regulatory point of view, as exchanging very risky assets for cash (or even a less risky asset) reduces the required capital. This

[11] We use a logistic function that controls for each bond's static characteristics and time-varying characteristics before the downgrade and time-specific variables for each downgrade. We also include ratings group, U.S. state of domicile, and year fixed effects.

Table 8.1. Probability of selling downgraded ABS

	(1)	(2)	(3)	(4)
	Investment to non-investment	Investment to non-investment	AAA to non-investment	AAA to non-investment
Panel A: coefficient estimates				
P&C dummy	0.548***	0.438***	0.830***	0.746***
	(0.155)	(0.165)	(0.222)	(0.234)
Revalue dummy		0.588***		0.840**
		(0.216)		(0.374)
Rating group (before downgrade) fixed effects	YES	YES	YES	YES
State fixed effects	YES	YES	YES	YES
Year fixed effects	YES	YES	YES	YES
Observations	6,691	6,354	2,487	2,357
Pseudo R-squared	0.120	0.124	0.129	0.138
Panel B: marginal effects				
P&C dummy	0.041***	0.033**	0.064***	0.058***
Revalue dummy		0.049**		0.078*

Notes: This table reports logit estimates for the probability that an insurer will sell its downgraded ABS within three months after the downgrade. The first two columns include all downgrades from investment to non-investment grades during the sample period 2005–2010. Columns (3) and (4) include only downgrades from AAA to non-investment grade. Panel A reports the coefficient estimates. Panel B reports the marginal effects of (i) the company being a P&C insurer (over being a life insurer) and (ii) the position being revalued by the company at previous year-end. All other variables are held at the sample means. In addition to the fixed effects, the control variables, included in all regressions but not reported for brevity, are logs of ABS issue size and maturity. Standard errors, clustered by insurer, are in parentheses. *, **, and *** refer to statistical significance at 10%, 5%, and 1% levels.

Source: Authors' calculation based on NAIC Schedule D's position and transaction data

forced selling of ABS seems to generate fire sale effects, as shown by Merrill et al. (2012).

In continuing to hold their downgraded ABS positions, life firms may have the advantage of limiting an unfavourable price impact and avoiding the realization of losses, but *additional capital may still be required.* It is precisely here that gains trading becomes important. As a life firm attempts to sell existing assets to shore up its capital, it has an incentive to *selectively sell* those that have the *largest unrealized gains.* Only by selling these assets can the unrealized gains be recognized and applied to its capital. Although life insurers engaging in gains trading have different asset classes from which to choose, we focus on investment-grade corporate bonds since they account for over half of life insurers' bond portfolio and a significant number of them carried unrealized gains even in 2008. To identify gains trading, we relate the probability that an insurer will sell its corporate bond position to the position's unrealized gain, relative to others in the insurer's portfolio. Table 8.2 reports the results.

We start by comparing the results during the crisis period for life insurers, shown in column (1), with those for P&C insurers, shown in column (3). Considering the first row, we find that life firms have a positive and

Table 8.2. Gains trading and probability of selling corporate bonds

Panel A: coefficient estimates

	Life	Property & casualty		
	(1)	(2)	(3)	(4)
	Crisis	Non-crisis	Crisis	Non-crisis
(1) Unrealized gain percentile	0.202*	−0.462***	−0.289***	−0.081
	(0.104)	(0.077)	(0.095)	(0.063)
(2) High ABS exposure dummy	0.311**	0.287***	0.213***	0.241***
	(0.145)	(0.086)	(0.079)	(0.074)
(1) x (2)	0.007	−0.285**	0.309**	0.050
	(0.147)	(0.126)	(0.151)	(0.109)
(3) Low RBC ratio dummy	0.366**	−0.053	−0.028	0.062
	(0.164)	(0.107)	(0.094)	(0.079)
(1) x (3)	−0.254	0.431**	0.158	0.212*
	(0.262)	(0.171)	(0.176)	(0.128)
(1) x (2) x (3)	0.597**	−0.055	−0.313	−0.300
	(0.294)	(0.292)	(0.327)	(0.184)
(4) Revalue dummy	0.646***	0.652***	0.181**	0.264***
	(0.122)	(0.173)	(0.075)	(0.058)
Rating group fixed effects	YES	YES	YES	YES
State fixed effects	YES	YES	YES	YES
Calendar quarter fixed effects	YES	YES	YES	YES
Observations	1 018 874	1 478 908	526 873	774 144
Pseudo R-squared	0.070	0.050	0.052	0.043

Panel B: effects of moving from the 25th to 75th percentiles of unrealized gain

	Life (mean selling probability = 0.042)			Property & casualty (mean selling probability = 0.054)		
	Crisis	Non-crisis	Difference	Crisis	Non-crisis	Difference
High ABS exposure = 0 & Low RBC ratio = 0	0.005**	−0.006***	0.010***	−0.005**	−0.001	−0.004
High ABS exposure = 1 & Low RBC ratio = 1	0.017***	−0.006***	0.023***	−0.002	−0.003	0.000

Notes: This table reports logit estimates for the effects of unrealized gain on the probability that an insurer will sell a corporate bond during (i) non-crisis and (ii) crisis periods. The dependent variable is a dummy that equals one if the insurer holding the bond at the beginning of the quarter sells the bond during the quarter, and zero otherwise. Panel A reports the coefficient estimates. Columns (1)–(2) and (3)–(4) are for life (P&C) insurers. In addition to the fixed effects, the control variables, included in all regressions but not reported for brevity, are logged bond age, logged bond maturity, logged bond issue size, (bond issuer) bankruptcy dummy, bond downgrade dummy, logged insurer's capital and surplus, insurer's portfolio holdings of risky assets, insurer's leverage, and insurer's ROE. Panel B reports the effects of moving from the 25th to 75th percentiles of unrealized gains, evaluated for (i) the crisis versus non-crisis periods, (ii) the insurers in the top quartile of exposure to ABS not revalued at the previous year-end, and (iii) the insurers in the bottom quartile of RBC ratio. All other variables are held at the sample means. Standard errors, clustered by insurance company, are in parentheses. *, **, and *** refer to statistical significance at 10%, 5%, and 1% levels.

Source: Weiss Ratings. Authors' calculation based on NAIC Schedule D's position and transaction data

statistically significant propensity to sell corporate bonds at higher levels of unrealized gains during the crisis period. Interestingly, the same coefficient is negative for P&C firms. When we compare the propensity of life and P&C insurers during the non-crisis periods (column (2) for life and column (4) for P&C), we also find a significant difference. In normal times, life insurers are actually less likely to sell bonds with high unrealized gains (possibly to avoid tax) while P&C firms' trading is insensitive to unrealized gains. Overall, life insurers appear to engage in gains trading *only* during the crisis period, while they tend to sell their corporate bonds with the *lowest unrealized gains* during the non-crisis period. No such behaviour is detected for P&C insurers, which are required to use MTM for downgraded ABS during the crisis.

We next investigate the impact of each insurer's exposure to ABS assets *held at amortized historical cost* and its capital constraints, as measured by the RBC ratio, on the propensity to engage in gains trading. We have argued that the interaction between the accounting rules and capital requirements is an important factor that may induce insurance companies to gains trade. In the fifth row of column (1), we find that life insurers with high ABS exposure and low RBC ratios appear significantly more likely to gains trade during the crisis. No such behaviour is detected during normal times (column (2)) or among P&C insurers (columns (3) and (4)).

The question then becomes whether such gains trading generates distortions in financial institutions' portfolio allocations and engenders price pressures in the market for the assets with unrealized gains. Our analysis shows that the answer to both questions is in the affirmative.

To maintain the same risk-return profile as in the pre-crisis period, both life and P&C insurers should reduce their portfolio allocation to ABS during the crisis, especially for insurers with relatively low RBC ratios as they are most sensitive to elevated risk and vulnerable to further market declines. We investigate whether regulatory accounting rules interfere in any significant way with this process by regressing the proportion of ABS held by each insurer on year dummies during the period 2007–2010 for both types of insurers. This allows us to analyse the general evolution of ABS holdings over the event period and to capture any differences in the behaviour of life relative to P&C insurers.[12] The results are shown in Panel A of Table 8.3.

We first investigate these dynamics for the entire sample of affected insurance companies (column (1)) and then separately for each of the RBC ratio quartiles (columns (2) to (5)). Starting from the entire sample, the ABS holdings of P&C insurers increase slightly (0.8 per cent of portfolio) in 2007 over the average holdings in the benchmark period but decrease markedly as the

[12] The benchmark period is the average ABS holdings of each company over the years 2004–2006.

Table 8.3. Implications of gains trading for portfolio allocation and reported RBC ratio

Panel A: portfolio allocation to ABS over time

		By RBC Ratio Quartile			
	(1)	(2)	(3)	(4)	(5)
	All	Q1 (lowest)	Q2	Q3	Q4 (highest)
Year 2007 dummy	0.008***	0.004	0.014***	0.003	0.011**
	(0.002)	(0.004)	(0.003)	(0.003)	(0.005)
Year 2008 dummy	−0.004*	−0.005	0.003	−0.012***	0.002
	(0.002)	(0.004)	(0.003)	(0.004)	(0.007)
Year 2009 dummy	−0.014***	−0.015***	−0.005**	−0.020***	−0.012**
	(0.002)	(0.003)	(0.002)	(0.004)	(0.005)
Year 2010 dummy	−0.018***	−0.018***	−0.007***	−0.019***	−0.017***
	(0.002)	(0.004)	(0.003)	(0.004)	(0.005)
Life dummy x Year 2007 dummy	0.013***	0.013**	0.013**	0.014***	0.005
	(0.003)	(0.005)	(0.005)	(0.005)	(0.006)
Life dummy x Year 2008 dummy	0.009***	0.014**	0.009	0.009*	0.001
	(0.003)	(0.006)	(0.006)	(0.005)	(0.008)
Life dummy x Year 2009 dummy	0.012***	0.017***	0.008	0.010*	0.011
	(0.003)	(0.006)	(0.006)	(0.006)	(0.007)
Life dummy x Year 2010 dummy	0.012***	0.013*	0.001	0.004	0.012
	(0.003)	(0.007)	(0.006)	(0.006)	(0.009)
Insurer fixed effects	YES	YES	YES	YES	YES
Observations	4,677	1,235	1,269	1,224	941
R-squared	0.089	0.091	0.092	0.188	0.051
Number of insurers	1,135	455	540	513	372

Panel B: differences between market-adjusted RBC ratio and reported RBC ratio

				Mean by ABS exposure quartile			
Year	Number of firms	Mean	25th Pct	Q1 (lowest)	Q2	Q3	Q4 (highest)
Life							
2004	496	2.087	0.389	1.582	2.465	2.430	1.855
2005	474	0.749	−0.082	0.626	0.957	0.738	0.674
2006	454	0.148	−0.242	−0.118	0.359	0.201	0.145
2007	432	0.002	−0.407	0.150	0.164	0.175	−0.480
2008	424	−3.372	−5.156	−0.540	−2.877	−3.669	−6.219
2009	414	0.537	−0.352	1.195	1.185	0.305	−0.533
2010	412	2.457	0.644	2.174	2.785	2.979	1.868
Property & Casualty							
2004	1,307	0.266	0.037	0.222	0.345	0.358	0.225
2005	1,320	0.012	−0.135	0.020	0.110	0.025	−0.051
2006	1,313	−0.024	−0.121	−0.040	0.030	−0.006	−0.040
2007	1,344	0.141	0.024	0.175	0.178	0.147	0.067
2008	1,390	−0.030	−0.256	0.257	−0.039	−0.113	−0.418
2009	1,390	0.479	0.114	0.520	0.473	0.549	0.338
2010	1,385	0.591	0.130	0.580	0.580	0.583	0.623

Notes: This table reports statistics on the implications of gains trading for insurers' portfolio allocations and reported RBC ratios. Panel A reports coefficient estimates from regressing the proportion of ABS in each insurer's portfolio on year dummies and their interactions with the life dummy. Years 2004–2006 are lumped together as the benchmark for evaluating the evolution of ABS proportions over the subsequent years. All regressions include insurer dummies to absorb the fixed effects of firm characteristics on ABS proportion. Column (1) reports the estimates for the entire sample. Columns (2)–(5) report separate estimates for each of the four subsamples created by independently sorting life insurers and P&C insurers by RBC ratio. To be included in these regressions, insurers must invest in all four credit rating groups (A and above, BBB, BB, and B and below). Standard errors, clustered by insurer, are in parentheses. *, **, and *** refer to statistical significance at 10%, 5%, and 1% levels. Panel B presents summary statistics for the difference between market-adjusted RBC ratio and reported RBC ratio for the sample of life and P&C insurers over time. In calculating market-adjusted RBC ratio, unrealized gains and losses on all securities held at historical costs are added to the statutory capital in the denominator of the RBC ratio.

Source: Weiss Ratings. Authors' calculation based on NAIC Schedule D's position data

crisis unfolds (−0.4 per cent in 2008, −1.4 per cent in 2009, and −1.8 per cent in 2010). The ABS holdings of life insurers follow a significantly different trajectory. In 2007, life insurers also increase their ABS holdings, albeit with a larger magnitude. In the subsequent years, unlike P&C firms, life firms do not seem to significantly reduce their ABS allocations. For example, life insurers do not decrease their ABS exposure in 2008 and only reduce it by 0.2 per cent (compared to the average during the benchmark period) in 2009. Moving to the results in columns (2) to (5), it is evident that the slow pace of reduction in ABS allocations of life insurers is concentrated among those with the lowest RBC ratios (column (2)), i.e. those that are financially weak and hence most sensitive to risk and further reductions in the value of their positions.

By failing to recognize changes in the fair value of assets, HCA may induce a wedge between financial institutions' *reported* capital ratios, e.g. the RBC ratios in the case of insurance companies, and the *hypothetical* ratios that might better reflect market conditions. We investigate this issue in Panel B of Table 8.3. For each insurer at each year-end, we calculate a *market-adjusted* RBC ratio by adding the unrealized gains and losses on all securities held at historical costs to the firm's reported statutory capital, the numerator of RBC ratio. In column (1), we present the mean difference between the market-adjusted RBC ratio and the reported RBC ratio for all life and P&C insurers. For P&C insurers, the difference is close to zero even when we look at the 25th percentile (shown in column (2)). The same cannot be said for life insurers: there are several years in which the differences between the market-adjusted and the reported RBC ratios are sizeable. In 2004 and 2010, the market-adjusted RBC ratio is larger than the reported RBC ratio, on average. The opposite is true in 2008, at the height of the crisis, where the reported RBC ratio of an average life insurer is larger than the market-adjusted RBC by 3.4 (5.1 at the 25th percentile). That is, a sizable fraction of life insurers that appear healthy actually have RBC ratios below 2, and may warrant some regulatory intervention.

We next investigate the relationship between the difference in insurers' market-adjusted and reported RBC ratios and their ABS holdings. We rank insurers in each type into quartiles according to their portfolio allocations, with lowest ABS exposures in column (3) and the highest in column (6). Focusing on life insurers in year 2008, in which the difference between market-adjusted and reported RBC ratios is most negative, we find a striking confirmation of our conjecture: the difference between the market-adjusted and the reported RBC ratios increases in the level of ABS exposure. In fact, life insurers with the lowest ABS holdings would have been practically unaffected had fair value accounting been used, while those with the highest allocation to ABS would have seen their RBC ratios decrease by 6.21 in 2008.

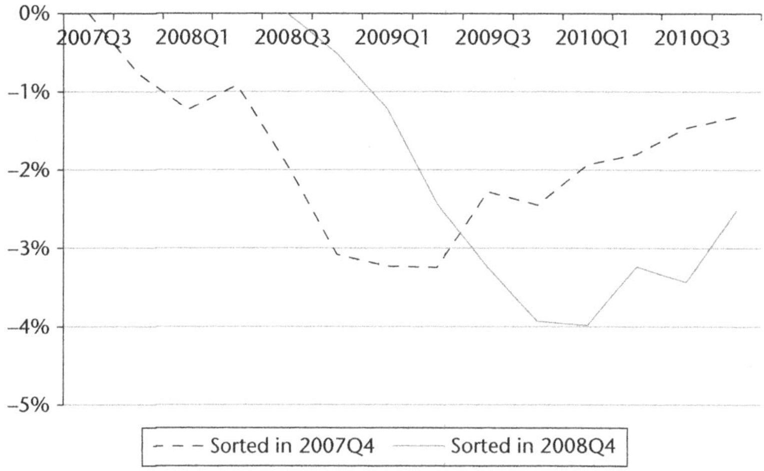

Figure 8.2. Price pressures and reversals of bonds targeted for gains trading

This figure plots the differences in cumulative returns of bonds with high average unrealized gains (top 25%) and those with low average unrealized gains (bottom 75%) across portfolios of life insurers at the end of 2007Q4 (dashed line) and 2008Q4 (solid line). Quarterly bond return is the log of change in prices on the last day when there are any trades of a bond from the previous quarter. Cumulative returns are tracked from the end of the sorting quarter to the end of 2010Q4.

Source: Authors' calculation based on TRACE and NAIC Schedule D's position data

Finally, we examine whether the selective selling creates enough pressure in the targeted corporate bonds to distort prices. In the case that such price pressures do occur, we can conclude that HCA—precisely because of its interactions with capital regulation—does not avoid fire sales and spillovers, as claimed by many. We do so by tracking the differences in the returns of bonds with high average unrealized gains (top 25 per cent) and those with low average unrealized gains (bottom 75 per cent) across portfolios of life insurers. We start from the quarter in which the unrealized gains are calculated and the pressure is induced. Figure 8.2 below shows the results. First, the selling pressures cluster over several quarters for the same bonds. Second, Figure 8.2 shows that there are significant price drops and price reversals eventually emerge: this is the conventional way of capturing fire sales. For example, bonds targeted for gains trading in 2007Q4 underperform other bonds in all but one quarter during 2007Q4–2009Q1. Price reversals started in 2009Q2 and continued slowly for many quarters. The cumulative underperformance is slightly over 3 per cent, much of which is erased by the end of 2010Q4.

8.2.4 *Risk-Taking Incentives in the Pre-crisis Period*

The evidence presented so far has focused on the regulatory capital and accounting channel through which systemic risk spreads during the crisis.

Our next objective is to explore the behaviour of P&C and life insurers in the years *leading up* to the crisis. Many have argued that the pre-crisis period was characterized by excessive risk-taking behaviour and 'reaching-for-yield' investments aimed at regulatory capital arbitrage (Rajan 2010; and Yellen 2011). Portfolio allocations in the pre-crisis period are important because the severity of the feedback dynamic during a crisis is linked directly to the amount of risk buildup before the crisis, when perceived low-risk conditions may lead institutions to excessively accumulate risky assets.

Drawing from Ellul et al. (2014), we investigate the selling behaviour of life and P&C insurers for the different types of assets they held both *during the pre-crisis years and post-crisis years*. Crucially, we also introduce in the analysis the RBC ratio difference in the multivariate analysis, again defined as an insurer's market-adjusted RBC ratio less the reported RBC ratio. Our objective is to explore whether the information contained in market prices provided useful signals to institutions to re-allocate their positions. Table 8.4 reports estimates for cross-sectional regressions of portfolio allocation changes (in per cent) for different types of risky assets (speculative-grade bonds, ABS, and investment grade bonds) from 2004 to 2007 (pre-crisis) in columns (1)–(3) and 2007–2010 (crisis) in columns (4)–(6).

Panel A includes all insurers, with P&C dummy to isolate the differences between P&C and life firms. Two main results are worth noting for the crisis period in columns (4)–(6). First, P&C insurers were significantly more aggressive in reducing the holdings of risky assets (speculative grade bonds and ABS) while increasing their holdings of investment-grade bonds compared to life insurers. Second, the RBC ratio difference had an impact but was mostly confined to the riskiest assets. This means that insurers that aimed to maintain the risk-reward tradeoff of its portfolio at pre-crisis levels should have reduced precisely their holdings of the riskiest assets. The results in columns (4)–(5) show that the insurers whose market-adjusted RBC ratios were below their reported RBC ratios were less aggressive in following this goal.

The first main result from the first three columns, that explores the *ex ante* incentives, is that relative to life insurers, P&C insurers reduced their holdings of risky assets (speculative grade bonds and ABS) and increased their holdings of investment-grade bonds during the 2004–2007 period. In other words, P&C insurers entered the crisis with a less risky balance sheet as compared to that of life insurers. Second, the RBC ratio difference has a statistically and economically significant effect on the allocation of ABS and investment-grade bonds. The effect of the RBC ratio difference on ABS holdings should be noted: larger market-adjusted RBC ratios compared to reported RBC ratios led to a *decrease of ABS holdings* (and *an increase of investment grade bonds* before the crisis). This effect is largely concentrated among P&C firms (Panel C compared to Panel B), a further confirmation that insurers that knew they had to apply MTM during

Table 8.4. Changes in asset allocation during pre-crisis and crisis periods

	Alloc. change (pre-crisis)			Alloc. change (crisis)		
	(1)	(2)	(3)	(4)	(5)	(6)
	Spec.-grade bonds	ABS	Inv.-grade bonds	Spec.-grade bonds	ABS	Inv.-grade bonds
Panel A: all insurance firms						
P&C dummy	−0.361***	−2.041**	5.950***	−0.605***	−2.656***	2.887**
	(0.118)	(0.838)	(1.197)	(0.215)	(0.504)	(1.183)
RBC ratio difference	0.033	−0.547**	0.727**	−0.230*	−0.683***	0.326
	(0.036)	(0.242)	(0.293)	(0.119)	(0.248)	(0.311)
Observations	1,750	1,750	1,750	1,793	1,793	1,793
Adjusted R-squared	0.199	0.090	0.153	0.022	0.667	0.487
Panel B: life firms						
RBC ratio difference	−0.012	−0.435*	0.580**	−0.146	−0.308	−0.145
	(0.040)	(0.259)	(0.289)	(0.097)	(0.239)	(0.289)
Observations	435	435	435	431	431	431
Adjusted R-squared	0.234	0.106	0.163	0.043	0.576	0.560
Mean allocation (%)	2.731	19.73	56.86	2.493	21.275	54.975
Panel C: P&C firms						
RBC ratio difference	0.145	−2.845***	5.240***	−1.389***	−2.707***	5.919**
	(0.112)	(0.872)	(1.327)	(0.534)	(0.838)	(2.374)
Observations	1,315	1,315	1,315	1,362	1,362	1,362
Adjusted R-squared	0.192	0.099	0.179	0.029	0.702	0.463
Mean allocation (%)	0.613	13.903	63.844	0.637	15.53	62.767

Notes: This table reports OLS estimates for the cross-sectional regressions of portfolio allocation changes (%) from 2004–2007 (pre-crisis) and from 2007–2010 (crisis) on P&C dummy, RBC ratio difference, and other control variables at the beginning of each period. The control variables included in all the regressions but not reported are RBC ratio, ln (capital and surplus), leverage, % risky assets, ROE, and allocation, which is the beginning portfolio allocation in the asset class. Columns (1) and (4) are for speculative-grade bonds, (2) and (5) for ABS, and (3) and (6) for investment-grade bonds. Panel A includes all insurers with P&C insurers dummied out. Panels B and C include only life and only P&C insurers, respectively. Bootstrapped standard errors, calculated using 1,000 repetitions, are in parentheses. *, **, and *** refer to statistical significance at 10%, 5%, and 1% levels.

Source: Weiss Ratings. Authors' calculation of market-adjusted RBC ratios using NAIC Schedule D's position data

a crisis moved away from riskier securities in the years before the onset of the crisis, and thus entered the crisis with a safer portfolio.

We next dig deeper into the assets that comprise the investment-grade portion of insurers' portfolios. In particular, we explore the behaviour of insurers in making 'reaching-for-yield' investments in the pre-crisis period. This process is aptly described by Admati and Hellwig (2013) in the context of banks—but the same concept can be applied to insurers—as follows: 'Banks

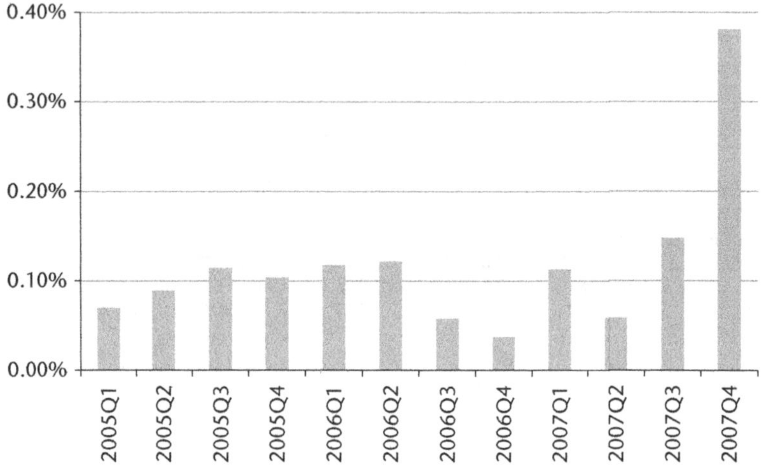

Figure 8.3. Difference in yields for bonds purchased by life versus P&C firms

This figure plots time series of difference in median yields for all ABS and corporate bonds purchased in each calendar quarter by life versus P&C insurers (life minus P&C). Only bonds rated in the A to AAA categories (NAIC Class 1) and with maturities between 2 and 5 years are included.

Source: Authors' calculation based on NAIC Schedule D's position and transaction data

have developed various techniques for "risk-weight optimization" that allow them to choose investments that are in fact riskier than the supervisors believe and have return prospects reflecting these risks so that, on average, returns are higher than the returns on investments that are in fact safer' (page 184). In our contexts, insurers may invest in riskier assets in the investment-grade classes, in order to maximize the weighted average yields of their portfolios, for a given amount of risk-based capital.

If the application of MTM during a crisis should lead to a more conservative investment approach pre-crisis, we expect P&C insurers to have engaged less in 'reaching-for-yield' behaviour compared to life insurers in 2005–2007. In Figure 8.3, we plot the time series of the *difference* of the median yields across all ABS and corporate bonds purchased in each calendar quarter, both at issuance and in secondary markets, by life versus P&C firms, roughly following the approach of Becker and Ivashina (2015). We focus on bonds rated A–AAA (NAIC Class 1) and with maturities between two and five years.

We find that in all quarters except one, life insurance insurers purchased ABS and corporate bonds that had higher yields than those purchased by P&C. The average difference over the pre-crisis period was 11 basis points, which is economically significant given that this is the highest rating class that carries little to no capital charge. Thus, life insurers, knowing that they will not face MTM and recognizing investment losses during the crisis, not only overweight ABS and speculative-grade bonds, compared to P&C insurers, but also engage in a greater degree of reaching-for-yield among investment-grade bonds. Overall, our evidence suggests that HCA may increase risk-taking incentives among financial institutions.

8.3 Regulations and Downgraded Securities

We next move to discuss the second aspect of how risk regulation may engender fire sales—by imposing constraints on financial institutions in the event of asset downgrades. We focus on the trading behaviour of insurance companies in corporate bonds and the consequent price dynamics. Insurance companies constitute an important part of the corporate bond market and, at the same time, face regulations that either prohibit or impose large capital requirements on the holdings of speculative-grade bonds. When corporate bonds are downgraded from investment to speculative grades, the required capital significantly increases, potentially forcing less capitalized insurance companies to sell the bonds. This forced selling, coupled with the lack of liquidity, is likely to generate significant and persistent price pressures, which are particularly problematic as insurance companies collectively hold between one-third and two-fifths of all investment-grade corporate bonds (see Schultz 2001). As insurers face shared regulation, the resulting *collective* need to divest the downgraded issues may be limited by a scarcity of counter-parties and associated bargaining power. Fire sale prices will obtain, leading to transaction prices significantly below fundamental values. Liquidity provision, then, has to come from outside of the insurance industry. The gradual emergence of outside investors in high search cost markets, like that for downgraded corporate bonds, will generate a slow reversal of transaction prices and an eventual realignment with fundamental values.

To empirically test the fire sale hypothesis in the corporate bond market as related to regulatory requirements, we construct a dataset of 1,179 bonds that were downgraded to speculative grade over the period 2001–2005.[13] Consistent with the theoretical predictions, we find that (even modest) forced selling by insurers produces significant price declines and reversals in downgraded bonds, as shown in Figure 8.4 below.

The median cumulative abnormal return in the first three weeks for downgraded bonds is more than 11 per cent, and that is largely reversed by week +16. It is precisely this persistent divergence of bonds' transaction prices from their fundamental values and the subsequent price reversals that constitute

[13] We combine information on these bonds with observations on insurance companies' holdings and transactions provided by the NAIC. We obtain data on the financial position and strength of *each insurance company* from Weiss Ratings, formerly part of the Street.com.

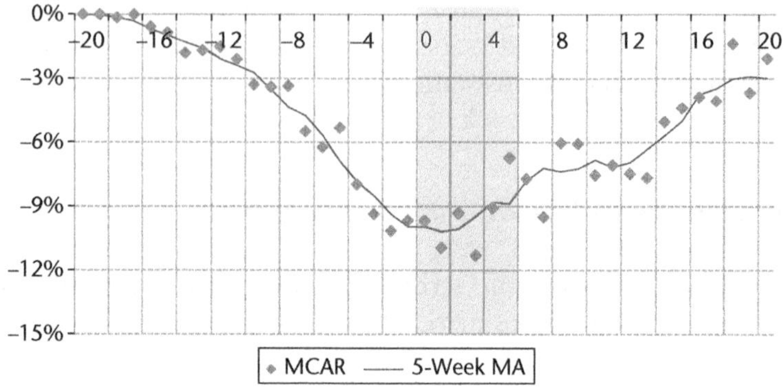

Figure 8.4. Median cumulative abnormal returns of downgraded corporate bonds

This figure plots the median cumulative abnormal returns (MCARs) by event week for corporate bonds that are downgraded from investment to speculative grades during the sample period 2001–2005. Week 0 is the downgrade announcement week. Abnormal returns are measured as the residuals from the market model in which observed bond returns load linearly on changes in maturity-matched Treasury bond yields, maturity-matched investment-grade corporate bond spreads, maturity-matched high-yield corporate bond spreads, and stock market returns. The estimation period is the period before week −30 for the abnormal returns prior to the event week and the period after week +30 for abnormal returns in and after the event week. MCARs are measured as across-bond across-transaction medians of cumulative abnormal returns for each week.

Source: Authors' calculation based on NAIC Schedule D's transaction data

fire sales. Ellul et al. (2011) present an important piece of evidence, suggesting that the fire sales are induced by risk regulation: the pattern of price decline and reversal is significantly more pronounced for bonds that are more widely held by regulatory-constrained insurance companies. For example, the median cumulative abnormal returns in the first five weeks after the downgrade is over −14 per cent for bonds held by insurers with low RBC ratios, but less than −8 per cent for bonds held by insurers with high RBC ratios; the price reversals stop around sixteen weeks after the downgrade for each. The departure from fundamentals is temporary in both cases, but larger in magnitude for bonds widely held by more constrained insurers. As we also observe that these same insurers demonstrate a larger probability of selling downgraded bonds, the evidence here points to a market imbalance generated by regulatory pressure.

We next proceed to test the fire sale hypothesis in a more rigorous way and model the probability that an insurer (holding the bonds at the quarter end preceding the downgrade) will sell the downgraded bonds during weeks 0 to +5 after the downgrade. The coefficient estimates and the marginal effects of our probit models are reported in Table 8.5.

The result in the first column of Table 8.5 is consistent with the fire sale hypothesis: P&C insurers are significantly more likely to immediately sell downgraded bonds. Panel B shows that the probability of selling is 2.64 per cent higher for P&C firms than for life firms. This effect is economically significant,

Table 8.5. Probability of selling during weeks 0 and 5 after downgrade

	(1)	(2)	(3)	(4)	(5)	(6)	(7)
	All	Life	Life	Life	P&C	P&C	P&C
Panel A: coefficient estimates							
P&C dummy	0.183***						
	(0.028)						
ln(RBC ratio)		−0.262***			−0.207***		
		(0.060)			(0.069)		
ln(RACR1)			−0.075			−0.245***	
			(0.065)			(0.071)	
Liquidity index				−0.028**			0.011
				(0.011)			(0.021)
State fixed effects	YES	YES	YES	YES	YES	YES	YES
Quarter fixed effects	YES	YES	YES	YES	YES	YES	YES
Observations	23,690	16,006	16,006	16,006	6,264	6,264	6,264
Pseudo R-squared	0.054	0.069	0.067	0.068	0.067	0.068	0.065
Panel B: marginal effects							
P&C dummy	0.026***						
ln(RBC ratio)		−0.031***			−0.035***		
ln(RACR1)			−0.009			−0.042***	
Liquidity index				0.001			0.002

Notes: This table reports probit estimates of the effects of regulatory constraints on the probability that an insurer will sell downgraded corporate bonds within five weeks after the downgrade. The downgrade is from investment to speculative grades, and the sample period is 2001–2005. The first column includes both life and P&C insurers. Columns (2)–(4) ((5)–(7)) include only life (P&C) insurers. Panel A reports the coefficient estimates. Panel B reports the marginal effects whereby all other variables are held at the sample means. In addition to the fixed effects, the control variables, included in all regressions but not reported for brevity, are logged bond age, logged bond issue size, dummy for being downgraded to BB class, logged insurer's capital and surplus, and insurer's portfolio holdings of risky assets. White's robust standard errors are in parentheses. *, **, and *** refer to statistical significance at 10%, 5%, and 1% levels.

Source: Weiss Ratings. Authors' calculation based on NAIC Schedule D's position and transaction data

given that the mean probability of selling for the entire sample is only 7.1 per cent.

We examine the effects of other constraint measures separately for life and P&C firms since the two types differ significantly in the nature of their business, liabilities, size, capitalization, and liquidity. Columns (2) to (4) report the results for life insurers, and columns (5) to (7) do so for P&C insurers. For most of the regulatory constraint measures, we find that the *more constrained* is the insurance company, the more likely that it will immediately sell the downgraded bonds. This finding holds separately for both life and P&C firms. The effect of regulatory constraint on selling probability is also economically significant. Considering the P&C sample as an example, if we increase a firm's RBC ratio (holding everything else constant) from the 25th percentile to the 75th percentile of the sample (hence making it less regulatory constrained), this company's probability of selling will decrease by 1.8 per cent (the mean selling probability for P&C insurers is 9.5 per cent). An interesting question, to which we will turn next, is the extent to which this increased likelihood of selling after the downgrade exacerbates the documented price deviation and subsequent reversal.

So far, we have shown that in the weeks immediately after the downgrade (i) the price drops and the net selling volumes are largest, and (ii) more constrained insurers are more likely to sell. These results point to the direction of regulatory-constrained insurance companies being behind the large price declines and subsequent reversals in Figure 8.4. In if the risk regulation is indeed primary in driving the fire sales, downgraded bonds held widely by constrained insurers should experience larger price declines and reversals. We test this hypothesis, using the RBC ratio and the predicted immediate selling probability as proxies for regulatory-induced selling pressure. We aggregate the insurer-level constraint variables into the bond-level variables by averaging across all insurers that hold the bond at the end of the quarter preceding the event. The downgraded bonds are then grouped by the average RBC ratio or by the average selling probability. The low (high) RBC ratio group includes bonds with the average holders' RBC ratio below (above) the median. The high (low) selling probability group includes bonds with the average holders' selling probability above (below) the median. Table 8.6 compares the price drops and reversals (calculated using the median cumulative abnormal returns or *MCARs*) between the high and low regulatory constraint groups.

Panel A shows that during the first five weeks after the downgrade, the *MCARs* are significantly more negative for the low RBC ratio group than for the high RBC ratio group (−14.11 per cent versus −7.89 per cent). This difference largely disappears after week +11. An almost identical pattern emerges for the split along the selling probability. However, *MCARs* for the high selling probability group remain significantly more negative than those of the low selling probability group through twenty weeks after the downgrade. This is likely due to the fact that selling probability reflects both information about the bond and the regulatory constraints. Panel B directly compares price reversals, as measured by the change in *MCARs* from the period between weeks +1 and +5 to later periods, across regulatory constraint groups. Price reversals seem to take place after week +11 and are significantly larger for bonds in the low average RBC ratio group than for those in the high average RBC ratio group. The results are similar, albeit less significant, for the split along average selling probability. Together, the results are strongly consistent with the fire sale hypothesis and the associated role for capital regulation.

These price patterns beg the question: why do agents holding downgraded corporate bonds, in our case insurance companies, sell around the downgrade? Given that the corporate bond market is notoriously illiquid, selling at such times is likely to exacerbate the price impact in the face of limited counterparties and high search costs. If other investors were to provide liquidity, we should not find similar price effects, but instead observe an adjustment of

Table 8.6. Cumulative abnormal returns of downgraded bonds by selling pressure group

Panel A: median cumulative abnormal returns by selling pressure group

	RBC ratio			Sell probability		
5-week period	Low group *MCAR*	High group *MCAR*	Low–high *MCAR*	High group *MCAR*	Low group *MCAR*	High–low *MCAR*
[1, 5]	−14.108	−7.884	−6.223***	−13.815	−7.274	−6.541***
[6, 10]	−11.678	−5.696	−5.982***	−12.730	−6.908	−5.822***
[11, 15]	−6.968	−6.107	−0.861	−7.111	−6.254	−0.857***
[16, 20]	−2.690	−2.855	0.166	−4.254	−1.853	−2.401***

Panel B: changes in median cumulative abnormal returns by selling pressure group

Difference between two periods	RBC ratio			Sell probability		
	Low group Δ*MCAR*	High group Δ*MCAR*	Low–high Δ*MCAR*	High group Δ*MCAR*	Low group Δ*MCAR*	High–low Δ*MCAR*
[6-10]–[1-5]	2.430	2.189	0.241	1.085	0.366	0.719
[11-15]–[1-5]	7.140	1.777	5.363***	6.704	1.020	5.684***
[16-20]–[1-5]	11.418	5.029	6.389***	9.561	5.421	4.139***

Notes: This table reports the median cumulative abnormal returns (MCARs) for downgraded corporate bonds grouped by the (regulatory) selling pressure faced by insurers holding the bonds. The downgrade is from investment to speculative grades, and the sample period is 2001–2005. MCARs are reported by 5-week period relative to the event. Week 0 is the downgrade announcement week. The bonds are grouped by either (i) the average RBC ratio, or (ii) the average predicted probability of selling during the first five weeks after the downgrade. For each bond, both measures are calculated by averaging across all insurers holding the bond at the end of the quarter immediately preceding the downgrade. The low (high) group includes downgraded bonds with each measure below (above) the sample median. Panel A reports MCARs for the 5-week period immediately after the downgrade and for three subsequent 5-week periods. Statistical significance of the differences is based on the rank-sum tests of difference in abnormal returns. Panel B reports changes in MCARs from the period immediately after the downgrade to each of the subsequent periods. Statistical significance of the differences is based on the median regression (LAE) estimates of difference-in-differences models, in which the differences are across the two selling pressure groups and across the two event periods. *, **, and *** refer to statistical significance at 10%, 5%, and 1% levels.

Source: Weiss Ratings. Authors' calculation based on NAIC Schedule D's transaction data

transaction prices to a revised fundamental value that properly reflects the information contained in the downgrade. A reasonable explanation for the lack of counterparties is related to the fact that a very large group of potential counterparties—other insurance companies—are prevented from providing liquidity. Fire sales caused by regulatory constraints seem to be the most appropriate explanation for such trading behaviour.

8.4 Policy Implications and Conclusions

The fire sale feedback mechanism has been identified as an important channel that can cause and amplify systematic risk in a financial crisis. The evidence shown in this chapter, using the U.S. insurance industry as a laboratory, provides support to this view and contributes to the body of knowledge by showing how risk regulations themselves can trigger or exacerbate fire sales. In this chapter, we have mostly identified fire sales that originate from the downgrades of assets held by insurers. Importantly, one has to consider that such downgrades are normally accompanied by a fall of the market values of those assets. The sales of a large financial institution, carried out mostly to improve its own regulatory metric, may end up causing a price and liquidity spiral from which other institutions may suffer.

The evidence we show in the chapter has a number of important policy implications for the current debate surrounding financial institutions' capital adequacy rules and systemic risk exposures. Before proceeding, we want to caution that the fire sales that we demonstrate here should be interpreted as an *unintended consequence* of capital adequacy regulation, which regulators should recognize exists in reality and whose effects may have been underestimated in policymaking. We do not, in any way, suggest that the capital regulation that may trigger the fire sales should be removed; rather, our goal is to raise awareness to ensure that the fire sale externality is considered in relevant regulatory discussions. In particular, asset fire sales may have significant consequences for the financial system when financial institutions are interconnected and when market participants, upon seeing such fire sales, make assessments about other financial institutions that are most likely at risk, perhaps because they hold similar assets. To this end, our evidence suggests a novel perspective on the implications of financial institution interconnectedness. While academic research has largely focused on interconnectedness arising from the funding structure (as in the case of inter-bank lending), we show that an important externality can also arise from the asset side of the balance sheet.

There are various ways that regulators can deal with the fire sale and interconnectedness externalities stemming from capital adequacy regulation. Perhaps it is relatively easier to state what regulators should avoid doing rather than what they ought to be doing. Regulatory forbearance may be one of them, as our evidence suggests that the expectation of such forbearance may affect *ex-ante* incentives and actions in ways that may compromise the original intent of the regulation. Take as an example the use of MTM: regulators can, for example, suspend the use of MTM for a temporary period during a financial crisis in order to halt the fire sale incentive. We think that this is likely ineffective because it stands on a view that ignores how MTM works in reality, adds an extra layer of complexity, is unlikely to solve the excessive *ex ante* risk-taking incentive, and therefore does not do away with the pro-cyclicality problem.[14] We show that even HCA, when interacting with

[14] Our argument is reminiscent of the one by Brunnermeier et al. (2009): '... we feel one of the few things worse than mark-to-market accounting is allowing it in the booms and suspending it in

regulatory capital requirements, can also engender fire sales through gains trading behaviour. Thus, suspending MTM is unlikely to produce any clear benefits.

Our findings are generally consistent with the view that, while MTM can certainly induce a fire sale externality during a crisis, as compared to HCA, one has to also consider the *ex ante* incentives: financial institutions using MTM may adopt a more conservative approach to their investments in normal years when the risk buildup takes place. The balance sheets of those institutions using MTM may, by virtue of holding less risky assets *entering into a crisis*, dampen systemic risk. Thus, it may be misplaced to focus exclusively on MTM as a major 'culprit' of the financial crisis[15] and ignore risk-taking incentives under different accounting regimes in normal times: for sure, any distortions engendered by MTM are not solved by simply replacing it with HCA.

While a fully-fledged MTM system has many benefits, including providing early warning signals that help both the individual financial institution to better manage its risk and regulators to perceive where threats to financial stability may arise, it also suffers from the fire sale externality that potentially leads to financial contagion. How should we enjoy the benefits of MTM while mitigating its downside? One suggestion is to apply MTM to both the balance sheet assets and liabilities in a consistent manner. So far, financial institutions have been using a piecemeal accounting approach when it comes to the valuation of assets and liabilities: some assets are valued at MTM while others are valued at HCA and, importantly, there are differences across assets and liabilities. Any arrangement based on the selective use of accounting measures is likely to generate unintended consequences and more so during times of crisis. Deteriorating fundamentals should impact both assets and liabilities and therefore financial institutions should categorically apply MTM to both sides of the balance sheet, and not selectively.

Another broad suggestion is to replace MTM with the so-called 'mark-to-funding' as suggested by Brunnermeier et al. (2009): the accounting measure used by an individual institution should depend on its funding horizon. MTM is imposed on institutions with short-term funding while some form

periods of market decline, or for assets to be simply shifted from the available-for-sale and trading books onto the hold-to-maturity (banking) book, where they can be valued differently, but where the banks have no real capacity to hold the assets to maturity'.

[15] In a September 2008 letter to the SEC, the American Bankers Association stated: 'The problems that exist in today's financial markets can be traced to many different factors. One factor that is recognized as having exacerbated these problems is fair value accounting.' On 3 October 2008, President George W. Bush signed the Emergency Economic Stabilization Act, giving the SEC the authority to suspend MTM accounting. A similar move was attempted in Europe as well when former French President Nicolas Sarkozy also reportedly sent a proposal to the European Commission recommending the suspension of MTM accounting. For example, former French President Sarkozy and others supported accounting changes at E.U. level.

of fundamental value is used in institutions with long-term funding. While mark-to-funding appears quite similar to the current statutory accounting rules where P&C firms (arguably, having short-term liabilities) face MTM while life firms (arguably, having long-term liabilities) use HCA, it corrects an important shortcoming of the current rules: the excessive risk-taking incentives associated with HCA are mitigated as fundamental values are used in place of historical costs. One major criticism of MTM is that it generates large changes in financial institutions' balance sheets that may not be justified by the underlying fundamentals. Importantly, such changes may be unrelated to the institution's ability to meet future commitments and its solvency. If so, this regulatory alternative is designed to link closely the institutions' future commitments with the valuation of its assets. Moreover, the mark-to-funding arrangement may alleviate liquidity black holes that can exacerbate the effects of fire sales for high-quality assets, as institutions with long-term funding have incentives to provide liquidity and buy undervalued assets.

Another way to mitigate the fire sale externality is to modify the capital adequacy regulation itself, rather than modifying the accounting rules. A popular proposal is to make the regulatory capital requirements countercyclical. Lower requirements during bad times should reduce the need to engage in fire sales while higher requirements in good times should limit excessive risk- taking. While this proposal seems reasonable from a welfare standpoint, its implementation may be tricky as the capital requirements should reflect risk and risk seems higher in bad times than in good times. In addition, further empirical evidence is needed to understand and appreciate how the interactions among various pieces of the regulation may affect *ex ante* risk-taking incentives.

Finally, our evidence also indicates that the system to assess capital adequacy through regulatory capital ratios that employ detailed, but necessarily imperfect, risk weights may be adding excessive complexity when simplicity may constitute a better approach (see Admati and Hellwig 2013; and Haldane 2012). This is a theme that runs through all the results shown in this chapter and has also directed significant attention to the work of credit rating agencies whose ratings are used for precisely this task. Such a complex capital adequacy system may be introducing distorted incentives and risks in the system. The evidence on 'reaching-for-yield' is an example of such behaviour, where life insurers facing HCA may have accumulated tail risk within the system in the years leading up to the crisis. It is potentially this accumulated tail risk in normal times that may heighten systemic risk during a crisis, and as a result, this behaviour should be the focus of regulators and policy makers.[16]

[16] Admati and Hellwig (2013) describe this environment as follows: 'The risk-weighting approach is extremely complex and has many unintended consequences that harm the financial

References

Admati, A. and M. Hellwig (2013): *The Bankers' New Clothes*. Princeton University Press.

Allen, F. and E. Carletti (2008): 'Mark-to-market Accounting and Cash-in-the-market Pricing', *Journal of Accounting and Economics*, 45: 358–78.

Brunnermeier, M., A. Crockett, C. Goodhart, A. D. Persaud, and H. Shin (2009): *The Fundamental Principles of Financial Regulation*. Centre for Economic Policy Research, London.

Becker, B. and V. Ivashina (2015): 'Reaching for Yield in the Corporate Bond Market', *Journal of Finance*, 70: 1863–1902.

Campbell, J. Y., S. Giglio, and P. Pathak (2011): 'Forced Sales and House Prices', *American Economic Review*, 101: 2108–31.

Coval, J. and E. Stafford (2007): 'Asset Fire Sales (and Purchases) in Equity Markets', *Journal of Financial Economics*, 86: 479–512.

Duffie, D. (2010): 'Presidential Address: Asset Price Dynamics with Slow-moving Capital', *Journal of Finance*, 65: 1237–67.

Ellul, A., C. Jotikasthira, and C. T. Lundblad (2011): 'Regulatory Pressure and Fire Sales in the Corporate Bond Market', *Journal of Financial Economics*, 101: 596–620.

Ellul, A., C. Jotikasthira, C. Lundblad, and Y. Wang (2014): 'Mark-to-Market Accounting and Systemic Risk in the Financial Sector', *Economic Policy*, 29: 299–341.

Ellul, A., C. Jotikasthira, C. Lundblad, and Y. Wang (2015): 'Is Historical Cost Accounting a Panacea? Market Stress, Incentive Distortions, and Gains Trading', *Journal of Finance*, 70: 2489–538.

Geanakoplos, J. D. and H. M. Polemarchakis (1986): 'Existence, Regularity, and Constrained Suboptimality of Competitive Allocation When the Asset Market is Incomplete' in W. P. Heller, R. M. Starr, and D. A. Starrett (eds.), *Uncertainty, Information and Communication, Essays in Honor of Kenneth J. Arrow*. Cambridge University Press, Cambridge, UK, 65–95.

Haldane, A. G. (2012): 'The Dog and the Frisbee', Federal Reserve Bank of Kansas City's 36th Economic Policy Symposium, 'The Changing Policy Landscape', Jackson Hole, Wyoming.

Laux, C. and C. Leuz (2009): 'The Crisis of Fair-value Accounting: Making Sense of the Recent Debate', *Accounting, Organizations and Society*, 34: 826–34.

Merrill, C. B., T. D. Nadauld, R. M. Stulz, and S. M. Sherlund (2012): 'Did Capital Requirement and Fair Value Accounting Spark Fire Sales in Distressed Mortgage-backed Securities?', Working Paper, Ohio State University.

Mitchell, M., L. H. Pedersen and T. Pulvino (2007): 'Slow Moving Capital', *American Economic Review*, 97: 215–20.

Plantin, G., H. Sapra and H. Shin (2008): 'Marking-to-market: Panacea or Pandora's box?', *Journal of Accounting Research*, 46: 435–60.

Pulvino, T. C. (1998): 'Do Asset Fire Sales Exist? An Empirical Investigation of Commercial Aircraft Transactions', *Journal of Finance*, 53: 939–78.

system. It allows banks to reduce their equity by concentrating on investments that the regulation treats as safe.'

Rajan, R. (2010): *Fault Lines*. Princeton University Press.

Sapra, H. (2008): 'Do Accounting Measurement Regimes Matter? A Discussion of Mark-to-Market Accounting and Liquidity Pricing', *Journal of Accounting and Economics*, 45: 379–387.

Schultz, P. (2001): 'Corporate Bond Trading Costs: A Peek Behind the Curtain', *Journal of Finance*, 56: 677–98.

Shleifer, A. and R. W. Vishny (1992): 'Liquidation Values and Debt Capacity: A Market Equilibrium Approach', *Journal of Finance*, 47: 1343–66.

Stiglitz, J. E. (1982): 'The Inefficiency of Stock Market Equilibrium', *Review of Economic Studies*, 49: 241–61.

Yellen, J. (2011): 'Remarks at the International Conference: Real and Financial Linkage and Monetary Policy', Bank of Japan, http://www.federalreserve.gov/newsevents/speech/yellen20110601a.htm

9

A Regulatory Framework for Systemic Risk in the Insurance Industry

Felix Hufeld

9.1 Introduction

The financial crisis of 2007/2008 and of the following years has shattered financial markets and, indeed, the general economy as a whole as few events have done before. Financial supervisors and regulators, central banks and policy makers in general were faced with an unprecedented level of interconnected events leading to a crisis of global proportions. Around the globe, billions of tax-payers' money had to be invested or put at risk to bail out individual financial institutions in order to stabilize and secure the functioning of financial markets and to restore the trust of non-financial corporates and of millions of private citizens in financial institutions, and the institutions themselves in one another. Following a period of immediate crisis management, it became apparent that there were many causes of the financial crisis as we witnessed it, one of them being the existence of 'systemic risk' largely driven by a combination of two factors:

First, events of seemingly limited impact in scale (size) or scope (geographic or business segment extension) may, in fact, jeopardize financial stability on a national or international level due to previously underestimated channels of infection and degrees of interconnectedness. In particular, the practice of packaging, structuring, and selling financial risk to investors around the world disseminated the originally limited risk to a huge number of investors around the world. These investors trusted the high ratings of these securities, which under stress turned out to be 'toxic', i.e. almost worthless. Not knowing who owned how much of these toxic securities, there was an almost complete breakdown of trust, particularly between the banks. As a result, the inability to access (bank) funding, the difficulty of trading on particular securities markets and severe valuation challenges—to name but a few challenges—created severe disturbances in financial markets around the world. Bundles of risk that were initially limited in scope became 'systemic'.

Second, it appeared that financial institutions—predominantly but not exclusively banks—could become so big and provide such critical functions to (international) financial markets that their failure would create unforeseeable and potentially unacceptable risks for the broader economy and society as a whole: the famous 'too-big-to-fail' problem. It was hence unavoidable that public, i.e. tax-payers' money was used to bail out individual companies for the sake of stabilizing the financial system and the economy in general. In that sense, certain financial institutions became 'systemic' as well.

From a public policy point of view, it was and is still, of course, obvious that keeping the upside, i.e. profits, private for financial institutions but 'socializing' the downside to society and the economy as a whole, particularly if it is systemic, is fundamentally unacceptable and creates significant moral hazard. Bold reforms both on an institutional, as well as on a regulatory level, were initiated to avoid such a situation ever happening again. At the famous G20 summit in Washington in 2008, the G20 leaders pledged 'to (...) ensure that all financial markets, products and participants are regulated or subject to oversight, as appropriate to their circumstances',[1] and tasked the Financial Stability Board and other global financial standard setters with working quickly to create appropriate financial regulation.

Not surprisingly, these reforms started with a strong focus on banks. One key element of such efforts was, and remains, the recognition of systemically important banks, notably on a global level[2]—*Global Systemically Important Banks (G-SIBs)*. Given the importance of inter-bank funding and the inherent interconnectedness of banks to one another, combined with the 'too-big-to-fail' challenge, it is obvious that the focus needs to be primarily on individual banks or banking groups as the predominant proxy to cope with systemic risk in the banking sector. Since the financial crisis, much progress has been made both in developing a solid designation methodology as well as policy measures of various kinds to identify and regulate G-SIBs.

[1] Leaders of the Group of Twenty 2008: p. 3.

[2] For the purpose of this chapter, it is sufficient to focus on the global aspects of systemic risk to discuss the conceptual challenges associated with it. It is understood that there is the possibility to enlarge the concept from a domestic point of view.

9.2 Systemic Risk in the Insurance Industry

Whilst it is obvious—due to the specifics of the banking sector—that focusing on individual banks or banking groups captures potential systemic risk appropriately, this is much less obvious in the insurance or the so-called 'Non-Bank-Non-Insurance (NBNI)' sector. The latter, which includes asset managers, funds, financial markets, central counterparties, etc. is probably more appropriately, or at least predominantly addressed to deal with systemic risk by focusing on specific activities or rules on how to participate or interact in a particular marketplace as such, as opposed to corporate entities—but this is not the focus of this chapter. To appropriately address systemic risk in the insurance industry, so it will be argued, a 'hybrid approach' will have to be applied. A hybrid approach considers the need to develop and combine two conceptually different regulatory frameworks in order to manage comprehensively the systemic risk that may emerge within or through the insurance sector. The two frameworks are largely driven by the distinction between direct and indirect systemic risk.

Direct systemic risk represents the potential consequences that the financial system would suffer, that may be caused by a single insurer or insurance group, with the causes of this detrimental impact lying immediately in the nature, activities, product features, etc. of the insurer itself. In combination with its size and degree of interconnectedness, it could directly create disturbances of systemic proportions to the financial system. Direct systemic risk is a first-round effect where the insurance undertaking itself imposes a systemic threat to the wider system.

Indirect systemic risk refers to the potential negative consequences for the financial system due to the activities of one or many insurers or insurance groups consisting of (collective) reactions to negative events or shocks to which they themselves have been exposed. This is a second-round effect where an insurance undertaking or multiple insurance undertakings are exposed to risk and their (collective) reactions create systemic consequences for the wider system.

What both characteristics of systemic risk have in common is that the scale of their potential impact is large enough to threaten the functioning of the financial system as a whole, or at least to such a serious extent that the risk must be considered 'systemic'. From a regulator's perspective, it is not only legitimate but a duty to monitor both characteristics. With respect to financial stability, a regulator's primary focus is not to fault or sanction misbehaviour but to provide or mitigate objective risk. Culprit and victim are not regulatory categories, at least not in this context. It is, therefore, immaterial whether a particular undertaking infects others because of activities that are potentially contentious, or whether it was merely exposed to other participants' activities or events within the financial system and its—or many undertakings—reactions may cause systemic risk as well. The distinction, however, between direct and indirect systemic risk becomes highly relevant when determining the appropriate regulatory and policy responses including, in some jurisdictions, answering the question: who is legally in charge, why and to what extent?

9.2.1 *Direct Systemic Risk—the G-SII Approach*

Direct systemic risk, as described above under Section 9.2, is a characteristic attributed to a specific insurance undertaking or group. Whether this characteristic is attributed or not is decided based on a designation methodology developed by the International Association of Insurance Supervisors (IAIS), which was applied for the first time by the Financial Stability Board (FSB) in 2013.[3] Currently nine insurance groups are designated as Global Systemically Important Insurers (G-SIIs).

G-SIIs are one class of G-SIFIs (Global Systemically Important Financial Institutions), which are defined by the FSB as '. . . institutions of such size, market importance, and global interconnectedness that their distress or failure would cause significant dislocation in the global financial system and adverse economic consequences across a range of countries'.[4]

The designation methodology applies an indicator-based assessment that is related to the methodology used for Global Systemically Important Banks (G-SIBs). However, the specific nature of the insurance sector has influenced the selection, grouping and weighting assigned to certain indicators. The selected indicators are grouped into five categories:

- size (weight: 5 per cent);
- global activity (5 per cent);
- interconnectedness (40 per cent);
- non-traditional and non-insurance activities (NTNI: 45 per cent); and
- substitutability (5 per cent).

Although the G-SII designation methodology uses activities as its primary indicator to identify systemic risk in an impact given default logic it is a corporate-centric approach with respect to the policy measures assigned to certain internationally operating insurance groups. The three main categories of policy measures for G-SII's are:[5]

- enhanced supervision, particularly on a group level;
- precautionary definition of recovery and resolution measures;

[3] FSB 2013a. [4] FSB 2010: 2. [5] IAIS 2013a: 13.

- capital add-ons to establish a 'higher loss absorbency (HLA)' capacity reflecting the specific systemic risk of the respective insurance group.

Whilst the two former policy measures could be (and, in fact, are) assigned to other non-G-SIIs as well, it is safe to assume that an HLA requirement will only be imposed on a G-SII.[6]

Obviously the concept of G-SIIs has been and continues to be a matter of much debate. The two prime challenges mentioned are:

1. Is there any systemic risk in the insurance business model and the overall insurance industry to begin with?
2. And if so, is higher loss absorbency as an extra capital surcharge the right remedy?

(1) Since 2011, the IAIS has maintained the position that neither '...long experience of insurance markets...' nor '...information arising from the global financial crisis...' provide '...any evidence of traditional insurance either generating or amplifying risk within the financial system or in the real economy. The potential for systemic importance is only considered to arise in any non-traditional or non-insurance activities'.[7]

This view is to be fully supported to the extent that direct systemic risk and the G-SII methodology are concerned. The idiosyncratic nature of insurance risk, the law of large numbers, diversification within an undertaking or a group balancing out risk in the collective body of the policyholders and over time, the long-standing and proven capability to predict cash-outflows even under stress, and the liability-driven investment approach, etc. do not suggest a direct systemic threat originating from traditional insurance or reinsurance.[8] Therefore, the key whether or not a particular insurance undertaking should be deemed a G-SII, critically depends on the definition of NTNI, with interconnectedness serving as an amplifier. Notwithstanding the fact that the NTNI indicators will need further refinement, as the IAIS intends to do, it is undeniable that *in principle* complex, internationally active insurance groups (IAIGs) can have NTNI activities as part of their business portfolio. Whether we consider outright activities in banking or derivatives trading (not used for hedging), to name just two examples, or features of insurance or insurance-linked products that substantially increase market or liquidity risk—even the most

[6] For the purpose of this chapter the possibility of extending such measures including HLA to 'D-SIIs' (Domestic systemically important insurers) will be neglected. The point here is that HLA needs to be based on the designation of some kind of systemic importance not otherwise captured in order to be justified whereas enhanced or group supervision and recovery and resolution can be imposed on a much larger group of undertakings based on other supervisory considerations.

[7] IAIS 2013b: 9; for reinsurance the IAIS published a report and concluded similarly on the systemic risk of traditional reinsurance (IAIS 2012: 5).

[8] See footnote 7.

conservative and traditional insurance business can *in principle* be associated with such NTNI activities and, hence, create transmission channels into the broader financial system of systemic proportions. After the AIG experience, there is no point in rejecting this possibility for reasons of principle. On the other hand, it has become clear in applying the G-SII methodology since 2013 that, by global standards, only very few IAIGs can be considered G-SIIs, much fewer than in the banking sector.[9]

The ongoing challenge remains, therefore, how to further refine the G-SII designation methodology in order to improve its capability to capture and mitigate or disincentivize the taking of systemic risk. There are a number of specific components that deserve particular attention, e.g.:

- **Process set-up:** given the rather small and possibly even decreasing number of G-SIIs, a more explicit and detailed design of quantitative and qualitative factors and their interaction as part of the overall multi-step designation process will be important.
- **Cut-off point(s):** an improved definition of the methodology used to identify at least two (G-SII vs. non-G-SII) or more buckets will be important in increasing certainty as to whether a 'marginal' undertaking should be 'in' or 'out'.
- **Relative versus absolute perspective:** to avoid both distortions stemming from very specialized business models, as well as offering credible incentives as a reward, if systemic risk is reduced, a more detailed approach on how to include absolute reference values or ancillary criteria as part of a qualitative assessment will be required. A bias towards a predominantly relative ranking needs to be avoided. The goal is to discourage insurers from becoming (more) systemic and to make it possible to eliminate the need for HLA, if the systemic risk has been sufficiently reduced, as it has been explicitly stated by the IAIS.[10]
- **Flexibility of policy measures:** in order to avoid unwanted cliff-effects on the policy measure side, a more staged design of policy measures with respect to G-SIIs or 'potential G-SIIs' could be envisioned. An appropriate treatment of G-SIIs needs to be ensured, even if one of the policy measures, HLA, may not be feasible.
- **NTNI:** as mentioned above in this Section, the hitherto principles based approach to NTNI will be refined and operationalized to allow a better-founded classification of certain product features and activities, e.g. the use of derivatives, not used for hedging purposes.

[9] For list of designated G-SIIs see FSB homepage (FSB 2013b, FSB 2014, and FSB 2015).
[10] IAIS 2013a: 27

- **Transparency:** enhanced disclosure to improve transparency, possibly including peer reviews or comparable procedural elements to both promote dialogue with the industry as well as market discipline should be considered.

The appropriate refinement of the G-SII methodology with respect to reinsurers still needs to be resolved and should be ready for application by the end of 2016. Whether or not reinsurers can in principle pose systemic risk has caused at least as much debate as for the same question regarding primary insurers. Based on the work done so far, the following regulatory considerations seem to be relevant:

- Reinsurers can create direct or indirect systemic risk basically for the same reasons that primary insurers can, i.e. there is no evidence or conceptual reason to assume that the traditional reinsurance business model can create systemic risk.
- The largest global reinsurers, however, can become rather complex and, like primary insurers, be engaged in NTNI business activities which follow very different risk patterns than the traditional reinsurance business model.
- There is, therefore, no reason to exclude reinsurers from applying the G-SII methodology in principle or to design a fundamentally different methodology.
- What is necessary, however, is to avoid a methodology that would more or less penalize size and/or interconnectedness where there is no sufficient proof of an underlying NTNI exposure. Size and interconnectedness on the reinsurance side, even more so than on the primary side, reduces (systemic) risk as opposed to creating it. Interconnectedness as such does not create any systemic risk in the insurance sector, neither for primary nor for reinsurers, but serves as an amplifier of systemic risk based on NTNI. The designation methodology needs to be reviewed accordingly, both in its quantitative as well its qualitative aspects.
- Reinsurance enables primary insurers to provide higher and more stable risk coverage to the real economy and society as a whole by spreading and diversifying risk on a global scale, which in turn helps to significantly reduce (indirect) systemic risk of primary insurers faced with massive catastrophes and the related losses incurred. In fact, combined losses in certain peak years in recent history which would have put the global (re-) insurance sector under very serious stress and truly systemic risk in earlier years could be digested rather smoothly thanks to much more efficient underwriting and reinsurance strategies.

- Even under strict loss given default conditions it is very difficult to construct a case where the collapse of one of the global reinsurers—with respect to its traditional reinsurance business—could create systemic risk: the short-term nature of reinsurance contracts, the limited quota share of any reinsurer within the reinsurance portfolio of primary insurers, the limited (and, in fact, decreasing) quota share of reinsurers in the total amount of risk-taking capital provided as non-insurance based reinsurance capital, the nature of premium payments by primary insurers, etc.—all of these features make it extremely unlikely that the default of even one of the globally leading reinsurers could trigger (direct) systemic risk.
- Without a sufficiently significant 'NTNI-hook', neither a primary insurer nor a reinsurer should be considered as directly systemically risky or a G-SII.

(2) The purpose of imposing an HLA capacity serves two goals: first, as already mentioned in this Section, to discourage insurers to become (more) systemic or to encourage them to reduce their systemic risk. Second, to reduce the probability of G-SII's distress or failure and its impact on the financial system by internalizing some of the cost to the financial system and overall economy that would otherwise remain externalities to the G-SII as well as to support earlier supervisory intervention to reduce the probability of distress.

Whilst the first purpose is obvious and does not cause a lot of debate, the second meets considerable resistance for at least two reasons: first, an HLA for G-SIIs necessarily requires an underlying, well-defined and at least a comparable global capital standard serving as a loss absorbency capacity (LA) upon which an HLA could be based—neither of which existed so far. Second, even if an HLA could be properly defined, it would be either entirely insufficient or, even more fundamentally, an alien and, hence, inappropriate concept for the insurance industry where minimum or prescribed ratios of solvency (PCR) are largely defined to back-up equivalent liabilities, predominantly based on technical provisions. In addition, there are concerns around the level-playing field vis-à-vis non-G-SII insurers.

The first concern is accurate. Unlike Basel II/III on the banking side, the insurance sector is currently lacking a framework to derive a global capital standard for IAIGs. To develop such a global 'Insurance Capital Standard (ICS)' is one of the key projects of the IAIS. It aims to deliver a version for implementation by end 2019. In the meantime, a simple, factor-based 'Basic capital requirement (BCR)' was developed at the end of 2014 that serves as a backstop and LA capacity for a first version of the HLA that was delivered at the end of 2015. It is well understood that the current combination of BCR and HLA can only serve as a first proxy. It will most definitely change and become more accurate over time. Eventually, the ICS—once developed—will replace BCR as a much more refined, i.e. market-oriented and risk-sensitive measure of risk. In the meantime, HLA will not be used as a supervisory tool let alone become 'hard law' anywhere in the world. But such a step-by-step approach is indispensible for serving as a secure path to make progress in developing complex regulatory concepts as a basis for an effective financial (insurance) system in general.

The second concern is more fundamental. Indeed, unlike banking, 'capital' in the insurance sector does not define various tiers of capital against which a bank—based on leverage—can build its business portfolio measured as risk-weighted assets. By contrast, an insurer accepts insurance liabilities which are prepaid by a continuous stream of premium-payments and the solvency ratio describes the minimum or prescribed level of funds, to ensure both secure fulfillment of technical provisions and coverage by own funds at all times. The solvency capital will be calculated and evaluated based on standard or internal models (in addition to many further statutory or regulatory requirements). However, it is for exactly that reason that not only the meaning of 'capital' is fundamentally different, the way in which prescribed levels of capital or solvency work is also fundamentally different: whilst the prescribed minimum level of capital in a bank balance sheet immediately limits scale and scope of its business and because the holding of capital is an expensive source of funding, banks tend not to hold too much excess capital if there is no specific strategic reason to do so. A bank that holds capital at a level close to the required minimum in a given year—supplemented by a multi-year outlook and appropriate stress-testing, is, from a regulatory point of view, in good shape and is not a reason for senior management or the supervisory authority to be concerned. This is quite different for the insurance side: insurers, due to the long-term nature of the business, regularly hold—in addition to adequate technical provisions to absorb potential losses—much higher levels of own funds, i.e. 'capital', than prescribed, let alone vis-à-vis required minimum levels. Solvency ratios of more than double the prescribed level are not exceptional. PCRs on a group level that fall below 150 per cent would raise questions from the supervisor, ratios that fall below 125 per cent, although still not necessarily leading into a recovery situation, would most definitely trigger some action on behalf of the supervisor. In other words, not just the nature of 'capital' means different things in banking and insurance, the limits or PCRs work quite differently as well—a difference that has not been fully appreciated even in a number of regulatory discussions so far. With respect to an HLA concept, it simply means that the actual solvency ratio which each and every insurance group, particularly IAIGs, holds way beyond the PCR will very likely always embrace and surpass the combined PCR and HLA, even if an HLA would be calibrated rather 'bity'. Otherwise, such an insurance group would already be a concern to a supervisor for entirely different reasons than systemic risk, i.e. 'conventional' reasons. In addition, it is safe to assume that IAIGs, let alone G-SIIs, apply internal models in one shape or form. In this context, the application of an HLA de facto serves as an 'early warning indicator' or intermediate threshold leading to some kind of enhanced supervisory attention or activity—but very likely not to a significant increase of the actual solvency ratio entertained by the G-SII. Such a regulatory framework—the application of intermediate thresholds as early warning indicators—is neither conceptually alien to the insurance industry nor unknown in the real world of certain supervisors. It may not (yet) be a universally applied concept but it is conceptually entirely appropriate and currently used in supervisory practice. This may be particularly relevant in relation to the use of internal models to contain the model risk, and to the danger of excessive variability of outcomes across the industry. In that sense, it might even help to promote a level-playing field, if other G-SIIs, and not smaller local players, are considered as the relevant peer-group.

The rationale described above, i.e. the different impact and functioning of HLA as a capital buffer in the insurance context as opposed to in banking, is just another way of saying that there is more than one good regulatory reason to consider such intermediate levels—of which an HLA for systemic risk would be just one possible justification. Intermediate levels, as an expression of proportionate supervision at the upper end for the most complex insurance undertakings or for those containing unwanted model variability, would be other justifications—without ever recurring to the debate of systemic risk.

With respect to the amount of HLA and its (in)ability to cover all possible systemic consequences measured in real money, it is impossible to predict—as it would be on the banking side as well. This, however, does not make the regulatory goal (to internalize externalities) obsolete—on the contrary. What legitimately remains is the need to calibrate an HLA properly and to improve the G-SII methodology in general. This challenge is very well understood by the experts within the IAIS and will be continuously considered, refined, and tested. Conceptually, however, there is no reason whatsoever in principle not to apply an HLA concept in the insurance industry.

9.2.2 *Indirect systemic risk—the general regulatory framework*

Indirect systemic risk, as already described above under Section 9.2, refers to the potential consequences that the financial system might suffer due to the activities of one or many insurers or insurance groups representing (collective) reactions to negative events or shocks to which they themselves have been exposed. Examples could be: the sudden devaluation of certain sovereign bonds; the default of one or several large issuer of covered bonds; a sudden and massive break-down of equity markets; or, indeed, a prolonged period of very low interest rates, possibly followed by a sudden spike in interest rates; or, of course, any combination of several of those or other new factors. It is always a second-round effect, where an insurance undertaking or multiple insurance undertakings are exposed to risk, and their (collective) reactions create systemic consequences to the wider system.

Elements of indirect risk based on an undertaking's exposure and possible reactions to external events or shocks have already been considered as part of the G-SII approach. In this context, however, being potential transmission channels, they still served as indicators or amplifiers in scrutinizing an individual insurance group's business portfolio and activities, particularly with respect to NTNI, in order to answer the question of whether this specific insurance group may pose a systemic risk to financial stability, i.e. stays still in the direct systemic risk approach. Conceptually, the first component of the two-pronged, hybrid approach coping with systemic risk in the insurance industry, as proposed in this chapter, aims to identify individual groups and remains in that sense 'corporate centric'.

The second component, described in this chapter, aims to address systemic risk which, although generally triggered by exposure to external shocks or events, only becomes 'systemic' due to its impact on multiple insurers and their possible collective reactions to it. Most examples of this, if not all of the above-mentioned, typically would affect many insurers at the same time, the number of which is almost impossible to determine in advance. It is exactly the simultaneous nature of such an impact that creates the potential for systemic risk, including, of course, many medium-sized or small insurers which would never be considered 'systemic' individually. This second component of the hybrid approach is, therefore, not corporate but 'activity- or market-centric'.

It is apparent that the first component of the hybrid approach, the G-SII methodology, is conceptually incapable of capturing systemic risk properly based on the impact on multiple insurers and on their collective reactions. It needs to be supplemented by a second component explicitly dealing with safeguards focusing on collective behaviour. This is the domain of general regulatory frameworks in any particular country, e.g. the *Versicherungsaufsichtsgesetz (VAG)* in Germany, in a supranational region, e.g. the *Solvency II Directive* in Europe, and globally: the *Insurance Core Principles (ICPs)*; *ComFrame* for IAIGs; and the ongoing work on developing a global capital standard *ICS*, to name just some of the many important examples.

On the other hand, however, general insurance regulation (as opposed to specific insurance regulation addressing direct systemic risk) traditionally focuses more on policyholder protection and less so on matters of financial stability. Of course, many traditional aspects of regulation serving policyholder protection also strengthen financial stability: requirements placed on solvency capital; valuation; risk management; fit and proper, technical provisions; risk margins; profit participation; surrender policies; types, classes and duration of investable assets; disclosure, etc. to name just a few examples. It is needless to state that policyholder protection is, and should remain, at the centre of insurance regulation. It is a fact, however, that a more systematic and explicit framework on how to address indirect systemic risk within general insurance regulation is still missing. Neither would it be appropriate to assume that a G-SII methodology alone would be sufficient to cope with systemic risk in its entirety. Nor would it be wise to assume that general insurance regulation with its traditional focus on policyholder protection will implicitly and comprehensively take care of indirect systemic risk. Both need to be done in combination; and both need to be dealt with explicitly.

There are several highly-relevant examples for potential indirect systemic risk, which cannot be dealt with as part of the G-SII approach but only through general insurance regulation, e.g.:

- **Diversification:** an obvious inroad to trigger indirect systemic risk through the insurance sector would be an overexposure of (many) insurers to a particular asset class, whether sovereign bonds of the home country, equity, high yield securities, project finance, or any other accumulation of assets with respect to type of risk, geography, etc. which, in case of default or extreme depreciation of such assets, could result in collective action of those insurers, contributing to systemic risk. Insurance regulation has developed various tools to ensure an appropriate level of diversification, including risk management and reporting requirements, direct maximum limits per asset class, or the provision of economic capital commensurate to the risk profile of the asset class. The future will tell which tools or combination of tools will serve best to ensure diversification. Whatever the tools may be, however, they address a key source of indirect systemic risk for insurers and they must be part of a general regulatory framework not restricted to G-SIIs.
- **Sovereign Bonds:** currently the risk of sovereign bonds (similar to the banking side) is only partially captured in some internal models but generally, when applying the standard formula, it is considered risk-free. In addition, no large exposure limits have been established so far. Obviously this can create unwanted overexposures and create systemic risk if all the insurers in a certain country were to be forced to drastically adjust asset values accordingly or fail to sell assets for an acceptable price.
- **Surrender Policies:** this example only serves as a placeholder for many similar regulatory safeguards (for example insurance guarantee schemes, actuarial safety margins calculated in the contract, requirements to lower

the insurance sum or the surrender value of an insurance policy), which do exist in certain jurisdictions and do not or do not sufficiently exist in others. They are the keys that allow any undertaking or supervisor to influence or prohibit certain surrender behavior which, if applied *en masse*, could incentivize or create run-like situations and create systemic risk. Just to rely on a traditional policyholder perspective will not suffice. It also demonstrates that the (short-term) behaviour of some policyholders may severely impair the legitimate (long-term) interests of other policyholders, which needs to be balanced under financial stability considerations.

- **Model risk:** the application of internal models in the insurance industry is an important step forward to capture the real risk represented by an individual undertaking and is obviously not limited to G-SIIs or even IAIGs. As much as the principle of modelling risk individually needs to be supported, it comes with a number of different types of model risk, e.g.: insufficient formulas; wrong or biased assumptions; excessive variability of outcomes; or the general trend to optimize results against a given regulatory system. In combination, such potential downsides of models may in sum create systemic risk if negative developments remain undiscovered by the supervisor for too long and if they occur in many firms as opposed to just one. Limitations for guided or constrained use of internal models is not a matter of G-SIIs but needs to be implemented as part of the general regulatory framework.

There are many more examples of regulatory components that need to be part of a general insurance framework but are highly relevant for financial stability. In reality, across the globe many of those elements may be addressed properly in some places whereas in others they may not be. What needs to be developed is a consistent framework of principles, and, possibly, key attributes and criteria for managing effectively indirect systemic risk based on collective behaviour.

Such a framework may include, but is not identical with, what is commonly called a 'macroprudential' perspective. The difference between the two approaches introduced in this chapter—G-SII versus general regulation—is not equivalent to the difference between a micro- and macroprudential perspective. The G-SII methodology, being a corporate centric and in that sense a microprudential tool, relies just as much on macroprudential analysis and insight. By the same token traditional, or even financial stability orientated, general regulations do not per se transform into macroprudential strategies just because the former concern all undertakings under their jurisdiction. Both regulatory approaches to address systemic risk include macro- and microprudential elements. Which combination of strategies and tools works best in order to formulate new regulatory and supervisory responses to tackle systemic risk needs to be determined through further work.

9.3 Conclusion

The existence of systemic risk—direct or indirect—is a key lesson from the financial crisis and cannot be neglected. This is true for all sectors of the financial industry, including, of course, the insurance and reinsurance industry. A very different task, however, is how to identify systemic risk and how to identify which regulatory and supervisory measures are appropriate.

With respect to the insurance industry, this chapter proposes to use a hybrid approach combining two different regulatory frameworks to deal comprehensively with systemic risk in the insurance industry. The G-SII approach modelled after the G-SIB methodology on the banking side is a legitimate and conceptually appropriate tool to address direct systemic risk in the insurance industry, including the application of capital surcharges. However, using *only* this approach would neglect indirect systemic risk largely based on the collective behaviour of many insurance undertakings. In fact, limiting policy measures just to G-SIIs, and possibly to D-SIIs, in certain jurisdictions would dangerously limit the effectiveness of insurance regulation and supervision with respect to preserving financial stability. In short: the G-SII approach in the insurance industry is correct and needs to be refined—but it is incomplete. Its relevance should not be overrated. Nobody knows how exactly the next financial crisis with systemic elements may emerge. But with respect to the insurance industry, it seems at least as likely that it may be triggered by collective behaviour of many insurers as opposed to very few G-SIIs. On the other hand, general insurance regulation has so far been neglected as an important potential tool with which to address (indirect) systemic risk and financial stability concerns in addition to traditional policyholder protection. General insurance regulation, nationally, regionally as well as globally, needs to be sharpened with a view as to how to consider financial stability issues as well. Only the combination of both approaches into a unified *hybrid approach* will ensure a comprehensive regulatory response to systemic risk in the insurance industry.

In doing so, the hybrid approach reflects the fact that preventing or mitigating systemic risk in the insurance industry is probably somewhere between the banking and the NBNI sector. Like banks, insurance groups under certain conditions can and should be deemed as possessing systemic potential risk but, due to the reasons described above, will only generate a rather limited list of undertakings. Large and important parts of (indirect) systemic risk—more akin to the NBNI sector—need to be captured by an activity or behaviour-centric focus through general insurance regulation. The hybrid approach combines both.

Bibliography

FSB (2010). Reducing the moral hazard posed by systemically important financial. institutions—FSB Recommendations and Time Lines, 20 October 2010.

FSB (2013a). FSB identifies an initial list of global systemically important insurers (G-SIIs), press release, Ref no 49/2013.

FSB (2013b). Global systemically important insurers (G-SIIs) and the policy measures that will apply to them, 18 July 2013.

FSB (2014). 2014 update of list of global systemically important insurers (G-SIIs), 6 November 2014.

FSB (2015). 2015 update of list of global systemically important insurers (G-SIIs), 3 November 2015.

IAIS (2012). Reinsurance and financial stability, 19 July 2012.

IAIS (2013a). Global systemically important insurers: Policy measures, 18 July 2013.

IAIS (2013b). Global systemically important insurers: Initial assessment methodology, 18 July 2013.

Leaders of the Group of 20 (2008). Declaration summit on financial markets and the world economy, 15 November 2008. (https://www.bundesregierung.de/Content/DE/StatischeSeiten/Breg/G8G20/uebersicht-dokumente.html).

Part 4

Open Questions Going Forward from the Insurance Sector

10

The Big Questions for the Insurance Sector

Findings from a Survey of Insurance Companies

Luca Pancaldi and Uwe Stegemann

10.1 Introduction

Are there systemic risks in the insurance sector? How does regulation account for them? How well do companies' internal risk management approaches perform? To explore these big questions for the insurance sector, we conducted a comprehensive survey of insurance industry executives. The aim of the survey was to establish a quantitative fact base of the industry's perspective on the systemic riskiness of the insurance sector and on the adequacy of current regulations and internal risk management processes.

The survey was conducted between July and October 2015 with the help of tools, frameworks, and resources of McKinsey & Company. Twenty-seven CFOs and CROs from the insurance industry participated. The respondents represented organizations with an aggregate total of more than three trillion Euros in assets. Participating organizations are headquartered in Europe, but many of them have global operations.

Participants answered 38 questions that were organized around four overarching categories:

- main sources of risk and expected evolution (5 questions);
- systemic risk in insurance (7 questions);
- risk management practices in the industry (18 questions);
- academic research and future research efforts (7 questions).

Questions were mostly of multiple-choice type, with the option to leave comments or remarks.

To capture the most comprehensive view possible of the industry, the section of the survey on 'Risk management practices in the industry' was designed around the McKinsey Enterprise Risk Management Framework, which includes five key areas of assessment: (i) risk insights and transparency; (ii) natural ownership, risk appetite, and strategy; (iii) risk-related decisions and processes; (iv) risk organization and governance; and (v) risk culture and performance transformation.

Figures reported refer to asset-weighted results if not otherwise indicated. In particular, equally weighted results are also exhibited in comparison to asset-weighted results when important differences arise between small players' and large players' responses to the survey.

10.2 Main Sources of Risk and Expected Evolution

There is a broad consensus that the current economic environment presents a higher risk than the past environment.

Eighty-six per cent of the insurers consider the current economic environment more volatile or significantly more volatile compared to the past. Moreover, 93 per cent of the respondents believe that the risks to financial performance in the future economic environment will be more volatile or significantly more volatile than the current economic environment (Figure 10.1).

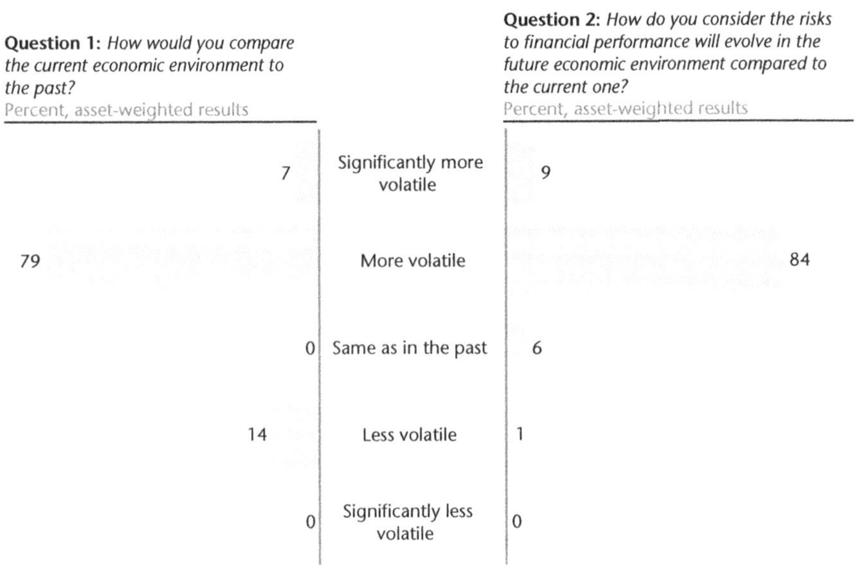

Figure 10.1. Perspective on the macroeconomic environment
Source: Enterprise Risk Management Survey for Insurers 2015

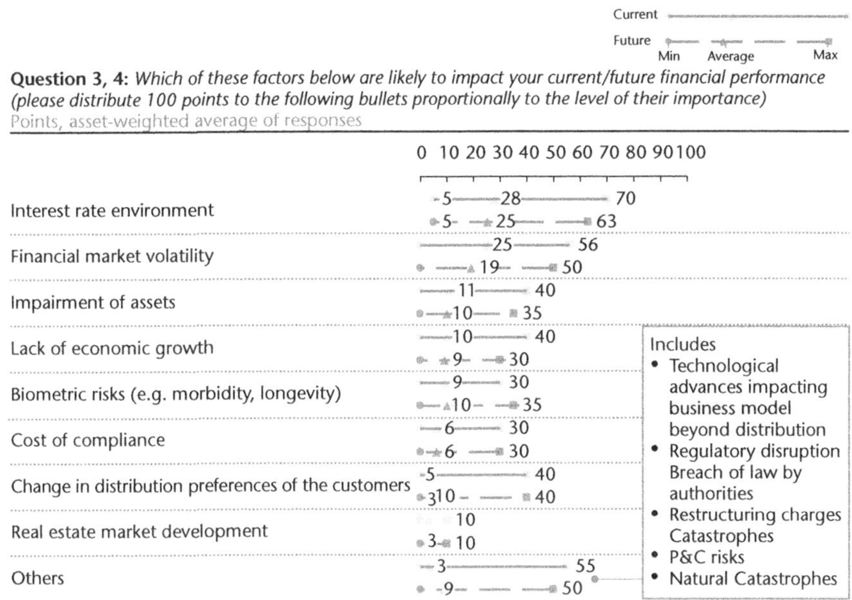

Figure 10.2. Current and future main sources of risk
Source: Enterprise Risk Management Survey for Insurers 2015

Insurers highlighted *interest rate environment* (asset-weighted average of 28 points among the main sources of risk today and 25 points among the main sources of risk in the future), and *financial market volatility* (25 points today and 25 in the future) as main factors that can affect current and future financial performance and can endanger the business given extreme circumstances (Figure 10.2).

Other concerns related to new trends included change in distribution preferences of customers and biometric risks (e.g. mortality, longevity) and potential future catastrophes/NAT CAT events. Another interesting trend emerging from the survey is an increasing concern about new risks related to technological advances that might impact the business model beyond distribution and regulatory disruption (e.g. Fintech).

10.3 Systemic Risk in Insurance

There is a broad consensus among survey participants that the insurance industry is not subject to systemic risk.

The consensus is very strong amongst large insurers—in an asset-weighted evaluation, 89 per cent of respondents saw a systemic risk event as not

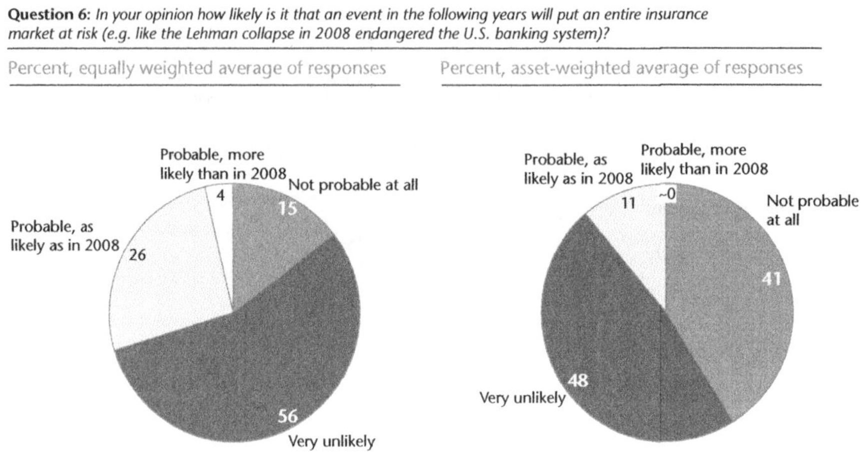

Figure 10.3. Systemic risk in insurance
Source: Enterprise Risk Management Survey for Insurers 2015

probable at all or very unlikely—as well as amongst smaller players (71 per cent of participants on equally-weighted basis denied the existence of systemic risk) (Figure 10.3).

Participants' comments highlighted their belief in the inherently higher stability of the insurance sector compared to the banking sector, in particular due to its significantly lower interconnectedness. Sovereign risks, NAT CAT risks, and loss of confidence regarding industry solvability are seen as main potential sources of systemic risk in the industry (Figure 10.4).

In this context, insurers disagree on how effective the current and evolving regulatory framework is in further mitigating systemic risk and preserving the financial stability of the insurance sector (Figure 10.5):

- In an asset-weighted evaluation, 34 per cent of the insurers consider the current regulatory framework[1] either not effective at all (20 per cent) or somewhat effective but with additional measures to be introduced (14 per cent). On the other hand, 56 per cent of the insurers consider the current framework sufficiently effective, and the remaining 10 per cent consider the framework highly effective.
- In an asset-weighted evaluation, 52 per cent of the insurers consider the global regulatory framework (ComFrame, ICS) not effective at all, while 40 per cent consider it to be sufficiently or highly effective.

[1] Which can include both local prudential regimes such as Solvency II and new systemic regulation depending on the size of the insurance companies and their designation or not as systemically important.

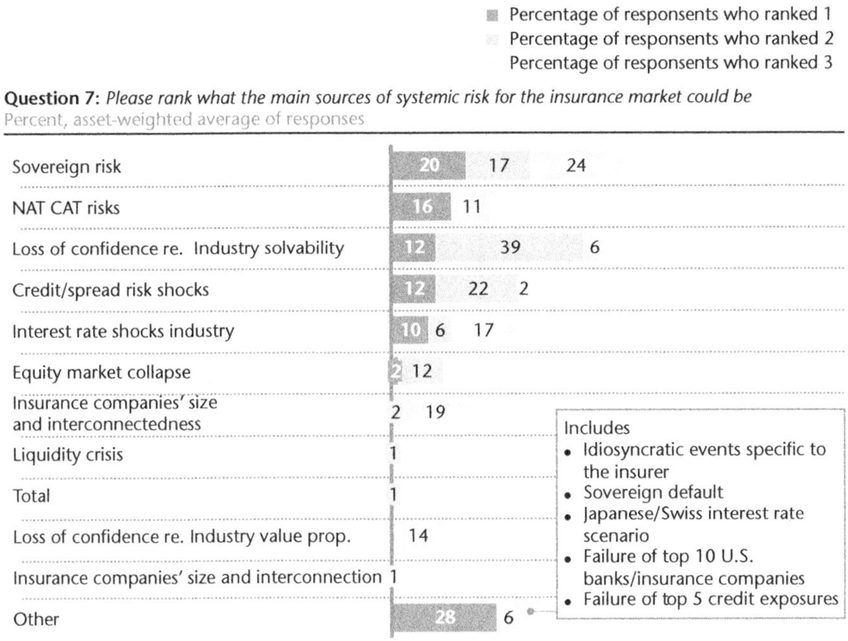

Figure 10.4. Sources of systemic risk in insurance

Source: Enterprise Risk Management Survey for Insurers 2015

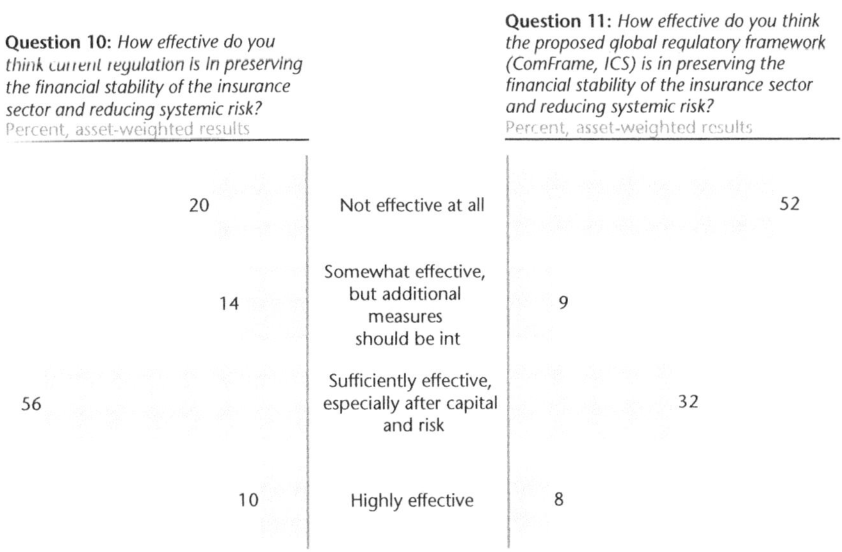

Figure 10.5. Effectiveness of the regulation

Source: Enterprise Risk Management Survey for Insurers 2015

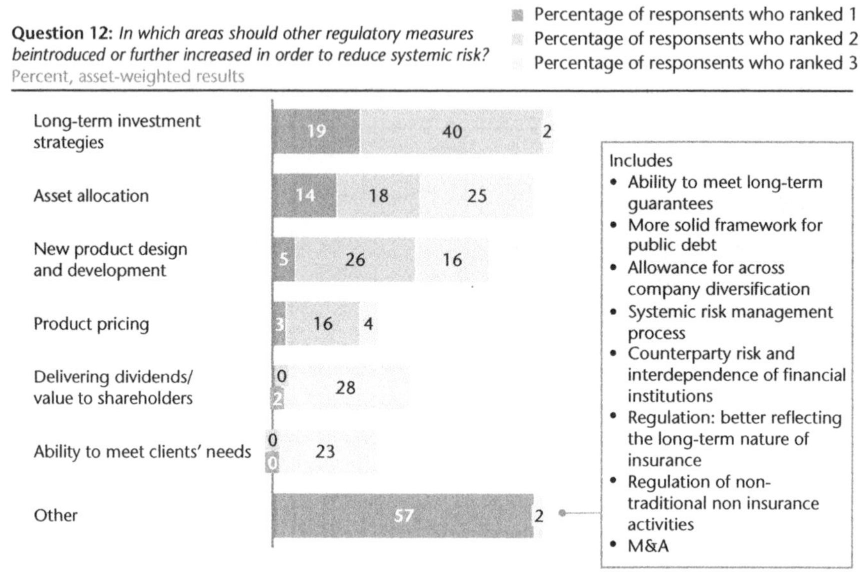

Figure 10.6. Key areas for additional regulatory measures to be introduced
Source: Enterprise Risk Management Survey for Insurers 2015

Another interesting message from the survey stems from the fact that large players are even more sceptical than smaller players about the effectiveness of current regulatory frameworks. *Long-term investment strategies, asset allocation,* and *new product design and development* are the three key areas where insurers see room for additional regulatory measures to reduce systemic risk (Figure 10.6).

Finally, many insurers complained about the heterogeneous nature of regulation and would like regulators to slow down its evolution and simplify requirements. A general desire was expressed for globally more consistent regulation.

10.4 Risk Management practices in the Industry

The riskier environment and evolving regulation have pushed the insurance industry to upgrade risk management capabilities and are continuing to force improvements in this area.

Insurers today are generally quite confident about the robustness of their risk management capabilities and perceive them to be already adequate. When asked to what degree their risk management framework needed improvement, 75 per cent of respondents indicated that little or no improvement was required. There is a greater confidence among the largest players and

A framework helps in assessing enterprices risk management.

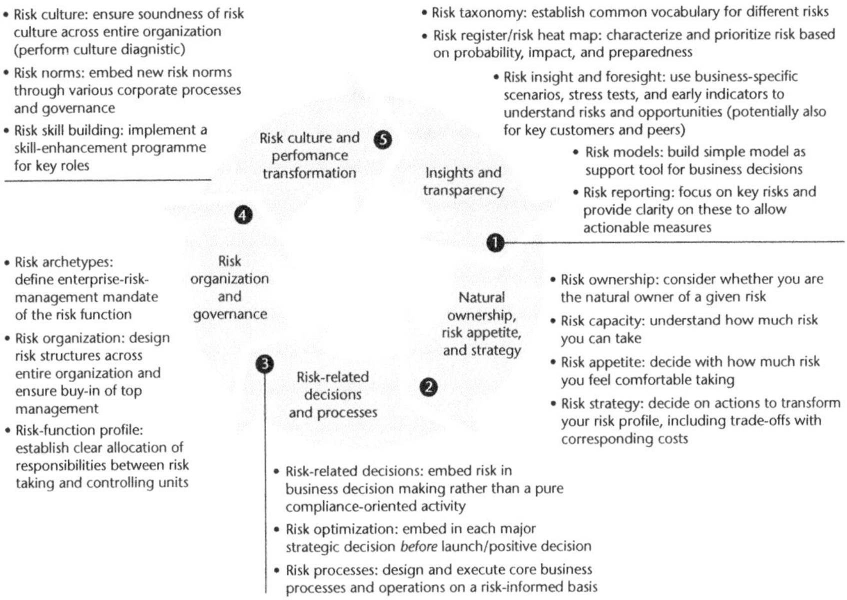

Figure 10.7. McKinsey ERM framework

a higher perceived need for evolving risk management practices among smaller institutions.

To go beyond these general perceptions, the survey deep-dived into each single element of the McKinsey Enterprise Risk Management (ERM) framework to identify which specific issues are of greatest concern today and require future investments (Figure 10.7).

The main areas cited as needing improvement differ slightly between the larger and smaller players participating in the survey (Figure 10.8).

For the larger players, the key area identified for attention (based on the asset weighted share of participants) was *risk transparency and insights*, specifically the three following issues:

1. *IT, data governance and analytics* (32 per cent);
2. *stress testing capabilities* (19 per cent);
3. *risk reporting* (18 per cent).

Another area highlighted for improvement, *risk organization* and governance (10 per cent), is related to the complexity that larger financial institutions and multi-national groups typically struggle with.

For the smaller organizations, *risk culture* is also important (first choice for 22 per cent of participants in the survey based on equally weighted results).

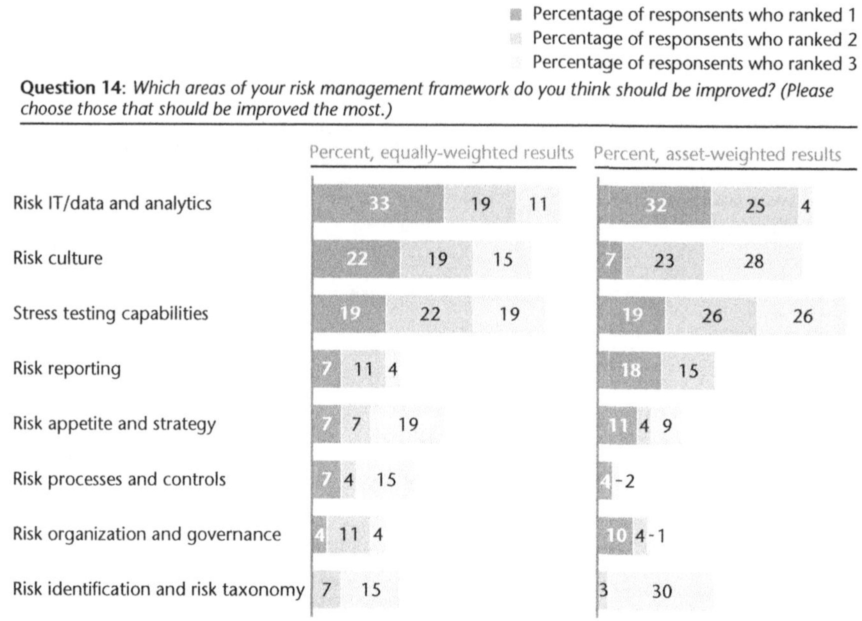

Figure 10.8. Key areas of improvement for insurers' risk management function
Source: Enterprise Risk Management Survey for Insurers 2015

More detail on the answers and improvement areas across the different elements of the ERM framework is reported below.

10.4.1 *Risk Insights and Transparency*

In the McKinsey ERM framework, risk insights and transparency include four main elements that were all (excluding risk identification and taxonomy) picked up in the survey as areas of concern where improvements are required. In particular:

- **Risk IT/data and analytics:** when asked which areas in this category needed improvement, respondents mentioned data governance and quality (25 per cent), and automation/speed of data gathering (24 per cent) as their main areas of concern. Comments on the survey and follow-up discussion with participants highlighted a perceived need for increased investment in the industry into *advanced analytics* and new techniques (e.g. *machine learning*) to enhance the quality of reporting and companies' ability to generate managerial insights from data.
- **Stress testing:** 47 per cent of participants indicated that although stress testing is performed and typically considered in decision-making

processes, only some risks are currently taken into account and modelled. Interviews and follow-ups with survey participants indicated that further developments in stress testing in the coming years will mainly focus on properly considering all risks in stress tests and on providing more useful insights from a managerial perspective.

- **Risk reporting:** quality and governance of reporting appears to be a key area of improvement and in particular for smaller players: risk reporting was deemed only partially structured and with no pre-defined escalation mechanisms in place by 28 per cent of participants (up to 48 per cent considering equally weighted results).
- **Risk identification and taxonomy**: respondents do not perceive risk identification and taxonomy as a first priority for improvement. No respondent rated this as a number one concern, while only 33 per cent of respondents ranked it as number two or number three. However, some risks are still perceived as not properly captured/measured. In particular, when asked about risks that need better measurement and transparency participants chose (i) cyber risks (first choice for 60 per cent of respondents), (ii) sovereign risks (first choice for 24 per cent of respondents) and (iii) behavioural risks (second choice for 63 per cent of respondents).

10.4.2 *Risk Appetite and Strategy*

Survey results show that, apart from the Regulatory Solvency Ratio and the Economic Solvency Level that are widely used, there is still a strong variance of indicators across risk appetite frameworks of insurers:

- The most commonly used metrics include: economic solvency level (96 per cent); regulatory solvency ratio[2] (87 per cent) value at risk (65 per cent); concentration (64 per cent); target credit rating (61 per cent); cash buffer (59 per cent); risk adjusted return on capital (54 per cent), earnings at risk (48 per cent). Some other metrics, still not common but becoming more frequent, are related to: operational risks, stress liquidity measures, conduct risks, etc.
- There is no common practice among participants of the survey regarding the cascading of the risk appetite down to business units. There is also no single preferred option: legal entity, business unit, risk type, and geography were all chosen as the primary axis for cascading by at least one respondent.

[2] With no indication at this stage if Solvency I or Solvency II.

Interviews with some CROs and CFOs from leading international insurance companies highlighted some trends in this field including: (i) higher level of integration of the risk appetite framework with strategic planning and budgeting and (ii) more structured and frequent cooperation between CROs, CFOs, and business leaders in the definition of the risk appetite framework.

10.4.3 *Risk Culture and Performance Transformation*

When asked about the level of accountability for risk-related matters in their organization, 38 per cent of respondents declared that risks in daily business are not always considered with the support of both qualitative judgement and quantitative tools.

With respect to frontline functions, participants indicated that risk is most engrained in people's minds in the following areas: investment management (first choice for 56 per cent of participants) and corporate and commercial non-life (22 per cent). Room to improve frontline risk culture seems to exist in retail life and non-life businesses.

Discussions and interviews with insurance leaders highlighted that some players are making significant investments in risk culture programmes, in particular launching dedicated actions to increase risk culture in retail businesses where third parties (i.e. brokers, IFAs) are often the main distribution channel.

10.4.4 *Risk-related Processes and Decisions*

In this area, the survey investigated in particular the use of derivatives and how they are leveraged to mitigate risk.

Almost half of participants (46 per cent) increased their use of derivatives after the crisis which is an interesting reality to be put into perspective with the indication that insurance companies were considering risks to financial performance in the future economic environment to be more volatile or significantly more volatile than the current economic environment. This could indeed indicate that derivatives are growingly seen as an important tool to mitigate financial risks. In particular, 42 per cent of those who increased their use of derivatives did so to mitigate risk predominantly through macro-hedging (37 per cent).

Insurers use different types of derivatives for different purposes:

- Interest rate derivatives are widely used. The main purposes for their use include: macro-hedging (87 per cent), micro-hedging (76 per cent), and management of financial balance sheet ratios (76 per cent, typically prudential capital ratios).

- FX derivatives are used mainly for micro-hedging (92 per cent) and accounting purposes (86 per cent).
- Credit derivatives are less common and used mainly for yield improvement (57 per cent) and assets' replication (52 per cent) purposes.

Finally, with regard to the potential impact of the failure of a large derivative counterparty, 95 per cent of participants claimed to be able to assess a counterparty exposure and resume operations within 48 hours (48 per cent in less than 24 hours). In 2008–2009, only 77 per cent of the participants think they would have been able to assess the exposure to an individual derivative counterparty and recover operations within 48 hours.

10.4.5 *Risk Organization and Governance*

The role of the risk management function in insurance organizations is clearly evolving. According to survey respondents, a stronger role of the risk management function is required in three areas particularly:

- life and non-life pricing (on a assets-weighted average basis, participants gave 26 points out of 100);
- asset allocation (20 points out of 100);
- capital allocation (16 points out of 100).

Another important trend is the centralization of more technical functions. In particular, three areas that today are typically fully centralized are (Figure 10.9):

- risk governance definition (79 per cent of participants);
- risk limit setting (50 per cent);
- capital calculation (46 per cent).

The centralization of risk modelling and reporting is ongoing, but they still sometimes remain totally or partially decentralized.

10.5 Academic Research and Future Research Efforts

Although the majority of participants (82 per cent—asset weighted) felt there is no lack of academic research in the insurance space, many pointed to potentially useful areas for future exploration.

Forty-two per cent of the respondents cited risk management tools and practices as the most important area for academic investigation, while 28 per cent pointed to the role of insurance in the macro-economy and in economic growth as the number-one priority for researchers (Figure 10.10).

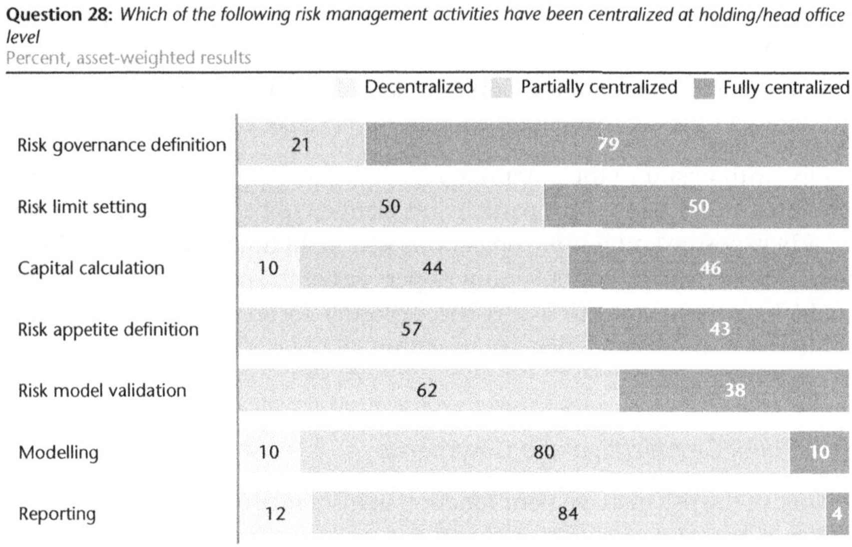

Figure 10.9. Level of centralization of risk functions
Source: Enterprise Risk Management Survey for Insurers 2015

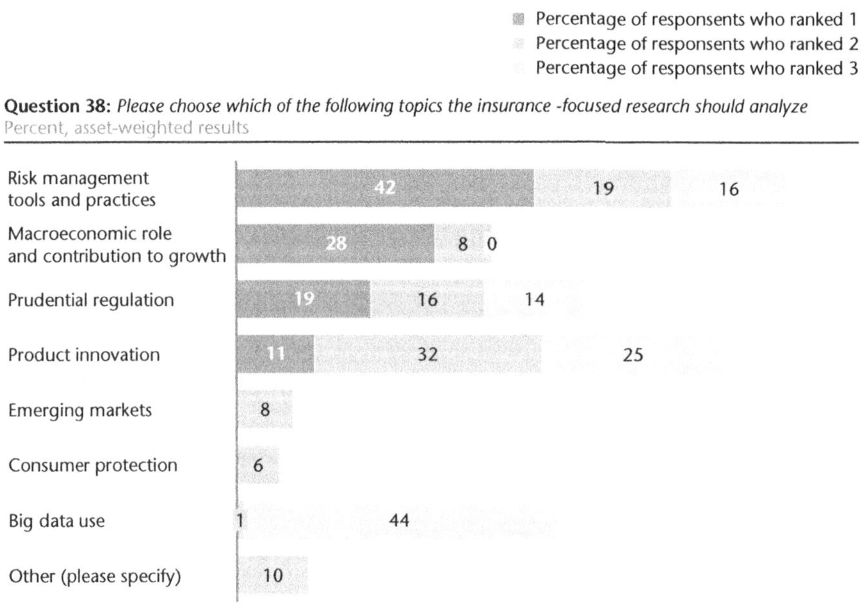

Figure 10.10. Areas where insurance risk research is needed
Source: Enterprise Risk Management Survey for Insurers 2015

Surprisingly, while big data was considered among the top three research topics by 45 per cent of respondents, none ranked it as a first priority, despite strong conviction that big data and analytics will be the next big game changer in the industry.

In terms of the audience that should be addressed by academic research, 47 per cent of the participants selected insurance companies' executives, and 39 per cent selected regulatory authorities.

Index